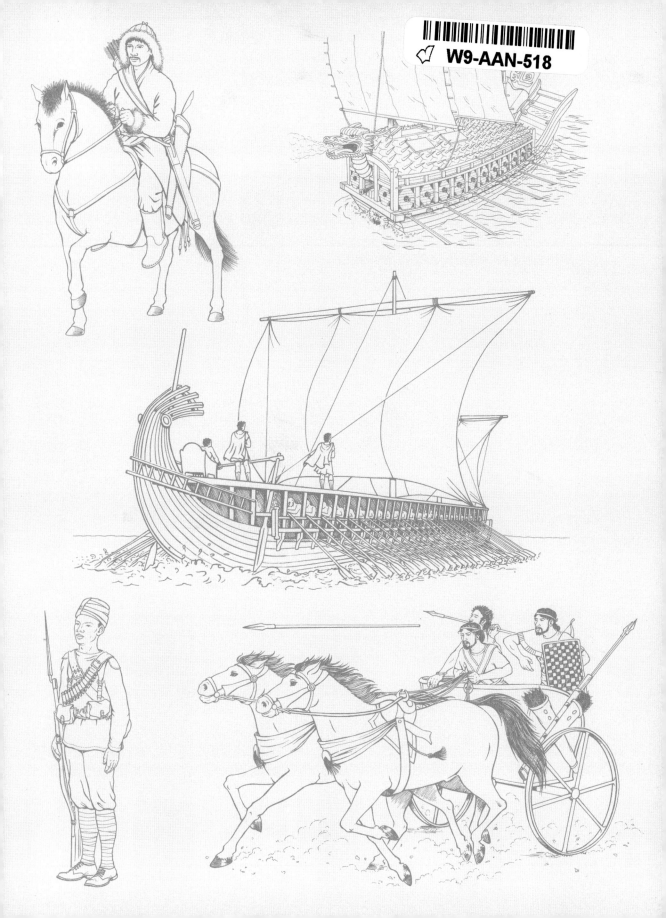

BATTLES
THAT CHANGED
WARFARE
1457 BC ~ AD 1991

BATTLES
THAT CHANGED
WARFARE
1457 BC ~ AD 1991

FROM CHARIOT WARFARE TO STEALTH BOMBERS

KELLY DEVRIES   MARTIN J. DOUGHERTY   CHRISTER JORGENSEN   CHRIS MANN   CHRIS McNAB

amber
BOOKS

This edition first published in 2011

Published by
Amber Books Ltd
Bradley's Close
74–77 White Lion Street
London N1 9PF
United Kingdom
www.amberbooks.co.uk

ISBN: 978-1-907446-69-6

Project Editor: Michael Spilling
Picture Research: Kate Green
Design: Jerry Williams

Printed in China

CONTENTS

INTRODUCTION

ONE OF THE MOST FAMOUS SCENES IN CINEMA IS FROM THE 1968 CLASSIC, *2001: A SPACE ODYSSEY*. A TRIBE OF PRE-NEANDERTHAL APES AWAKEN TO THE APPEARANCE OF AN ALIEN BLACK MONOLITH. IT TRIGGERS IN THESE APES AN AGGRESSION THAT IS INTENSIFIED WHEN ONE APE PICKS UP A BONE TO USE AS A WEAPON AND IMMEDIATELY GAINS VIOLENT DOMINATION OVER THE OTHERS. THE MESSAGE IS SIMPLE: HE WHO HAS THE BETTER MILITARY TECHNOLOGY DOMINATES HIS ENEMIES.

The origin of war among men has been and will continue to be disputed. What is not debated is the link between technology and war. While the idea suggested in *2001*, that the army with the best technology wins, has frequently proven historically inaccurate, this has not prevented almost every state that has ever existed from seeking to build their technological arsenal, to run an 'arms race'. And once they have acquired these arms, their use in military conflict against a neighbour almost always follows.

It has been difficult for anthropologists and archaeologists to determine when the first military technology was invented. Some theorize that warfare is a man-made activity, learned and not inherent, and, therefore, that early military technologies were invented as agricultural implements and devices and not

With a knife and helmet, if he was lucky, the Neo-Hittite archer (fifteenth century BC) would depend on his bow and speed to protect him during a battle or a siege. The quality of his bowmanship would depend on his familiarity with his weapon, and skill was the product of years of use and practice.

as tools of war. Others believe the opposite: that man has always been aggressive and bellicose and – like the apes in *2001* – has worked on technology for solely military uses since the very beginning of human existence. Certainly, by the beginning of the Stone Age (Neolithic or Early/Middle Palaeolithic times – c.70,000 BC) people had started to use spears, fire, and stone clubs to protect themselves against animals and other men.

By the end of the Palaeolithic Age (35,000–12,000 BC), cave paintings show that Neanderthal and Cro-Magnon man had also begun to integrate their weaponry in their strategy and tactics, thus creating the first organized warfare. By this time, military technology was offensive only and designed for use by one individual against another. These weapons fit into three categories: clubs, stone axes and thrusted spears, which were used for short-range warfare; thrown spears or javelins for medium-range warfare; and thrown stones for long-range warfare.

SLING AND BOW

The Mesolithic Age (12,000–7000 BC) brought the first significant technological changes in arms and armour. The most important inventions of this time were the sling and the bow. This increased the long-range firepower, both in the range of missile fired and in the damage caused by its impact. They also allowed their users to be further away from opponents and, if desired, to remain concealed while using them. Finally, when used together in a group, slings and bows could unleash a heavy barrage of missile fire. For anyone hit by a slingshot, the result could be lethal. Indeed, the biblical story of David and Goliath exemplifies the fatal result of such a missile fired accurately, even from a small, irregular soldier against a much larger, more professional foe. The Mesolithic period also saw the invention of the mace and the rudimentary dagger, which replaced the club and stone axe in short-range warfare, although the thrusted spear still seems to have remained the most preferred weapon for this type of combat. In addition, cave paintings depict the introduction of protective clothing (proto-armour) worn by late Stone Age warriors.

FROM STONE TO METAL

The Bronze Age saw no change in the types of weapons, only in the material used to make them. Man began experimenting with the use of copper as early as 6000 BC in Anatolia, but it another 2000 years before the extraction and smelting of metals produced bronze strong enough and cheap enough to replace traditional stone tools and weapons. Spears, javelins, arrows, maces and axes were now all fitted with bronze heads, which could be easily sharpened. Archaeological remains from Ancient Mesopotamia and Egypt show that the metallic axe also became the most frequently used weapon of these civilizations. Daggers became a more viable short-range weapon, especially when lengthened (as bronze now made possible) to produce a sword, which could be used both to pierce and slash an enemy. Stronger, more protective armour – helmets, shields, breastplates and greaves – was also introduced.

Finally, during the Bronze Age, chariots appeared and were used primarily as a means of transportation to and around the battlefield or as mobile missile-launching platforms. At the battle of Megiddo, probably fought in 1457 bc – although this date is disputed – Egyptian forces led by Pharaoh Thutmose III used their fast two-wheeled chariots to sweep across the battlefield and find the weak spots in the Canaanite rebel troops.

Assyrian chariot, eighth century BC. The Assyrians experimented with chariots pulled by as many as four horses. Note the yokes, which severely limited the load each horse could pull; the horse collar was invented many centuries later.

The Bronze Age became the Iron Age sometime around 1200 BC, and once more the material composition of both offensive and defensive armaments changed, although the types of weapons remained the same: the spear, sword and axe were the primary short-range weapons; the javelin was the primary medium-range weapon; and the sling and bow were the primary long-range weapons. The only major changes came with the introduction of the staff-sling, which was capable of throwing a large stone or a dart more than 200m (656ft), and in the length of the spear, which expanded during the Macedonian period to a length of more than 7m (23ft). This latter weapon (known as a *sarissa*) became the characteristic personal weapon of the armies of Philip II of Macedon (382–336 BC) and Alexander the Great (356–323 BC), who used it to conquer Greece, Persia, the Middle East, Egypt and the western portion of India. Philip and Alexander also employed new siege technologies.

Principal among these was the *ballista*, a catapult that derived its impressive power from torsion springs made of very tightly wound sinew ropes. Introduced as a defensive military technology in the fourth century BC, Philip and Alexander turned the *ballista* into a besieging machine, the effectiveness of which was demonstrated in the latter's conquest of the island city of Tyre in 332 BC.

FROM ROMANS TO KNIGHTS

From the beginning of their history, Roman armies too were characterized largely by the use of a single weapon, the *pilum*. Made of a strong but pliable iron, a *pilum* when thrown would bend upon impact – which

These are fairly typical legionaries of the first century BC, each forced to carry his equipment with him on the march. Each soldier is armed with two pila, which were needed in battle. Amongst the equipment carried would be entrenching tools, a bedroll, a cloak, and cooking implements, plus rations for several days in the field.

meant that it could not be returned by an enemy, or, if it actually pierced an opponent's armour or shield, would hinder his fighting or defensive capabilities. It could also function as a short-range thrusting weapon. Combining this military technology with the unit cohesion brought about by their training and discipline made Roman soldiers the most feared warriors of the ancient world, besting among others the Greek phalanx when the two faced each other at the battle of Cynoscephalae in 197 BC.

However, even the Romans could not control the world forever, and the Empire began to crumble from internal conflicts and outside invasions. Of the invaders, none were more impressive than the Huns, who

made their appearance in Europe in the fourth century but achieved their greatest victories in the fifth century under Attila (406–453). His dominance of both the Eastern and Western Roman Empire came from the speed and power of horse archers, who shot recurved compound bows as they swept past their opponents on the battlefields of Thrace, Anatolia, Greece, Hungary, Germany, France and Italy.

The Western Empire failed, but the Eastern Empire transformed into the Byzantine Empire, in part not by adopting the tactics and technology of their most feared opponents, but by developing their own heavy cavalry, the *cataphracti*. Armoured from head to foot in mail, the Byzantine *cataphracti* moved relatively slowly but were virtually invulnerable, especially when led by skillful and intelligent generals, such as Belisarius, as at the battle of Ad Decimum in AD 533, when they defeated the Vandals and reconquered North Africa.

It is thought that the heavily armoured medieval knight may have descended from the Byzantine *cataphracti*, although the link is probably not as direct as some historians have theorized. Still, few military entities dominated warfare for as long as the medieval knight, who often encased not only himself but also his horse in armour. By the beginning of the fifteenth century, mail armour had begun to give way to steel plates until, in the middle of that century, everyone who could afford to do so, wore a complete plate armour and helmet. This move may have been simply a response to

These two early Japanese arquebuses date from the mid-sixteenth century. They proved decisive at battles such as Nagashino (1575) and Sekigahara (1600).

the fashion of the day, although at least in Scotland, France and the Low Countries, it could also have been a result of the effectiveness of the English longbow archers. Starting in 1298, at the battle of Falkirk, the English began to realize the importance of large numbers of these soldiers as they defeated William Wallace's (c.1270–1305) Scottish army.

GUNPOWDER

It was not until the invention of gunpowder weapons that the dominance of the armoured horseman in Europe was effectively ended. Unlike most other military technologies, it took a long time to develop gunpowder, as well the weapons that eventually utilized it to propel projectiles at a speed, and with a lethality, that rivalled even the longbow. Probably introduced into Europe in the third decade of the fourteenth century, it was not until the end of that century that guns began to make an impact on siege warfare, and not until the middle of the fifteenth century that they began to influence the results of battles. One of the earliest battles to be determined by gunpowder weapons was fought at Castillon in 1453, when a French army led by a former gunner, Jean Bureau, defeated an English force and ended the Hundred Years War.

Yet, it may not have been gunpowder weapons or longbows that were solely responsible for ending the domination of the medieval knight in European warfare. The fourteenth century also saw a rise in the effectiveness of infantry on the battlefield. In early-fourteenth century battles, infantry forces or dismounted

This Scottish musketeer from the 1640s carries a matchlock musket with bandolier containing powder. He has a dirk (dagger) at his belt. Musketeers would often use their muskets as clubs in close combat.

cavalry and infantry forces defeated the cavalry-dominated forces they faced at: Courtrai (1302, Flemings over French); Arques (1303, Flemings over French); Kephissos (1311, Catalan Company over Frankish Greeks); Bannockburn (1314, Scots over English); Mortgarten (1315, Swiss over Austrians); Boroughbridge (1322, English over English rebels); Morlaix (1342, English over French); and Crécy (1346, English over French).

This trend would continue throughout the fourteenth, fifteenth and sixteenth centuries, invariably giving rise to specialist infantry units who hired themselves out to whoever could pay. In particular, they found employment in the numerous wars fought in Italy during this period, with the Swiss pikemen becoming the most famous for their military skills and discipline. These were exhibited especially well at the Battle of Novara of 1513, when the Duchy of Milan, whose army was primarily composed of mercenary Swiss infantry, defeated the French and Venetians.

Europeans were not the only ones to witness the changing nature of warfare due to new military technologies. In the Far East, the Japanese, Chinese and Koreans were all affected by new means and methods of fighting wars.

While gunpowder had been invented in the region and used there in warfare for many centuries, it was not until after the introduction of guns, at about the same time as in Europe, that the traditional arms, armour and tactics of Asian wars began to change. For example, at the Battle of Nagashino, fought between the armies of Oda-Tokugawa and Takeda in 1575, the handguns fired in volleys by the Oda-Tokugawan soldiers defeated numerous charges made against them by the Takeda heavy cavalry.

Gunpowder weapons also altered the way naval battles were fought, leading the Koreans to build the first ironclad vessels – the famous turtle ships. Their value was immediately recognized when a turtle ship defeated and sank a Japanese warship at

Members of a reanactment society fire matchlock muskets during an English Civil War reenactment. The bandoliers containing both powder and shot are visible. Traditionally, there were 12 such vials, and they were referred to as the 'Twelve Apostles'.

Soldiers from an early-nineteenth century British foot regiment prepare to fire a volley. Well-trained foot soldiers of the Napoleonic era could cause at least five per cent casualties amongst their enemy at a range of 150m (492ft).

spiessen (*Arms Drill with Arquebus, Musket and Pike*), which first appeared in 1607 and was reprinted and translated numerous times afterwards, or the development of the New Model Army by Oliver Cromwell (1599–1658) and other Parliamentarian theorists during the English Civil War, they were mostly in the adoption of new tactical and training techniques using the older weapons. They were effective, though, as the English demonstrated by standing solidly in support of their French and Dutch allies against the Spanish at the Battle of the Dunes in 1658. Had the English not shown such discipline in the engagement, the Spanish, according to most historians, would certainly have won.

WEAPONRY IN THE INDUSTRIAL AGE

It is from the middle of the nineteenth to the end of the twentieth century that history saw the greatest number and diversity of military technological improvements. Of course, industrialization provided a major incentive, as did the greater flow of money from governmental and private concerns into the purchase of new and better

Sacheon in 1592 despite Japanese marines constantly firing artillery and arquebuses at it.

From the sixteenth to the nineteenth century, there were few significant changes in military technology. Gunpowder artillery pieces became more standardized in sizes and types, and their carriages both on land and at sea became more sturdy and shock resistant – although they always wore out before the guns they carried. Handguns were also improved through the addition of better trigger mechanisms: from the match to the matchlock, then to the wheellock and finally to the flintlock. However, all guns continued to sacrifice accuracy for ease and speed of loading, as rifling was known and understood but considerably slowed the process of loading the weapon. Nor did improvements in metallurgy, which had

seen the introduction of iron casting in the early sixteenth century, or gunpowder, which had seen the adoption of different powders for different guns at the same time, change much from then until the middle of the nineteenth century. When military technological improvements were made, such as in the widespread printing and availability of Jacob de Gheyn's manual, *Wapenhandlingen van roers, musquetten end*

A typical bronze cannon of the sixteenth century had a barrel length of 1.25m (4ft). These weapons were woefully ineffective compared to the cannons that came to dominate the battlefield in the eighteenth and nineteenth centuries.

weapons – or, as it is often known, 'the arms race'. On the other hand, major technological improvements have been made in all aspects of human life during the past 150 years, so the changes in military technology may simply have been a product of modernization.

The earliest of these changes were improvements to conventional weapons. The handheld gunpowder weapon improved significantly. The problem with accuracy was solved by a change in loading technology. Breech-loading had long been used for larger artillery pieces, but it primarily involved removable chambers filled only with gunpowder, while the projectile – a stone or metal ball – was loaded into the smooth-bore barrel. Removable chambered guns continued into the eighteenth century, although their use diminished with the improvement in loading techniques that minimized any difficulties loading the gunpowder directly into the cannon's muzzle.

The breech-loading of handguns had also been known, at least as early as the reign of King Henry VIII, although during the sixteenth and seventeenth centuries they

were made for only the most wealthy or elite patrons. It was not until the end of the eighteenth century that a breech-loaded handgun became more viable. In 1770, a Milanese gunsmith, Giuseppe Crespi (1665–1747), designed a pivoted breech to ease the loading of handguns, in this case Austrian carbines. Ten years later, Swiss inventor Durs Egg (1748–1831) copied the design and made breech-loading carbines for the British Board of Ordnance. In 1811, a variation of the breech-loader crossed the Atlantic to be patented in the United States by John Hancock Hall and William Thorton, leading to Hall's supervision of the manufacture of such weapons at America's primary military arsenal, Harper's Ferry Armoury.

THE NEEDLE GUN

Other arms' inventors used this innovation in their own work. In 1828, a German, Johann Nikolaus Dreyse (1787–1867), placed a fulminate primer in the middle of the gunpowder cartridge – which by this time had become the standard means of loading gunpowder into a handgun – and to ignite it used a long firing pin, known as the

Following their victory in the Franco-Prussian War of 1870, Prussian soldiers pose with captured French artillery. Along with the machine gun, artillery came to dominate the battlefield in the static warfare of the early twentieth century.

Hiram Stevens Maxim, posing with an early model of his fully automatic machine gun. Maxim invented the Maxim Gun in 1881, and it was to revolutionize warfare for the next 50 years.

'needle', which gave his gun the nickname 'needle gun'. Seven years later, Casimir Lefaucheux (1802–52), a French gunsmith, patented a paper cartridge with a percussion cap attached at the rear so that when loaded from the breech, it could be more easily set off by a trigger hammer (especially after further improvements were made to the invention in 1850 by fellow Frenchman, CH Houillier).

Rifling had also developed during this period until opposed spiral grooves had become standard. Also, in 1838, a special bullet was made with a raised band that could match the grooves, greatly increasing the accuracy of the gun. This bullet was also the direct ancestor of the Minié ball, introduced by Captain Claude-Etienne Minié (1804–79) in 1849, which not only fitted snugly into rifled grooves, but was also made to expand with the blast until its flight was completely controlled by these grooves, thus producing the straightest trajectory ever achieved.

The armies of Europe quickly adopted the rifles that resulted from these innovations for their infantry units: France, Prussia and Austria by 1841, Britain in 1851, and Russia and Belgium a short time later. The United States was far slower in its adoption of this small-arms technology, although by the end of the American Civil War in 1865, almost all regular army soldiers were equipped with rifled needle guns. By then, the Prussian Army, led by Helmuth von Moltke, had completely changed its battlefield tactics to include the new weapons, winning stunning victories over Denmark in 1864, Austria in 1866 and France in 1870–71. At Sadowa (Königgrätz) in 1866, their military value was especially borne out as the Prussians crushed the Austrians, whose forces had been slower to adapt to the needle gun.

Breech-loading technology was also reintroduced to larger artillery during this time, resulting in increased power and greater accuracy. Indeed, it was found that

the cast-iron barrels, which had not changed for centuries, were simply too weak to contain the force of the increased projectile power. A number of inventors set out to improve barrel strength, with several actually succeeding, though none were as successful in publicizing their improvements as Alfred Krupp (1812–87). In 1844, at the Berlin Exhibition, he first displayed his cast-steel artillery barrels and breastplates, winning the Gold Medal. In 1851, at the Crystal Palace in London, he showed a more complete artillery piece, a three-pounder steel gun that was mounted on a mahogany carriage and displayed in a Prussian war tent. And in Paris, in 1855, he exhibited a larger steel cannon, a twelve-pounder.

Still, Krupp had received only a few orders – from Egypt and Prussia – until 1867, when Napoleon III put on the Champs de Mars exhibition. Krupp went all-out for this show, with a 45-tonne (50-ton) cannon that could fire a 450kg (1000lb) projectile. He presented this piece to King Wilhelm of Prussia. Several more were purchased over the next few years and these, together with similar large artillery pieces purchased from other manufacturers, formed the core of the Prussian army's artillery division. Ironically, it was these

pieces that the Prussians used to crush the French at the battle of Sedan, fought in 1870, and at which Napoleon III – the host of the 1867 Champ de Mars exhibition – was captured. Unfortunately for Napoleon, he had neglected to purchase at the exhibition any guns similar to those used by the Prussians to defeat him at Sedan.

THE MACHINE-GUN

The ability for increased firing speed had been a by-product of the improvement in gunpowder weapons, and this led to a race to produce the first effective machine-gun. Dr Richard Jordan Gatling's (1818–1903) famous 1862 gun, which carried his name as the 'Gatling gun', was the first to make a substantial military impact. Gatling placed ten 11.4mm (.45in.) calibre barrels around a revolving circular core and mounted the whole on a light wheeled carriage. A man who had moved from the southern to the northern United States before the United States fell into the Civil War, he hoped to make an impact for the North in the Civil War, but it was not until after the war, in 1866, that the government made its first large purchase of the guns.

From that point until the end of the 1870s, Gatling manufactured machine-guns not only for the United States, but also

INTRODUCTION

British tanks cross entrenchments on the Western Front, 1918. Tanks were originally conceived as infantry support vehicles, designed to break the stalemate of the bloody, static trench warfare of World War I. However, with the development of German blitzkrieg ('lightning war') tactics in 1939, the tank truly came into its own.

for almost all the nations of Western Europe.

The Gatling gun, however, was not without its problems. It jammed frequently and was difficult to clear when it did, and the need to turn a large crank continually to operate the gun was a burden. A more reliable machine-gun was sought. Another American, Hiram Maxim (1840–1916), worked on a solution to these problems in the 1880s, and came up with a novel idea: use the recoil of the gun as a means of reloading it. He devised a machine-gun that allowed the spent cartridge to be rapidly replaced with a new one. Its speed and power were surprising, and because it had fewer moving parts, it jammed less often and could be cleared more easily when it did. It also did not rely on the strength or endurance of its user for its continual operation. Maxim's gun made an immediate impact. Used in the European colonial wars – where the Gatling gun had also found its primary use – the Maxim machine-gun mowed down opponents in Asia and Africa who could not afford the expensive technology. There is no better example of this than the battle of Omdurman in 1898, when an Anglo–Egyptian army led by Major-General Sir Herbert Kitchener

(1850–1916) decisively defeated a Mahdist rebellion led by the successor to 'Abd Allah (1845–85) in the Sudan.

Krupp steel cannons and Maxim machine-guns were representative of the growing influence of larger weapons that could deal death to a larger number of soldiers. When European soldiers turned their large artillery pieces and machine-guns against each other on the battlefields of World War I, death tolls rose into the millions. Moreover, many of those deaths can be blamed on leaders who, despite having purchased the weapons in very large numbers and being fully aware of their devastating potential, forced their men to face their firepower unprotected.

SUBMARINES, GAS AND TANKS

Following a similar military rationale, World War I also saw the introduction of the submarine, poison gas and tanks. Each was influential in altering military strategy and tactics. By this time, the submarine had been around for more than a century, but throughout the late eighteenth and nineteenth centuries, it had always been seen as more of a novelty than an effective military technology. Submarines had scored a few victories, such as the CSS *Hunley* successfully sinking the USS *Housatonic* in Charleston Harbor, South Carolina, in 1864, but almost always at the cost of the lives of the submariners, as indeed was the case with the *Hunley*.

However, advances in submarine technology during the following half-century meant that, by the outbreak of World War I, they were a viable, if not entirely proven, military technology. The Germans were especially adept at using them. At the beginning of the war, their fleet of 29 U-boats (*Unterzeebooten*) were quick to prove their worth. In September 1914, submarine *U9* sank three British

warships, the *Aboukir*, *Cressy* and *Hogue* – the so-called 'Live Bait Squadron' – without taking damage itself. Although the ships themselves were not a great loss to the British – they were obsolete and being withdrawn from active service – the conflict nevertheless led the German Navy to construct a huge U-boat fleet that plagued allied supply shipping throughout the war.

All military technology is designed either to kill or protect from being killed. However, no weapon may have killed with less discrimination than the poison gas and chemicals pumped over the battlefields of Europe during World War I. Several different poisonous chemicals were used,

A French infantryman mans a bell in the trenches of the Western Front, 1917 – a rudimentary alarm system to warn against gas attack.

INTRODUCTION

US Air Force personnel use a bomb loader to load
Mark 117 280kg (750lb) bombs on a B-52
Stratofortress aircraft during Operation Desert Shield,
1991. Although the destructive power of heavy
bombers is unmatched in conventional warfare, such
technologies have proved ineffective against guerrilla
tactics in places such as Vietnam and Iraq.

mostly in gaseous form, and unless soldiers
had good, tight-fitting gas masks, there was
little to keep them from suffering the lethal
consequences. Even if they were to escape,
there were often significant side effects. On
22 April 1915, during the Second Battle
of Ypres, the deleterious results of this
military technology were clearly seen after
the German Army released 152 tonnes (168
tons) of chlorine gas over a 6.5km (4-mile)
front, killing more than 6000 in a matter of
minutes and wounding even more. As a
result, a poison-gas ban was signed at the
end of the war, which, fortunately, has been
mostly adhered to since.

Far less lethal at the time of World War
I, but far more enduring as a military
technology, was the tank. A weapon entirely
conceived of and invented during this war,
the tank was derived when military
engineers tried to produce a mobile artillery
platform with enough protective armour to
allow it to fight in enemy troops in close
proximity. Early models were slow and
clumsy, often becoming stuck in mud or
trenches. But, needing something to break
the stalemate that had existed on the
Western Front since virtually the start of
the war, armies on both sides pushed
through its development. Eventually, late in
1917, the British Army had enough tanks
to try out in battle and, at Cambrai
(25 November to 6 December), their use
helped to bring victory to the allies.

WORLD WAR II TO THE GULF

Increasingly, armies were using larger and
larger machines to fight wars. Advancing
technology also allowed war to be
conducted more effectively at sea and in the
air. Still, the distance between bases and
targets could be too great to enable effective
air strikes. One proposal was to put runways
on ships that could move planes much
closer to their destinations. It was expensive
and risky, but the future of aircraft carriers
was written on 7 December 1941 when six
Japanese carriers delivered planes close
enough to destroy much of the United
States Pacific fleet at Pearl Harbor, Hawaii.

World War II introduced many other
military technologies that changed the
strategy and tactics of warfare. With radar
and sonar, planes and ships could be
detected from further away than previously
thought possible, giving targeted sites time
to prepare for an attack. Jet aircraft
increased the speed of flight for airplanes,
while helicopters could land in smaller
areas. And the atomic bombs dropped on
Hiroshima and Nagasaki at the end of the
war introduced the reality of nuclear
warfare, with its mass death, widespread
devastation and lethal, long-lingering and
horrific aftereffects.

Rockets were also introduced during
World War II. These were missiles made to
deliver explosives over long distances,
although the earliest types could not be
guided or controlled. For example, the V-1
rocket fell to earth simply when it ran out of
fuel. By 1945, research in missile

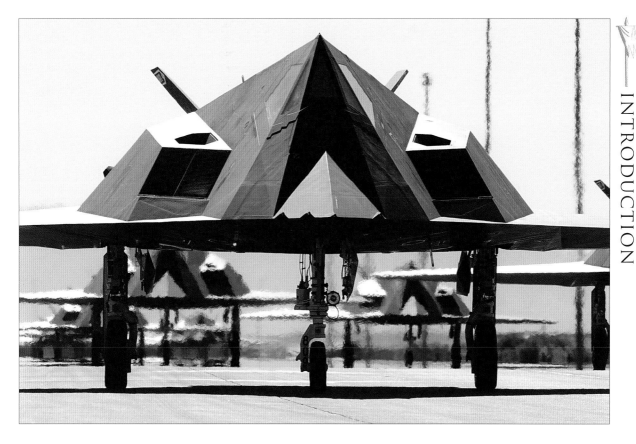

technology had gone in two directions: larger guided missiles, including, eventually, intercontinental ballistic missiles, among others; and smaller guided missiles that could be fired from smaller vehicles or even by hand. One of the more successful examples of the latter was the anti-tank missile, which by 1970 had become a viable, though very expensive, battlefield weapon – one, in fact, that helped the Israeli Army prove their worth against Egyptian tanks at the Battle of Mitla Pass during the Yom Kippur War of 1973.

Of course, new military technologies have continued to be produced and older military technologies have been continually updated. The proliferation of nuclear weapons produced a cold war between the two superpowers of the late twentieth century, when the United States and the Soviet Union threatened their use against each other. Fortunately, neither side ever carried out that threat, effectively creating a 'balance of terror' because the leaders of the two states worried about their own as well as

their allies' inability to recover from the effects of a nuclear war.

Still, warfare did not end with the end of the cold war, and new weapons have continued to appear. One of the more interesting of these is undoubtedly the Stealth Bomber. Developed by the United States from the 1970s to1990s as a means of avoiding radar detection, the Stealth Bomber went through a number of designs, most of which produced planes that were either: good at avoiding detection but not very good aircraft; or good aircraft that were only marginally more difficult to detect than normal planes. They also remained untested until the Persian Gulf War, when US Stealth Bombers performed their missions virtually undetected by Iraqi radar.

TOYS, BUT NOT FOR BOYS
'He who has the most toys wins' used to be a slogan that promoted male consumerism during the 1990s. But it could also be a definition of the arms race that has existed from the very beginning of human history.

This view of the nose of the F-117 gives a good perspective on the aircraft's radar-defeating design. The angular layout plus radar-absorbent materials serve to scatter radar waves and prevent an effective lock-on by enemy surveillance and targeting systems.

This race has gone from stones being thrown and wielded, or bones being used as clubs, to the intercontinental nuclear missile launched from a submarine that is able to lie hidden far below the sea's surface until only a few moments before firing. But, with this particular technology controlled almost completely by only one power, the United States, has the race actually been won? Consider this: in the Vietnam War and the Second Gulf War – the aftermath of which is continuing even at the time of writing – it has been the smaller, less complicated military technologies, such as landmines and Improvised Explosive Devices (IEDs), that have succeeded, while larger, more sophisticated military technologies have failed.

MEGIDDO
1457 BC

MEGIDDO IS THE FIRST BATTLE TO HAVE BEEN RECORDED IN A METHODICAL MANNER. IT IS NOTEWORTHY FOR THE EXTREME RISKS TAKEN BY THE EGYPTIAN COMMANDER IN MAKING HIS APPROACH MARCH. THE GAMBLE PAID OFF AND RESULTED IN A COMPLETE VICTORY FOR THE EGYPTIAN ARMY AND ITS DISCIPLINED CHARIOT FORCE.

WHY DID IT HAPPEN?

WHO An Egyptian army under the command of Pharaoh Thutmose III (d. 1425 BC) versus a Canaanite army under Durusha, king of Kadesh.

WHAT The Egyptians took a risky and unexpected route to the battlefield and achieved surprise.

WHERE Near the ancient city of Megiddo, Canaan; now in Israel.

WHEN 1457 BC (some sources suggest other dates).

WHY The Canaanites had rebelled against their Egyptian overlords.

OUTCOME After being defeated in the field, the rebels fled into the city and were besieged.

Thutmose III was a child when his father, Thutmose II, died, in 1479 BC. His stepmother Hatshepsut (d. 1457 BC), who was also his aunt, became regent over all the dominions of Egypt until such time as Thutmose was old enough to assume the throne. However, Egyptian politics were complex, and within a couple of years Hatshepsut was declared 'king' despite being a woman.

Although Thutmose was not deposed, the young pharaoh was sidelined. In theory, he and his stepmother ruled as co-regents and shared power. In practice, his position was nebulous and he was kept out of the way while Hatshepsut ruled. Thutmose was married to Hatshepsut's daughter, further consolidating his claim to the throne, yet for the first 22 years of his reign he did not rule. As Hatshepsut consolidated her hold on power in Egypt, there was a period of growth and security, which the nation needed. Trade routes were re-established and the economy grew vastly. This was the beginning of the wealth for which ancient Egypt is now famed.

Meanwhile, Thutmose studied and became widely respected for his learning. He also gained renown as commander of the army, and made a name for himself as a good general who was also wise in victory.

Finally, Hatshepsut died and Thutmose emerged from the shadows. He indulged himself in a certain amount of spite aimed at his stepmother, ordering her image to be removed from temples and her statues to be destroyed. However, he had urgent matters to occupy his attention.

News had arrived in Egypt that trouble was brewing in Canaan. The region

Although depicted as Pharaoh in this relief sculpture, Thutmose III had little power in the early years of his reign. After the death of Hatshepsut, his stepmother, he became a strong and effective leader.

EGYPTIAN CHARIOT

Chariots were invented in Canaan, and were still experimental at the time of Thutmose III's Megiddo campaign. It is possible to date some Egyptian sculptures quite accurately by their depiction of chariot wheels. Although Thutmose' chariots still used rather fragile four-spoked wheels, they were effective in action. At Megiddo, the Egyptians used their chariots as the advanced shock troops to disorientate and harass the Canaanites before they were fully formed for battle.

The driver did not fight but concerned himself with handling the vehicle while the warrior shot his bow at the enemy. At closer quarters, the warrior had a javelin to throw and could then fight with sword or mace. He protected himself and his driver with a shield when necessary. The light frame of the chariot was little protection from arrows or javelins, but rapid movement provided a good defence by making the vehicle a hard target.

contained many small kingdoms and states, most of which were Egyptian vassals. The area had been strongly controlled in the past, but in recent times Egyptian influence had begun to be replaced with that of foreign princes. Now word came that a confederation of princes were in open revolt, under the leadership of Durusha, king of Kadesh.

The revolt was probably triggered by the death of Hatshepsut. The death of a ruler often resulted in a period of reorganization or even political infighting. In such circumstances, mounting an effective response was not always possible, so for the Canaanite princes seeking their independence this was the best opportunity they were likely to have.

However, Thutmose had two advantages. First, there was no real period of dislocation. As co-regent, power fell to him in a manner that felt natural to the Egyptians – after all, he had been pharaoh for the past two decades! In addition, Thutmose was commander-in-chief of the army, and had been for many years. Thus he was ideally placed to meet this challenge to his rule.

Within a very short period, Thutmose mobilized his army and set out across the Sinai Desert in the direction of Canaan with about 20,000 men. His army was well provisioned, and the route was scouted to

ensure that water and other supplies could be located along the way. The army marched along a well-established road through the desert, which had been improved recently when Thutmose himself campaigned in the region.

CHARIOT ARMY

The main strength of Thutmose' army was its chariots. The horses of the time were too weak for cavalry work, though scouts and messengers sometimes rode. The invention of the stirrup, which would allow cavalry to become a truly effective battle-winning weapon, was some centuries off. The prestige and capabilities later associated with cavalry rested with the chariot corps.

The chariot was invented in Canaan, the land into which Thutmose now marched. Drawn by two small horses, the war chariot of the time was a fairly small vehicle composed of a wooden frame and basketwork sides. Experimentation was still in progress regarding the best position for the axle. Wheels had four spokes, which was later found to be inadequate. Eight- and finally six-spoked wheels were eventually used, but in the time of Thutmose III the chariot had relatively fragile wheels. The pharaoh's army contained a mobile chariot workshop – the ancient equivalent of an armoured formation's armoured recovery vehicles and field workshops.

LOCATION

CANAAN

✚ Megiddo

EGYPT

The city of Megiddo has been the site of three major battles, two of them in biblical times. Tradition also has it that it will be the site of the battle of Armageddon at the end of the world.

Each chariot had a crew of two men. The charioteer drove the vehicle, freeing his companion to fight from the small deck. The warrior was equipped with a mace or short sword plus a shield, a bow and a javelin.

The army also contained infantry and archers, and was organized into combined-arms divisions of 5000 men. These contained standard-bearers and support elements as well as fighting units. This level of organization enabled the army to cover ground quickly and efficiently, resulting in a much more rapid response to the situation than Thutmose' enemies were expecting.

The army marched from the frontier fortress of Tjel in Egypt to Gaza, a distance of 241km (150 miles), in 10 days. From

there, it took 11 days to cover the 129km (80 miles) to Yehem. This slower pace was probably due to a combination of greater caution and a need to forage for supplies in the rich surrounding lands.

Although the king of Kadesh and his rebel allies were surprised and alarmed at the speed of the Egyptian response, they announced that they would await Thutmose' host in the vicinity of Megiddo. This was commonplace for the time; there were rules and formalities associated with the conduct of a campaign, and these were – at least sometimes – followed.

Thutmose now had a difficult choice to make. North of him stood the Carmel Ridge. At 600m (1969ft) high in places, it presented a major obstacle to his army. Beyond it was the plain of Esdraelon, where the city of Megiddo stood and battle awaited. There were three passes through the ridge, of which two – the northerly and southerly passes – offered a slow but relatively safe approach to the plain.

The central route, the Aruna Pass, was an altogether different prospect. Much more direct, it offered the chance for a rapid approach but placed the army in jeopardy. The pass was so narrow that, in places, men would have to go in single file and chariots would need to be manhandled over obstacles. An ambush in the pass would be devastating, and even if one did not materialize, the army would be strung out. It would take time to assemble into fighting formation. If the lead elements were attacked while re-forming, they might be defeated before reinforcements could clear the pass.

COUNCIL OF WAR

Thutmose held a council of war, as was not uncommon at the time. This was a curious business in that as pharaoh, Thutmose was the absolute authority and could not be spoken to directly by his subordinates, who were nevertheless charged with giving their opinions without fear. The result was a situation in which Thutmose' officers each 'spoke in his presence' but not directly to him.

The pharaoh's officers were opposed to the central route, arguing that it was far too dangerous, and wanted to choose one of the

The land of Canaan as it is today. The hills of Galilee are to the north, across a barren plain. The observer is at Samaria, which was for a time the capital of the Israelites who came to dominate the region.

The Egyptians were highly organized in both peace and war. They built great monuments such as the Temple of Amun at Luxor, and fought in well-disciplined formations.

THE OPPOSED FORCES

EGYPTIANS (estimated)	
Total:	**20,000**
CANAANITES (estimated)	
Total:	**20,000**

other passes. Ultimate authority on earth he might be, but a wise pharaoh did not ignore the counsel of his officers, especially when their advice was unanimous. Leaving aside the possibility that they might be right, disregarding their advice was politically (and upon occasion, personally) dangerous.

Yet Thutmose did so. He was resolved to take the central pass. However, instead of ordering his commanders to follow him, he simply stated that he was going to take the Aruna road, alone if necessary. The officers could do nothing but immediately declare that they were going to do likewise.

EGYPTIAN ADVANCE

At first light the following day, the Egyptian army moved into the pass of Aruna, and in the next 12 hours the whole army moved through it

successfully. Meanwhile, Durusha of Kadesh had deployed his army. He predicted that Thutmose would take the southerly route, and was waiting in prepared positions near Taanach.

Durusha's position was good. If the Egyptians came via the southerly pass, they would have to fight in

Massed ranks of Egyptian infantry. Uniformity of equipment and regularity of formations are hallmarks of a well-organized and disciplined military force.

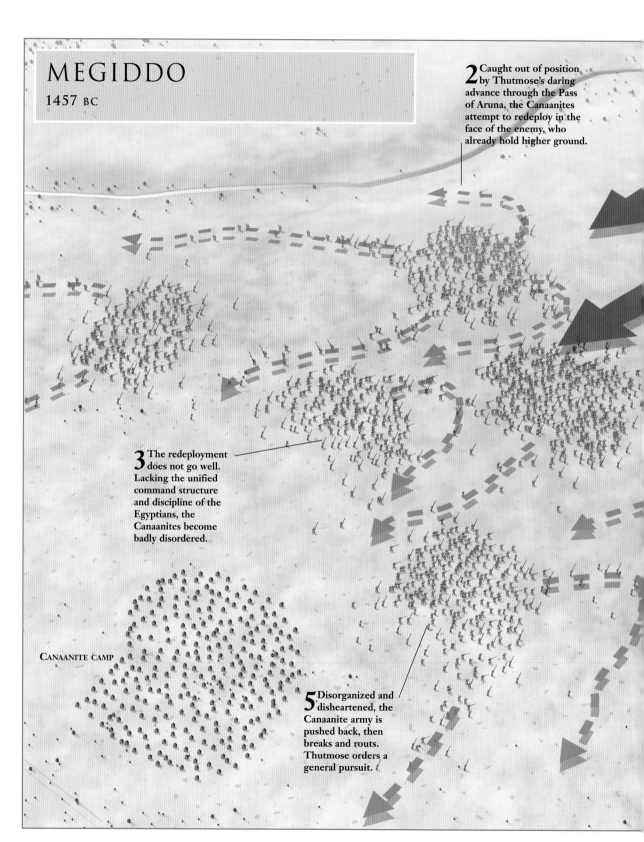

MEGIDDO
1457 BC

2 Caught out of position by Thutmose's daring advance through the Pass of Aruna, the Canaanites attempt to redeploy in the face of the enemy, who already hold higher ground.

3 The redeployment does not go well. Lacking the unified command structure and discipline of the Egyptians, the Canaanites become badly disordered.

CANAANITE CAMP

5 Disorganized and disheartened, the Canaanite army is pushed back, then breaks and routs. Thutmose orders a general pursuit.

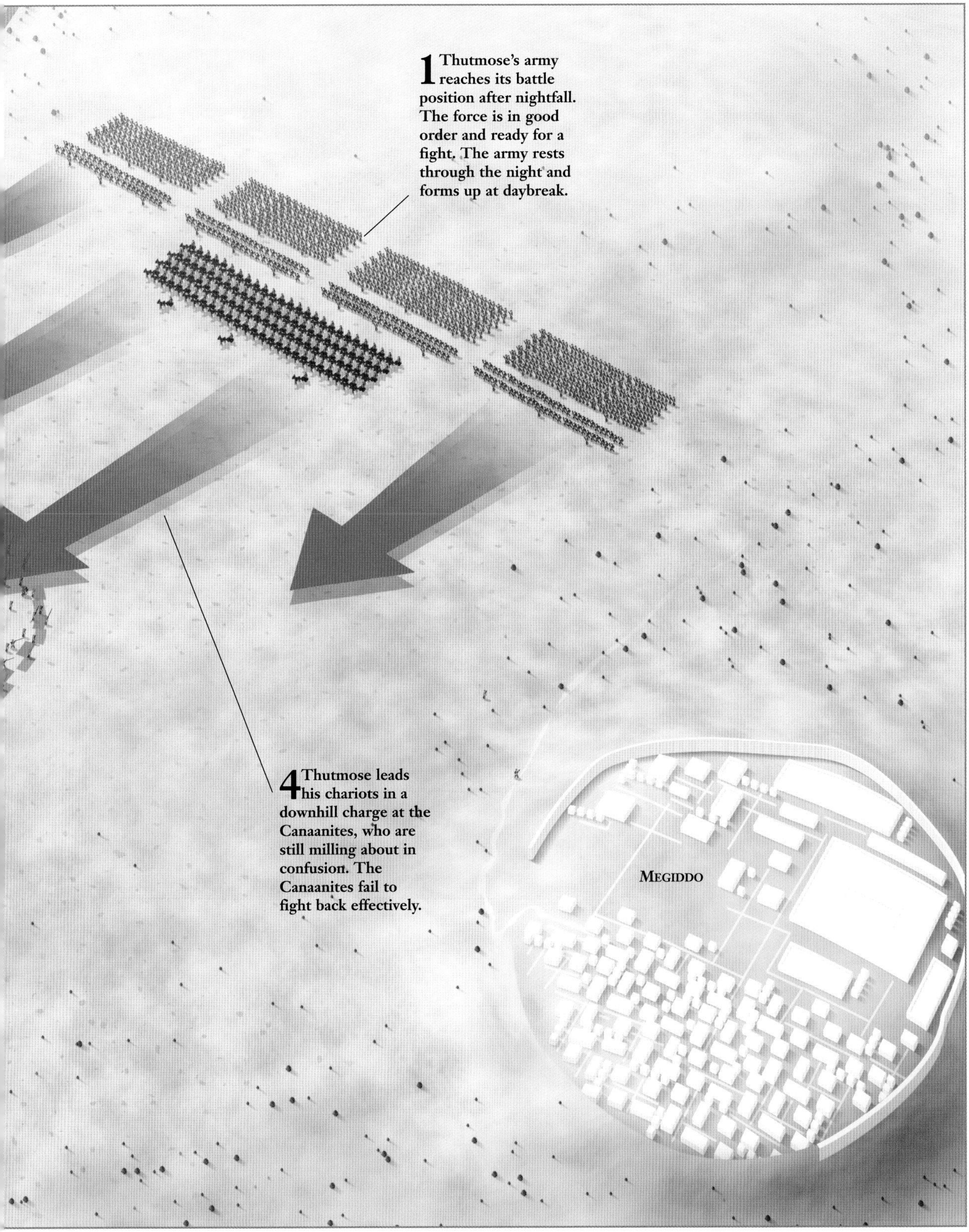

1 Thutmose's army reaches its battle position after nightfall. The force is in good order and ready for a fight. The army rests through the night and forms up at daybreak.

4 Thutmose leads his chariots in a downhill charge at the Canaanites, who are still milling about in confusion. The Canaanites fail to fight back effectively.

MEGIDDO

its mouth against a prepared enemy on ground of the latter's choosing. If they went north, there would be plenty of time for scouts to bring word, as this entailed a long detour. Durusha's army would be able to redeploy to meet them without being compromised.

Instead, the Egyptians emerged from the Aruna Pass and deployed on the plain of

This diagram shows the process by which early, solid chariot wheels were made from the trunk of a tree. A plank is cut from the centre of log. The plank is then halved: one half forms the middle plank of the wheel. The other half is further divided to form the two remaining sections.

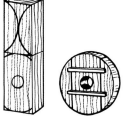

Esdraelon, appearing on Durusha's flank and causing alarm in the enemy camp. The Canaanite princes under Durusha's command were not a unified army in the way that the Egyptians were, and their response was uncoordinated and panicky. No scouts had been posted to watch the central pass and now the seriousness of that mistake was becoming apparent.

The two armies reached their battle positions in the dark, with only a little light from the new moon to see by. This was seen as a good omen by the Egyptians, as Thutmose' family were favoured by the moon goddess. Thutmose himself made sacrifices to Amon and to Montu, god of battle, before retiring to his tent.

Canaanite chariots were more advanced than those of the Egyptians. Notably, they had better wheels that broke less often. They were used in much the same way as those of the Egyptians.

THE BATTLE

The Egyptian account of the Battle of Megiddo suggests that the forces under Durusha's hand were huge, containing several million infantrymen, hundreds of thousands of chariots and the oddly precise figure of 330 kings. In all likelihood, the Canaanite force was no larger than that of the Egyptians. It was composed of the individual contributions of a large number of nobles and princes, and it is unlikely to have possessed good enough logistics to support a very large number of troops.

Durusha's forces, however big they may have been, were still redeploying as the

Opposite: The Egyptian god Amun had many aspects at different times. Amun was credited with the victories of Pharoahs, who raised great temples to him in the hope of continued success.

Egyptians prepared to attack. Never very well organized, the Canaanites were thrown into chaos by the conflicting orders of the various princes and were further confused by arguments among the many contributors to the host about who was senior to whom, and about who was to blame for the whole debacle anyway.

The Egyptian army was much better organized and was drawn up on higher ground than its enemies. Its left flank was close to the city of Megiddo; its right was anchored on a hill by the Kina Stream. Thutmose himself commanded the centre, where he had concentrated his chariots for the decisive blow.

The pharaoh wore a blue leather crown rather than a battle helm. He stood in his command chariot, which was decorated in gold and shone in the dawn sunlight, and gave the signal for his chariots to advance. The chariot was at that time mainly used as a mobile firing platform, and it was as mobile archers that the Egyptian charioteers made their first attack. Advancing rapidly downhill, they closed to short bow range before opening fire. Behind them, the infantry crashed their weapons against their shields, and trumpets added to the din.

CHARIOT ATTACK

Thutmose' chariot force advanced confidently and began pouring arrows into the disorganized Canaanites. The Egyptians' rapid approach was alarming, and no coherent response could be made to their shooting. In the Canaanite force, disorder turned to demoralization and then quickly to rout.

Seeing the Canaanite army breaking up and men fleeing, Thutmose' chariots followed as closely as they could, and the pharaoh ordered his infantry to make a general pursuit. However, many of the infantry paused to loot the enemy camp, and so a large segment of Durusha's army

The ruins of Megiddo. The city stood in a strong, high place and was protected by good fortifications. These almost proved the undoing of the defeated Canaanites, who could not get into the city.

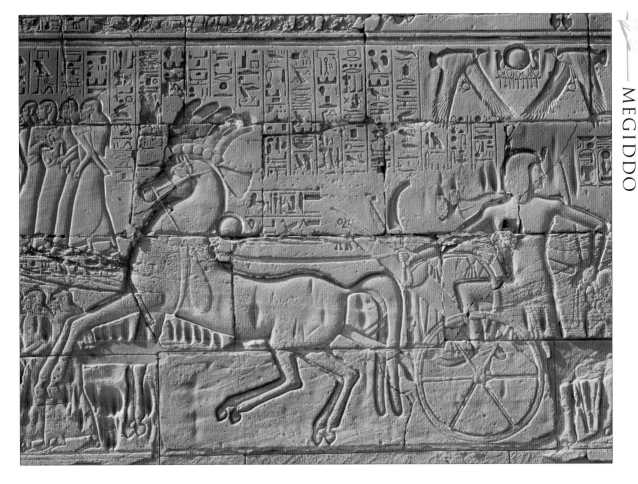

was able to reach the city of Megiddo. However, the gates were closed when Durusha arrived, and there was the possibility that his army would be pinned against the city and utterly smashed. Many of the Canaanite troops did manage to get inside while the Egyptians were rifling their belongings in the camp. The lord of Megiddo as well as the king of Kadesh himself were hauled up the wall on ropes made of clothing.

THE SIEGE OF MEGIDDO

The Egyptians laid siege to Megiddo, throwing up fortifications consisting of a moat and wall right around the city to ensure that no one escaped. With his enemies bottled up, Thutmose campaigned across the region for seven months, leaving a segment of his force to watch Megiddo. After a number of successes, including the capture of Damascus, Thutmose returned

to Megiddo and took its surrender. It was commonplace at the time to put the defenders of a city to the sword when it fell, but Thutmose spared Megiddo. His mercy was rewarded with oaths of loyalty from the former rebels, though some of the leaders were taken to Egypt as hostages.

Durusha of Kadesh was able to escape somehow, but it mattered little to the outcome. The revolt had been put down and governors installed in the region. With the challenge to his authority dealt with, Thutmose returned to Egypt and took up the reins of power in earnest. It was almost a year since he had set out on this, his first campaign as sole ruler. Throughout the campaign, Thutmose referred to it as his first. It seems that even in those early days he expected to lead many more. He had commanded two military campaigns while co-regent and would eventually lead no less than 17 as pharaoh.

This sunk-relief depiction of a charioteer at the Temple of Amun dates from later than Thutmose's campaign. The chariot uses six-spoked wheels, which supplanted other designs.

SIEGE OF TYRE
332 BC

THE PHOENICIAN CITY OF TYRE WAS ONE OF THE BEST-FORTIFIED CITIES IN THE ANCIENT WORLD, AND SUBDUING IT WAS VITAL TO ALEXANDER THE GREAT'S PLANS FOR CONQUEST OF THE PERSIAN EMPIRE. THE MOST CHALLENGING OF MORE THAN 20 SIEGES CONDUCTED BY ALEXANDER, THE SEVEN-MONTH SIEGE AND CONQUEST OF TYRE DISPLAY MACEDONIAN MILITARY SKILLS AND SIEGE TECHNOLOGY AT THEIR BEST.

WHY DID IT HAPPEN?

WHO Alexander the Great (356–323 BC) led a Macedonian and Greek army of about 30,000 men, aided by an allied fleet provided by several Phoenician cities and Cyprus, against Tyre, a major Phoenician city subject to Persia, with a population of about 50,000.

WHAT Macedonian siege of Tyre, which resisted Alexander in his effort to control the eastern seaboard of the Mediterranean.

WHERE Tyre (modern Sur, southern Lebanon), at that time an island about 4.4km (2.75 miles) in circumference, approximately 0.8km (0.5 miles) off the Phoenician coast.

WHEN January to August 332 BC.

WHY Alexander's conquest of Persia was impossible without control of the sea. Since he did not have sufficient naval force to meet the Persian fleet, he set out to eliminate the naval threat by conquering the Persian-held seaports of the eastern Mediterranean coast, including Tyre.

OUTCOME After seven months of increasingly desperate resistance, Alexander took Tyre, killing most of the male population and enslaving the women and children.

By ancient tradition, the first catapult was invented in 399 BC at Syracuse on the island of Sicily. King Dionysius I, threatened by Carthaginians and other enemies, brought together a group of engineers to create an arsenal of weapons to protect his city-state. One of the first of these was the non-torsion artillery piece, the *gastraphetes* (Greek for 'belly-bow'). In essence, the *gastraphetes* was little more than a large, powerful and flexible bow. Its flexibility came from the bow itself, which was made of wood, horn and animal sinew: a wood core covered by a tension layer of sinew in front and a compression layer of horn in the back. The whole was then sealed with strong glue made from boiled animal

hides, hooves and sinews. A bowstring – also made of animal sinew, 'from the shoulder or back, and from all animals except pigs', according to one ancient Greek source – gave the missile its ballistic power.

THE BELLY BOW

In many ways, the *gastraphetes* was like the contemporary hand-held composite bow, which by this time had been known for several centuries. However, the major difference between the composite bow and the *gastraphetes* was its power: the latter's came from its elaborate stock apparatus. The *gastraphetes* was mounted on a heavy stock made in two sections. The lower section (or case) was attached solidly to the

This sculpture portrays Alexander the Great at the Battle of Issus, fought in November 353 BC. Wearing his lion's head helmet, he is mounted on his famous horse, Bucephalus, rider and steed attacking a Persian foe, whose own horse has fallen.

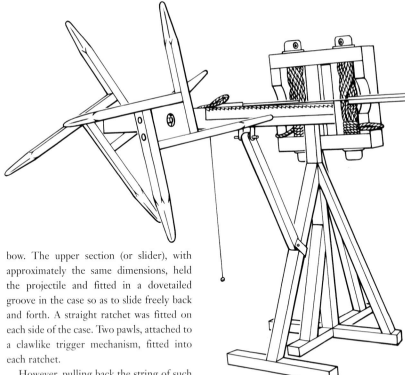

TORSION CATAPULT

The Ancient Greek interest in technology means that several descriptions and a few illustrations of torsion catapults exist. They all describe a machine in which a bolt or ball was placed onto a thick bowstring fastened to the end of two wooden arms anchored in springs of tightly twisted sinew ropes (hence the name 'torsion catapult'). The entire apparatus was mounted on a strong wooden base with a stock holding a slider and a trigger mechanism. Originally the string was retracted using ratchets, but in later catapults winches replaced the ratchets, as depicted here.

bow. The upper section (or slider), with approximately the same dimensions, held the projectile and fitted in a dovetailed groove in the case so as to slide freely back and forth. A straight ratchet was fitted on each side of the case. Two pawls, attached to a clawlike trigger mechanism, fitted into each ratchet.

However, pulling back the string of such a powerful bow was a problem. The solution was to attach a concave withdrawal rest to the end of the stock, which the operator put against his stomach. With the front of the bow placed against the ground and the rest against his stomach (or belly), he could raise the slider and attach the string to the trigger, load a missile and fire the *gastraphetes*. Thus, one man was able to withdraw the bowstring and discharge a projectile with much greater power than was possible with the traditional bow.

It is estimated that the *gastraphetes* added 50–100m (164–328ft) range to the hand-drawn composite bow, estimated to have been 500m (1640ft) at maximum range. It also added a ballistic force to a missile that few pieces of ancient armour could withstand, although the force was probably still too weak to breach most fortification walls. At the same time, however, this added power affected the *gastraphetes'* accuracy so that its main use became against siege engines or groups of soldiers.

IMPROVED DESIGN

The technology of the *gastraphetes* spread quickly throughout the ancient world and improvements in its basic design quickly

followed. By 360 BC, winches had been added to the stock, making it even easier to draw the trigger string and further strengthening the bow, increasing its ballistic force. A base was also added, which increased its size and improved its stability. Still, the 'belly-bow' artillery continued to be limited in force and power, both of which remained dependent on the strength and flexibility of the single bow. If these were exceeded, the bow broke. In addition, while some *gastraphetes* were equipped to fire stone balls, most fired only heavy, arrow-shaped bolts, which also limited the extent of their impact in battle or at siege.

To add to the catapult's power, it had to be adapted for greater force of discharge and for a change in missile type and size. Two bow arms extended from torsion springs replaced the single, flexible bow arm. Undoubtedly, artillery operators of the time were aware that it was the sinew that made it so resilient. Therefore, by stressing the role of the sinew, in the construction of tightly twisted springs, they could increase the force of artillery shot. By anchoring rigid bow arms in these springs, they could achieve a marked increase in range and power.

LOCATION

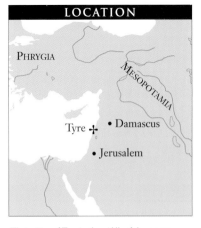

The position of Tyre in the middle of the eastern coastline of the Mediterranean Sea gave it control of almost all maritime traffic in that region, with its wealth determined by the trade or piracy.

THE OPPOSED FORCES

MACEDONIANS (estimated)
Macedonian and Greek
infantry: 30,000
Phoenician and Cypriot
triremes: 200
Marines and rowers: 40,200
Total: 70,200

TYRIANS (estimated)
Men of military age: 15,000
Tyrian triremes (it is unclear
how these were manned): 80
Total city population: 50,000

The remainder of the torsion catapult differed little from the non-torsion *gastraphetes*, as it had the same heavy sinew string, slider, winch, ratchet apparatus and trigger mechanism. However, the springs were a significant piece of new technology, which gave much more power when shooting missiles. By now, these were almost always stone balls generally weighing 13–26kg (29–58lb), although stones as large as 162kg (357lb) have been found. When the string was drawn back on a torsion catapult, the tension of the springs was applied to the bow arms, which sprang forward, discharging the missile. The power achieved was unprecedented. These weapons could breach fortification walls and were devastating against any armoured soldier on the battlefield.

At the time Alexander besieged it, Tyre was one of the largest and wealthiest cities in the Eastern Mediterranean. Following Alexander's conquest, the city never recovered its former size or wealth.

ALEXANDER THE CONQUEROR

It is thought that Macedonian engineers made the first torsion-spring catapults between 353 and 341 BC and that Philip II (382–336 BC) used them soon afterwards in his conquest of Greece. He then passed the technology on to his son, Alexander the Great (356–323 BC), who used it in his conquest of Persia, the Middle East, Egypt and India. Alexander seems to have been particularly impressed by his catapults' power and used them successfully to take towns that would otherwise have been almost impossible to conquer. That both Philip II and Alexander the Great were interested in using and developing siege weapons may come as a surprise to some. But, while both have been fairly judged to be excellent battlefield tacticians, they may, in fact, have displayed even greater genius in their campaign and siege strategies.

In 359 BC, Philip II assumed the Macedonian kingship, but because his inheritance was disputed he was forced

In this romantic portrayal of Alexander, drawn and coloured by Hugo Vogel in 1879, the great general sits atop the parapets of Tyre watching with satisfaction as the city is sacked.

immediately to go to war. He quickly built an army of disciplined, well-trained infantry and cavalry, which soon defeated much larger armies. Within three years, he had despatched his Macedonian enemies and conquered all neighbouring territories. His armies moved into Greece, a land of great military power, though only when the various city-states were united. They had so united when Persian forces under Darius and Xerxes invaded more than a century before, but since then war had raged throughout the Greek peninsula, and there was no unified force to repel Philip. By 337 BC, he stood unchallenged.

Along the way, Philip had made numerous enemies, including, it seems, his son. While it does not appear that Alexander was complicit in his father's assassination in 336 BC, he certainly profited from it. The usual inheritance crisis followed Philip's death, but Alexander swiftly quelled any opposition, and by 334 BC he had conquered Anatolia and crossed the Bosporus Strait to Asia.

The Persian king was still in control of Asia Minor and the Middle East when Alexander began his conquests of those regions. However, Persia was a far cry from the empire that it had once been. A century of civil war had ravaged the land, ruined the economy and destroyed both the military and its leadership. The new king, Darius III, was extremely insecure in his rule, having captured the throne only a year before Alexander's invasions, and was necessarily suspicious of all potential rivals.

This led to a further lack of discipline among soldiers whose allegiance to their king paled by comparison with the loyalty enjoyed by Darius and Xerxes on their ill-fated campaigns into Greece the previous century. This was particularly evident in the first two engagements with Alexander's forces, at the Battle of Granicus, 334 BC, and the Battle of Issus, 333 BC, where, even though outnumbered, the Macedonian king's phalanxes made easy work of the

once-vaunted Persian army. Darius retreated to central Persia to try to regroup. Instead of following after him, however, Alexander surprised his generals by turning his army south along the Mediterranean coast and directing them against the various city-states that had dominated the area for centuries. Of these, Tyre was seemingly the most secure.

AN UNASSAILABLE CITY
Founded perhaps as early as the third millennium BC, ancient Tyre was a large

city, its citizens prosperous from extensive trade and shipping. At the time of Alexander's siege, in 332 BC, Tyre was built both on an island and on the coast adjacent to it. The island part of the city was virtually impregnable, or so thought the many Mediterranean merchants who trusted their merchandise to the safety of the Tyrian warehouses there. This did not mean, however, that the town was never attacked. In fact, the city's wealth tempted several ancient magnates to try to besiege it. Most, like the Assyrian King Shalmaneser V

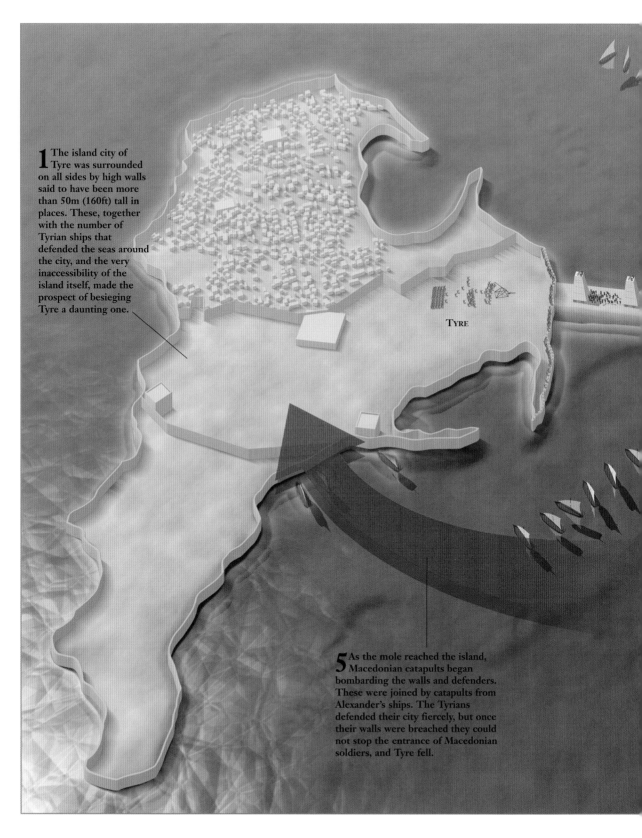

1 The island city of Tyre was surrounded on all sides by high walls said to have been more than 50m (160ft) tall in places. These, together with the number of Tyrian ships that defended the seas around the city, and the very inaccessibility of the island itself, made the prospect of besieging Tyre a daunting one.

TYRE

5 As the mole reached the island, Macedonian catapults began bombarding the walls and defenders. These were joined by catapults from Alexander's ships. The Tyrians defended their city fiercely, but once their walls were breached they could not stop the entrance of Macedonian soldiers, and Tyre fell.

3 As Alexander's mole neared completion, he had two large siege towers erected and moved to the end of the mole to protect the workers. The Tyrians sent a fire-ship against these towers and destroyed them.

2 In 332 BC, Alexander's army appeared on the shore opposite Tyre and asked for the city's peaceful surrender. After this was refused he began building a mole, perhaps 500-600m (1650–1980ft) long, between the shore and the island. Alexander also blockaded the island with his fleet.

4 As the Tyrians began to suffer from Alexander's blockade, they sent their fleet to attack his Macedonian, Greek and Phoenician ships. The Tyrian ships fail to defeat Alexander's blockading vessels and were ultimately destroyed in the engagement.

SIEGE OF TYRE

332 BC

SIEGE OF TYRE

As the mole neared the walls of Tyre, work became more dangerous for the soldiers and labourers. Then two large siege towers were destroyed by a Tyrian fire ship and Alexander was forced to stop construction until defences could be built to shield the workers.

(reigned 727–722 BC), who besieged Tyre for five years (724–720 BC), and the Babylonian Nebuchadnezzar (reigned 605–562 BC), who besieged it for 13 years (586–573 BC), discovered that trying to starve the Tyrian islanders into surrender was extremely difficult and costly. A direct attack on the strongly fortified island itself seemed nearly impossible.

Of course, the impossible did not deter Alexander the Great. Undoubtedly, he could have bypassed Tyre and proceeded on to Egypt, his furthest western goal. The Tyrians surely would have posed no military threat – although their fleet, allied with the Persians, was quite impressive. But Alexander's conquests were not simply about neutralizing military threats to his empire: he wanted to conquer the world, and Tyre was part of that world.

The question was how to do it. Alexander knew that the most effective siege was one that did not have to be waged, so,

initially, he sought surrender by negotiation: the Tyrians could live and thrive as they had always done, so long as they submitted to him without conflict. The land-based citizens quickly did so, but the islanders, believing their fortifications unassailable, did not.

Their fortifications were indeed impressive. Sturdy walls – reputed to reach 50m (164ft) in height – surrounded the entire island. Archaeological remains suggest that this was certainly an exaggeration. But it reflects the awe inspired in ancient writers who had seen the challenge facing Alexander. More important than their actual height, however, was the fact that the walls were built directly onto the island's coastline, with the sea butting against them. This meant that Alexander could not set up his impressive artillery on the land, and with the island lying 1km (0.6 miles) from the shore, even the largest artillery pieces could not reach it.

THE MACEDONIAN MOLE

Then, Alexander's engineers came up with a novel idea: they would build a mole to the island. This was, of course, easily said, but less easily done. Indeed, the enormity of this feat cannot be overstated. The mole had to

be deep enough to extend to the sea floor, wide enough to enable several catapults to be lined up on it, and, of course, long enough to reach from the shore to the island. In addition, those building the mole would be virtually unprotected from the ravages of the sea or from attacks launched from Tyre's walls and ships.

It was decided that the mole would be built using stakes driven deep into the seabed, with mud, wood and stones filling the spaces in between. It was also quite wide – it may have been as much as 500–600m (1640–1968ft), although this is probably an exaggeration – and was constructed by a combination of conscripted labour and all of Alexander's soldiers. According to the Roman historian Quintus Curtius, the sight of Alexander's soldiers labouring brought taunts from the Tyrians on the walls facing the mole. However, such mockery did not distract Alexander's disciplined troops from doing their duty. Indeed, Alexander himself lent a hand, and may even have joined his engineers in directing the construction work.

Work on the mole progressed slowly and, at least early on, without difficulty. But as the depth of the channel between island and shore reached three fathoms (6m/20ft), the work became more difficult and more dangerous. Catapults on the walls and on Tyrian vessels – the technology was also known there, although most historians believe that they had not developed beyond *gastraphetes* – fired continually on the unprotected builders, whose armour was too cumbersome and hot for construction work of this kind.

Alexander responded by building two large siege towers at the end of the mole. Torsion catapults were placed on top of these towers, and archers filled the lower decks. The Tyrians sent in a large fire ship, filled with sulphur and pitch, and with the stern heavily weighted so that the bow rose onto the mole next to the towers. Surprisingly, this worked, and both towers were destroyed, leaving the mole unprotected once more. In response, Alexander stopped construction long enough to widen and reinforce the mole's sides. Breakwaters were also added.

These changes did the trick. The Tyrians continued their assaults against the mole, but none were now effective. Fire ships and

Alexander's lighter penteconters, *with their single bank of oars, proved faster and more manoeuverable than the Tyrian multi-banked* quinqueremes, quadriremes *and* triremes.

catapult attacks from the walls and ships did less damage than previously, while more drastic attempts at disrupting Alexander's siege also failed: divers sent underwater to dismantle the wooden substructure could not pull tree branches from the mud and stones, and heavy stones fired from the town simply became part of the mole. In the meantime, Alexander's blockade of the city had grown as allies began sending ships to assist him. Eventually, the Tyrians attempted to break through this blockade with their own fleet, sending three quinqueremes, three quadriremes and seven triremes against them. But the Macedonian and allied ships, as capably led as the other parts of Alexander's military forces, outmanoeuvred, surrounded and defeated the heavier Tyrian vessels.

THE FALL OF TYRE

The inhabitants of Tyre could now rely only on their still formidable walls for protection against the Macedonian attackers. But the mole had reached the island and Alexander now had a platform to set up his torsion catapults. They fired continually on the wall. Elsewhere, his ships, now completely in charge of the sea, added to these attacks by using rams and firing their own catapults

Above: The core soldier of Alexander the Great's army was the Macedonian hoplite. Protected by a bronze helmet, torso armour and shield, and armed with a long lance – the sarissa *– and a short sword, the hoplite proved formidable on the battlefield but was also willing to lend a hand in the construction of a fortification or, at Tyre, the mole.*

SIEGE OF TYRE

Another view of the ruins from Tyre's ancient civilization confirms the size and wealth of the city. Alexander was forced to capture it to ensure the naval and logistical support of his armies in the Middle East and Egypt.

against other walls. The Tyrians had to split their defences between these locations. Still, they fought on, recognizing by this time that surrender would not save their lives. They added wooden towers to their walls; used long bladed poles to cut the ropes of rams; threw grappling hooks onto siege towers and catapults; poured hot sand and nets over Macedonian soldiers; and constantly repaired breaches in the walls. Indeed, so determined was their desperate fight that, according to Diodorus of Sicily (90–30 BC), Alexander even considered raising his siege of the city.

But, seven months into the siege, the Macedonian emperor had spent too much time and money to turn back. Finally, a breach in the southern side of the town was

made – quite far from the mole – and the Tyrians could not repair it before Alexander took advantage of the situation. Sailing his heavy Macedonian infantry to the site, he led them into the fight. Few in the ancient world could defend against a disciplined, well-trained, well-armed onslaught, led by one of the greatest generals in history, and certainly not the exhausted, poorly trained citizens of Tyre. The city quickly fell.

There is little doubt that Alexander the Great's leadership determined the outcome and assured the defeat of Tyre. His perseverance against reputedly impregnable defences seemed to know no limitations. His willingness to try all sorts of conventional and unconventional methods of attacking this island city had never previously been witnessed, nor would it be again until Caesar besieged Alesia in 52 BC. But Shalmaneser V and Nebuchadnezzar had seemed in their time equally determined to defeat Tyre, and they had both failed. Could it be, then, that Alexander's military technology, including his numerous torsion catapults, played the decisive role in his victory?

Left: At the siege of Tyre, both sides used screens to provide cover from missile fire. The screens allowed both the Tyrians and Macedoneans to move missile weapons and siege engines around while offering some protection to their crews.

Opposite: Despite Alexander's failure to conquer India and his death at a young age of 33, he is generally regarded as the greatest ancient military leader, as depicted in this Donata Creti (1671-1749) portrait.

CYNOSCEPHALAE
197 BC

THE BATTLE OF CYNOSCEPHALAE MATCHED THE TACTICAL FLEXIBILITY OF THE ROMAN LEGION AGAINST THE FIGHTING POWER OF THE MACEDONIAN PHALANX. WHILE NOTHING COULD STAND AGAINST THE HEAD-ON ATTACK OF THE PHALANX, GOOD TACTICS COULD DEFEAT IT.

WHY DID IT HAPPEN?

WHO A Roman army of about 26,000 men under the command of Consul Titus Quinctius Flaminius (c. 228–174 BC), opposed by an approximately equal number of Macedonians under Philip V (238–179 BC).

WHAT Manoeuvres by both sides led to an encounter battle that pitted the frontal power of the phalanx against the flexibility of the legion.

WHERE Southeast Thessaly, Greece.

WHEN 197 BC.

WHY Rome was concerned at the expansionist intent displayed by Philip V, and moved to counter his ambitions.

OUTCOME A crushing defeat for the Macedonians despite some local successes.

The phalanx, composed of large numbers of infantrymen armed with very long spears, was a powerful but unwieldy instrument. It had evolved as much as a result of social and economic conditions as military ones.

During the *polis* (city-state) period, no city could afford to maintain a large standing army, and nor could a general muster of the populace be away from the city for any length of time. The citizen-soldiers who fought for each city were also its economic lifeblood. While they were away at war, farms and businesses came to a standstill. Thus it was necessary to resolve conflicts as quickly as possible and get everyone back to work.

The result was a unique military system, in which the phalanx was the arm of decision. Formed of virtually every man who could be mustered, the phalanx was essentially a great block of pikemen that advanced towards its enemies and destroyed them quickly. Other troops did exist, including archers, slingers and cavalry, plus light infantry who guarded the flanks of the phalanx, but service in these units (even the cavalry) was of low status beside a place in the phalanx, which carried with it the fortunes of the city.

It required relatively little training for a man to be able to take his place in the phalanx, though handling the long pike was a tricky business. Many of the phalangites never even levelled their pikes at the enemy. Those in the front ranks used their weapons; the rest provided depth and 'pushing power'.

The advance of a phalanx was virtually unstoppable so long as it took place on relatively even ground and the formation retained its cohesion. Once broken up, or if attacked from the flank, the phalanx was vulnerable. Indeed, sometimes enemies got inside a phalanx from flank or rear and were able to cause a great deal of damage with knives and short swords among troops who were jammed close together and whose

A forest of spears. A frontal view of a Macedonian speira, *the unit making up the larger infantry phalanx. The ranks behind the front five would hold their counterweighted pikes aloft until required to fill a gap, and in the hope of deflecting incoming missiles.*

helmets (if they were rich enough to own one) restricted vision such that the threat might not even be noticed.

This problem aside, conventional wisdom had it that the only thing that could stand against a phalanx was another phalanx. The usual format for phalanx battles was that suitable ground would be chosen and the two forces would form up then advance against one another. Light troops might cause a minor nuisance, but this was rarely relevant to the outcome.

As the two phalanxes clashed, each presented a great wall of spear points to the other, driven home with all the force that thousands of men could muster. Several ranks could present their weapons over the shoulders of or between the men in front. Those behind kept their weapons vertical, which is said to have afforded some protection from missile weapons. Its appearance would certainly have been intimidating, making the enemy formation seem gigantic. The rearward men had an additional function – they kept the front ranks moving forward.

Once the charge had begun, a man could not turn aside even if he wanted to do so. Hemmed in by spear shafts and with hundreds of his fellow citizens shoving him forward, he could only fall down and be trampled to death – or else charge home like a true Greek warrior and hope to survive. Casualties in the first clash were always high among the front-rank men, yet this was the position of honour and front-rank positions were highly sought-after.

Assuming that one side did not panic and break before contact, and did not disintegrate at the first clash, the two formations would be locked together in something resembling a gigantic rugby scrum. The matter was now decided by the side that could shove the other harder. The effects of being driven bodily back were both physical and psychological.

Obviously, the side whose spear points were driving forward had an advantage in terms of causing casualties, but men moving forward can also keep on their feet better than those who are being driven back. Men who fell might be trampled, stabbed with daggers or done to death with the butt ends of pikes by the enemy rear ranks. The pike

had a spike on its reverse end for this purpose. With the weight of the long shaft behind it, this spike could tear through even a bronze breastplate.

In addition to its physical dangers, being shoved backwards was an indication that the formation was losing, and at some point morale would waver. As men broke away from the rear, the ability of the phalanx as a whole to resist would be diminished. The end would come suddenly, with the enemy suddenly surging forward to complete the ruin of the phalanx. Casualties as the unit broke were always heavy.

LOCATION

Cynoscephalae was an 'encounter battle', in which the goal was the destruction of the enemy force rather than a terrain objective. The battlefield was chosen by chance as much as by the generals involved.

This dramatic depiction of a Macedonian phalanx gives some indication of what the legionaries had to face. Each man in the front rank stands in a veritable forest of spearpoints.

THE OPPOSED FORCES

ROMANS (estimated)

Total:	**26,000**

MACEDONIANS (estimated)

Phalangites:	15,000
Other infantry:	10,000
Total:	**25,000**

A phalanx battle was thus often resolved in a matter of minutes, and it was graphically obvious who had won. Treaty negotiations would follow and the matter could be considered closed. The only way to prevent defeat in this sort of battle was to have a better, bigger, and/or stronger phalanx – or not to fight on these terms.

In the time of Alexander the Great (356–323 BC), the phalanx became more flexible, operating in smaller units with support from other troop types. This practice was continued after Alexander's death and formed the basis of Greek and Macedonian practice in warfare for many decades, for the simple reason that it worked. Although not the clumsy sledgehammer it had been, the phalanx of later Macedonian armies remained a fairly inflexible, though powerful, weapon. On its

own terms, it could defeat virtually anything other than a similar phalanx.

The phalanx was thus the main tool under the hand of Philip V of Macedonia as he set out to rebuild Macedonian influence in Greece and the Balkans. He achieved some minor successes but came into conflict with Rome in what became known as the First Macedonian War (214–205 BC). The Romans were at the time involved in a death struggle with Carthage; they were content to contain the situation and prevent Philip from providing assistance to the Carthaginians. A peace was agreed in 205 BC, which lasted for just five years.

SECOND MACEDONIAN WAR

Philip again began annexing territory, some of it from city-states allied with Rome. He was warned off but continued to expand his power until Rome was forced to act. An ultimatum was presented – Philip was to accept Roman overlordship or face the consequences. Whether the Romans thought Philip would acquiesce in their demand, which would convert Macedonia into a Roman province, or this was simply a way to generate a pretext for war is unclear. In any case, the proposal was rejected and the Second Macedonian War (200–196 BC) was begun.

The Romans were not unprepared. Their forces, under the command of Consul Titus Quinctius Flaminius, were based in Thebes, and as soon as war broke out they advanced on Pherae in Thessaly. Philip, meanwhile, had concentrated his forces at Larissa to the northwest and moved to meet his enemies.

The Macedonians' main capability was provided by their phalanx, which was around 15,000 strong. On the other hand, the Roman force was built around a solid core of professional legionaries, with allied and auxiliary troops including war elephants, Numidian cavalry and Cretan archers.

Scouts on both sides located the enemy and a brief clash took place near Pherae, in which the Roman cavalry defeated their opposite numbers. Nothing decisive was achieved and contact was broken as both forces turned aside to forage.

Titus Quinctius Flaminius was a talented leader who was young for his position but extremely effective. His success in Greece was as much due to his political abilities as his generalship.

CONTACT REGAINED

After a period of groping about in the hills in very poor weather, both sides were somewhat disordered and unsure of exactly where the enemy was. Another minor encounter took place when some Roman cavalry stumbled upon the Macedonians' camp. Things initially went well for the Romans, who received reinforcements and were able to force Philip to take up a defensive position on the ridge known as Cynoscephalae.

However, the success did not last and the Roman detachment was forced to withdraw after a time. Philip led his army down the ridge to where the Roman army was arrayed. His force was not in good order as a result of trying to deploy in contact with the enemy.

A Roman legion versus a phalanx: the legionaries throw their spears in an attempt to disrupt the phalanx. They then close with the formation, trying to get into hand-to-hand combat range, where the superior sword-fighting skills of the Romans will tell.

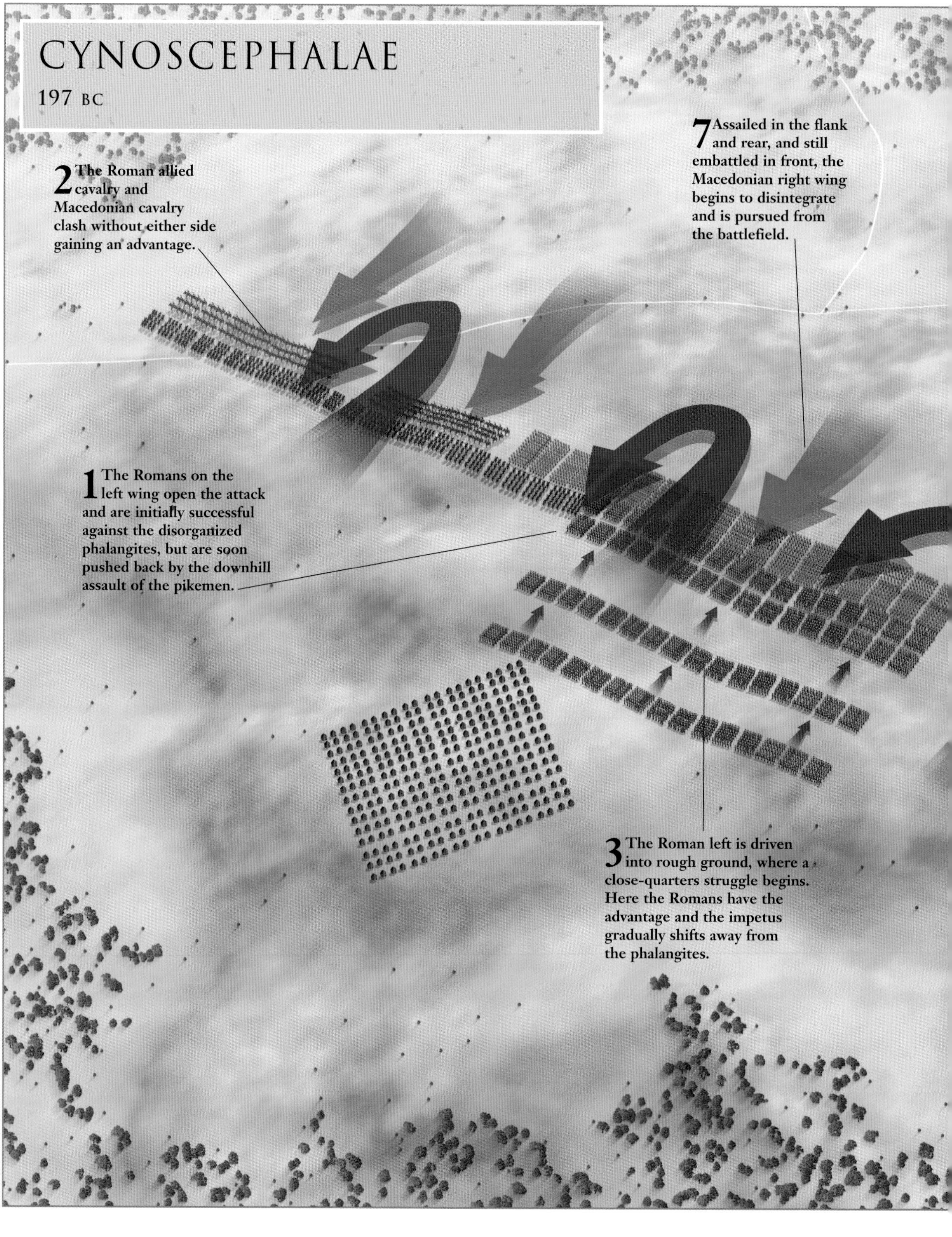

CYNOSCEPHALAE

197 BC

7 Assailed in the flank and rear, and still embattled in front, the Macedonian right wing begins to disintegrate and is pursued from the battlefield.

2 The Roman allied cavalry and Macedonian cavalry clash without either side gaining an advantage.

1 The Romans on the left wing open the attack and are initially successful against the disorganized phalangites, but are soon pushed back by the downhill assault of the pikemen.

3 The Roman left is driven into rough ground, where a close-quarters struggle begins. Here the Romans have the advantage and the impetus gradually shifts away from the phalangites.

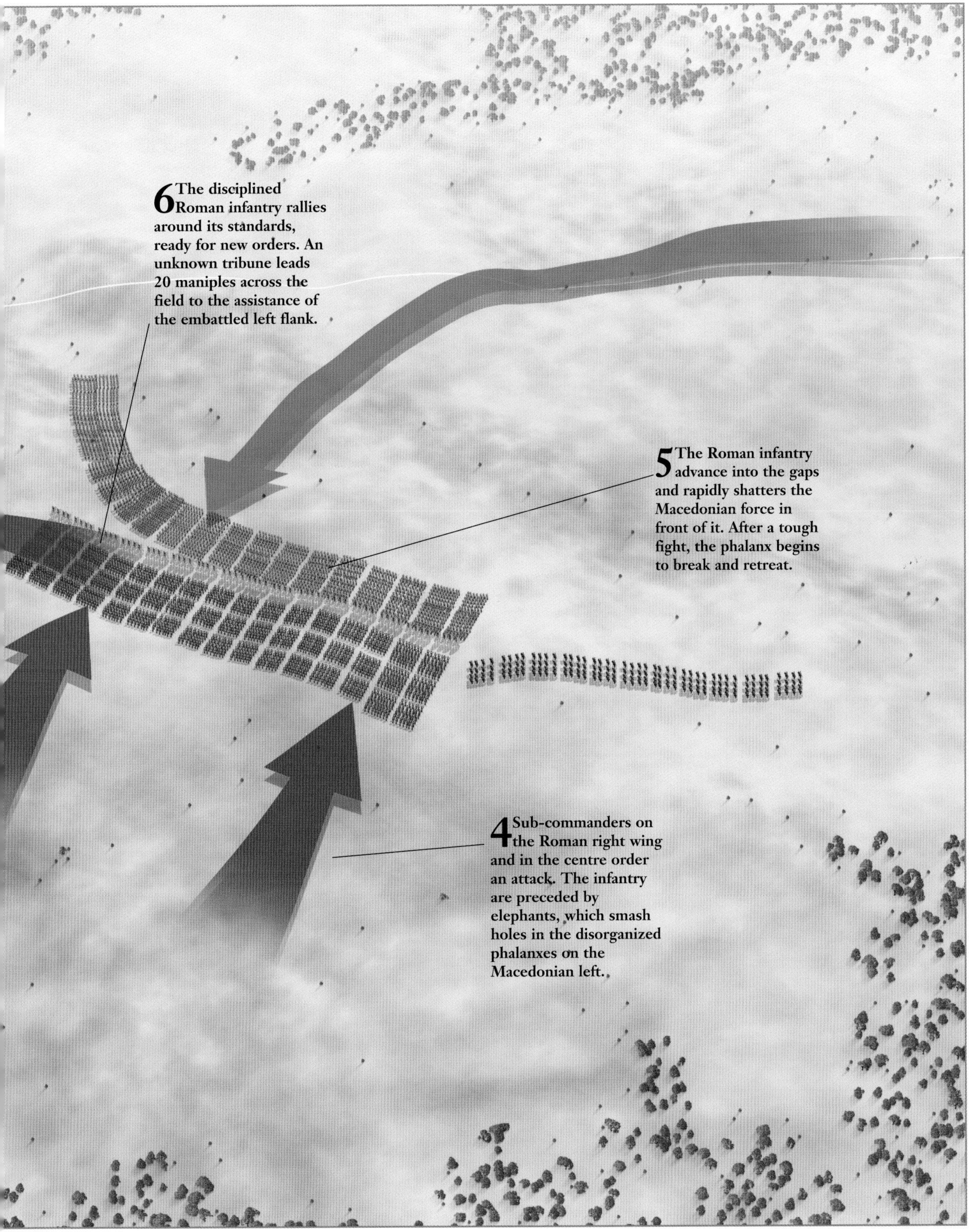

6 The disciplined Roman infantry rallies around its standards, ready for new orders. An unknown tribune leads 20 maniples across the field to the assistance of the embattled left flank.

5 The Roman infantry advance into the gaps and rapidly shatters the Macedonian force in front of it. After a tough fight, the phalanx begins to break and retreat.

4 Sub-commanders on the Roman right wing and in the centre order an attack. The infantry are preceded by elephants, which smash holes in the disorganized phalanxes on the Macedonian left.

Philip V of Macedon had a difficult relationship with Rome. At times his kingdom was a Roman ally, but suspicions between the two inevitably led to more troubles.

THE BATTLE OPENS

Flaminius had gained time to deploy to his satisfaction, and attacked with his left wing, composed mainly of light infantry. They were assisted by the detachment that had previously been sent to reinforce the troops fighting on the ridge. The Macedonian phalangites had a significant advantage in head-on combat of this sort. Advancing downhill against troops with much shorter weapons, Philip's men were able to shove the Romans back.

Cohorts of the Roman army were subdivided into three groups: Principes, Hastati *and* Triarii, *each screened by* Velites (*light troops*). *The* Hastati *opened the fight, with* Principes *and* Triarii *rotating in turn into the front line to ensure that men did not become exhausted.*

Flaminius' retreat took his left wing into rough ground, where the phalanx was at a disadvantage. As the massed ranks broke up and the advance lost momentum, the phalangites dropped their pikes and drew their sidearms – a mix of swords and long daggers. Now the fighting was on approximately equal terms, with both sides using hand weapons.

The phalanx continued to force its way forward, largely due to its mass and momentum. However, this is what the Romans trained for all the time, and it was much more to their liking than being stabbed with long spears from several metres away.

SUCCESS ON THE RIGHT

With the Roman commander-in-chief hotly engaged on his army's left, the centre and right were under local command. In some armies this might have been a problem, but the Romans had a clear and efficient command structure. More importantly, sub-commanders were encouraged and even expected to act without waiting for orders.

The Romans had a few elephants available, and these were sent at the advancing enemy on the right. The infantry followed. Had the Macedonians been in good order, they might have withstood the attack. Unfortunately, they were not. As a result, the war elephants punched deep into their disordered ranks, opening up dangerous gaps, which the infantry was able to exploit.

In this sort of close-quarter fight, individuals and small combat teams counted for more than large formations. The Romans were well-trained, capable soldiers who were confident in their own abilities and the support of their comrades. They quickly smashed the Macedonian force in front of them and sent it fleeing up the ridge.

A TRIBUNE'S INITIATIVE

The Roman army had started out as a phalanx-type force, which meant that it sometimes suffered for a lack of flexibility.

The result was a subdivision of the legion into maniples of about 120 men, each with its own commander and insignia. More importantly, the legionaries were trained to rally as a unit, and thus remained under the control of their officers even when recovering from a rout or, as in this case, when disorganized after combat.

The result was that even though it had just been through a hard fight, the Roman right was able to quickly throw itself into some kind of order, ready to respond to new commands almost immediately. However, this capability would have been of little use but for the initiative of a tribune who saw that the Roman left wing was struggling.

Greeks respond joyfully to the announcement that Rome has liberated them from Macedon. Flaminius' campaign was launched in response to empire-building by Philip V.

Tribunes were effectively 'spare officers' in a Roman legion. Most of the time, they functioned as staff officers and carried out administrative and routine duties, but they were also available to command detachments and carry out whatever other tasks needed the oversight of an officer. Although not directly in the chain of command, they could give orders where necessary, and in this case the intervention of a tribune was decisive.

The tribune (whose name is not known) ordered a number of maniples in the advancing Roman right wing to wheel and advance along the ridge, falling on the flank and rear of Philip's thus-far-successful right phalanx. As many as 20 maniples (more than 2000 troops) are recorded as having been redirected in this manner, smashing into the enemy rear in a disciplined but highly aggressive onslaught.

ROMAN VICTORY

Faced with hard-fighting enemies in front and assailed in the rear, and with its flank supports rapidly disappearing over the ridgeline, the Macedonian right collapsed

This reconstruction of the decisive battle of Pydna (168 BC) demonstrates how the broken ground disrupted the Macedonian phalanx, allowing the Romans to close with the phalangites and use their superior swordsmanship to good effect.

of the Second Macedonian War, a treaty concluding the conflict the following year. Philip was permitted to retain his throne, as this suited Roman foreign policy, but he had to pay a huge indemnity and disband most of his army and navy. In addition, Rome declared that many city-states which had formerly been vassals of Macedonia were now independent or allied to Rome, essentially ending the days of Macedonia as a major power.

Trouble between Rome and Macedonia would flare up again, and legion and phalanx would clash once more at Pydna in 168 BC. The result then would be the same – the phalanx was potent in a head-on collision but was too unwieldy to survive once drawn into rough ground or when fighting more flexible troops who could evade the initial charge.

The casualty figures at Cynoscephalae speak for themselves – about 13,000 Macedonians were slain for just 700 Roman losses. The day of the phalanx was over and the legion was in the ascendant. To this day, the legion's combination of fighting power and flexibility remains an ideal many militaries can only aspire to.

A Macedonian phalangite's back and breastplates. Armour of this sort was heavy and could restrict movement but offered the soldier good protection from arrows and spearpoints. His long pike prevented most other weapons from getting close enough to be effective.

into rout. Huge numbers of casualties were inflicted as the phalangites tried to fight their way free; Flaminius ordered a short pursuit to cement the victory. Afterwards, the Roman force rallied and was combat-ready once again, long before its foes had even stopped fleeing.

The collapse of the Macedonian army at Cynoscephalae effectively marked the end

THE HUNS' CAMPAIGN AGAINST EASTERN ROME

AD 441–444

IN THE FOURTH CENTURY, RIDING OFF THE CENTRAL ASIAN STEPPES CAME AN ARMY OF NOMADIC WARRIORS, THE HUNS. FAMOUS FOR THE SPEED AND BREADTH OF THEIR CONQUESTS, INFAMOUS FOR THEIR RUTHLESSNESS, THE HUNS WERE ACTUALLY DIVERSE PEOPLE WHO WERE UNITED BY CHARISMATIC LEADERS, THE MOST FAMOUS OF WHOM WAS ATTILA. THEY WERE ALSO UNITED BY THE WEAPONS THEY USED, NOTABLY THE RECURVED COMPOSITE BOW.

WHY DID IT HAPPEN?

WHO A large Hunnic army led by the famous Attila (406–53) and his brother, Bleda (c.390–445), campaigned throughout the Eastern Roman Empire.

WHAT The Huns marched through Southeastern Europe on a campaign that took them virtually to the walls of Constantinople.

WHERE The Eastern Roman Empire from the Danube River throughout the Balkans and into Anatolia.

WHEN From 441 to 444 AD.

WHY Breaking a peace treaty with the Huns by suspending his tribute payments, Emperor Theodosius provoked a campaign that devastated much of his empire.

OUTCOME The numerous victories of the Huns forced the Romans to negotiate the Treaty of Anatolius, which, among other things, markedly increased their tribute payments.

Anglo-American military historians revere the longbow used by medieval English archers as one of the most important weapons the world has ever known, frequently describing the weapon as 'invincible' and 'decisive'. In fact, the longbow had a very limited chronological and geographical impact on warfare. No one apart from the English used it, and even they used it effectively only from about 1330 to 1450. Other states, though, did hire English longbow companies to fight in their armies. For example, they fought on all sides in the Italian Wars of the fourteenth century and in Charles the Bold's Burgundian forces in his wars against French King Louis XI (1423–1483) in the 1460s and 1470s (sometimes called the War of the Public Weal), against the Liégeois in 1466–68 and against the Swiss and Lorrainers in 1475–77.

Of far greater influence, and for much longer, was the recurved composite bow. Appearing first in the ancient world – although it is uncertain exactly when – and popular among nomadic tribes, especially those of the Steppes in Central Asia, the recurved bow was first effectively used during the barbarian invasions of the Late Roman Empire. Late Roman authors commented on the accuracy and power of the weapon used by Visigothic archers, and accord them an important role in deciding victory for the Visigoths at the battle of Adrianople in AD 378 and throughout the rest of their conquests.

The large number of arrowheads found in Visigothic graves in Spain suggest the bow was widely used. From these, it can also be determined that the Visigoths shot a short arrow with an iron head, of varying shapes,

Theodosius II, Emperor of the Eastern Roman Empire, built the great circuit of walls around Constantinople. Some have suggested that this gave him the confidence to try and withstand the Huns. Others claimed it bankrupted his treasury and forced him to suspend the Empire's tribute payments to them.

from a bow of only around 150cm (5ft) in length.

THE HUNS

It is not certain when or where the Huns originated or why they moved out of their homelands to attack their neighbours in the fourth and fifth centuries. The best theory – though it is unsupported by solid evidence – is that they originated in the Steppe regions of Siberia and Mongolia, and were pushed out by those who would later be called the Mongols. The Huns first appeared in the west at the end of the fourth century, when it is reported that they attacked Germanic tribes living to the north and west of the Danube. In desperation, these barbarians then crossed the river into the Roman Empire, the Huns following after them. Immediately, the Romans seized upon the fearsome military skills of the Huns and hired large numbers as mercenaries. It was a decision that the Roman Empire would quickly come to regret. The Huns' style of warfare was not entirely unknown to either the barbarians or the Romans, although neither had ever seen it used on such a large scale. Primarily fighting as cavalry and mounted archers, the Huns used a speed and agility against Roman forces not seen for centuries. Ammianus Marcellinus's famous description of the Huns, although exaggerating some of their characteristics, shows a contemporary Roman perception of their new enemies:

They are not well suited to infantry battles, but are nearly always on horseback, their horses being ill-shaped, but hardy; and sometimes they even sit upon them like women if they want to do anything more conveniently. There is not a person in the whole nation who cannot remain on his horse day and night. On horseback they buy and sell, they take their meat and drink, and there they recline on the narrow neck of their steed, and yield to sleep so deep as to indulge in every variety of dreams. And when any deliberation is to take place on any weighty matter, they all hold their common council on horseback. … Sometimes, when provoked, they fight; and when they go into battle, they form in a solid body, and utter all kinds of terrific yells.

They are very quick in their operations, of exceeding speed, and fond of surprising their enemies. With a view to this, they suddenly disperse, then reunite, and again, after having inflicted vast loss upon the enemy, scatter themselves over the whole plain in irregular formations: always avoiding the fort or an entrenchment.

Initially hired in relatively small numbers to fight the other barbarian tribes attacking the Roman Empire, the Huns began to increase their presence just as the Romans began to lose unity and power. Defeat at Adrianople was devastating, but their inability to rebuild their forces speedily and protect their people made that single victory all the more important. When other invaders could also not be stopped, the Roman Empire began its historical fall. Even as members of their armies, the Huns could not help, for they quickly took on the role of invaders themselves. By AD 405, a large number of Huns, perhaps the majority of those within imperial borders, had turned

THE HUN ARCHER

The recurved bow was of composite construction in that the stave was a combination of wood, horn and sinew. The sinew – generally taken from a deer or other strong, fast animal – was softened in boiling water to be moulded into the required shape. Strips of sinew were glued with a strong but flexible adhesive onto the outside of a wooden piece cut to the desired length of the bow. Strips of horn were then glued to the inside. The combination of materials, the sinew strong in tension and the horn strong in compression, produced a highly effective, springlike stave. Recurved bows were built so that their arms, when in the relaxed state, bent forward.
Nocks, cut with a groove in them to fit the bowstring, were then glued to the tips of the arms. In order to string the bow, its arms needed pulling back and the bowstring, made of flax or hemp, linked between the two. At that point, the arms took a recurved shape – hence the name 'recurved bow' – and when the string was retracted, it could deliver an arrow with very impressive ballistic force. Because even small recurved bows could deliver a powerful shot, they could also be used from horseback. Late Roman sources describe Visigothic armies with both infantry and cavalry archers, although the foot archers were more numerous, as was true for the Vandals. But the Huns, enemies to both the Romans and the other barbarians, used their recurved bows primarily as mounted archers.

LOCATION

HUN TERRITORIES

Chersonesus ✣   Constantinople ●

EASTERN ROMAN EMPIRE

The Huns controlled lands to the north of the Danube River; the Eastern Romans, the lands to the south. A battle fought in the Chersonesus Valley brought victory to the Huns in the campaign of 441–444.

THE HUNS CAMPAIGN AGAINST EASTERN ROME

against the Romans and the citizens of the Empire.

These Huns are said to have fought with a confidence and a ferocity rarely seen in soldiers prior to this time. According to the contemporary military theorist Vegetius, they were far better than contemporary Roman soldiers. In part, this was due to the Huns' training and discipline: they were able to perform military manoeuvres on the battlefield with a speed and dexterity that could only have come from years of being on horseback. But it was also due to the use of the recurved bow by Hun mounted archers. However, the Huns were actually not a single tribe but a number of diverse tribes from the Steppes. That they were to come together under one leader is actually quite impressive considering their bellicose historical reputation. The Romans seem to have been effective in uniting them as

---

Attila 'the Hun' has become the legendary archetype of a barbarian, inspiring centuries of artistic flourish. This painting has Attila leading his cavalry. The arms and armour are incorrect, especially as none of the horsemen is shown using a bow.

mercenary troops under Roman command, indicating, perhaps, a willingness to be led, even by non-Huns, when the results were profitable. However, as the Romans discovered, the Huns did not remain loyal to their employers if the relationship ceased to be profitable.

HUN TACTICS

The Huns' main fighting force was light cavalry, all carrying composite bows, and some also carrying spears and swords. This cavalry would not ride directly into an opposing force as in a charge, but around them, firing as they passed. These mounted archers were especially skilful, able to shoot their bows with great accuracy from either side of their horses at full gallop. They would also fire across the rear of their horses, in order to protect themselves and their companions as they withdrew from an attack or in case of retreat.

Their bows were not overly powerful and could not shoot arrows capable of penetrating their opponents' armour, although their barbed arrows were devastating and often fatal against unarmoured enemies or the unprotected

parts of armoured soldiers. The Huns' bows were integral to these tactics and so, too, were their horses. Hunnic horses, known as 'Steppe ponies', were light, short and fast. They could also travel for long distances without tiring, although Ammianus Marcellinus remarks that most Hun cavalry soldiers travelled with several horses during times of war, allowing them to change mounts frequently to preserve their horses' strength.

The Huns' horses were also almost exclusively mares, as the milk of a mare could sustain the life of the warrior on campaign and they were easier to control than stallions. It is also thought that the Huns' horses may have been the ancestors of the modern Mongolian horse, the mares standing an average of 127cm (50in) high and capable of being productively milked four to five times a day.

BLEDA AND ATTILA

The leader of the Huns with the most ruthless reputation was Attila (AD 406–453). He came to power at some point after AD 434, when he and his brother, Bleda (c. AD 390–445), inherited the leadership of

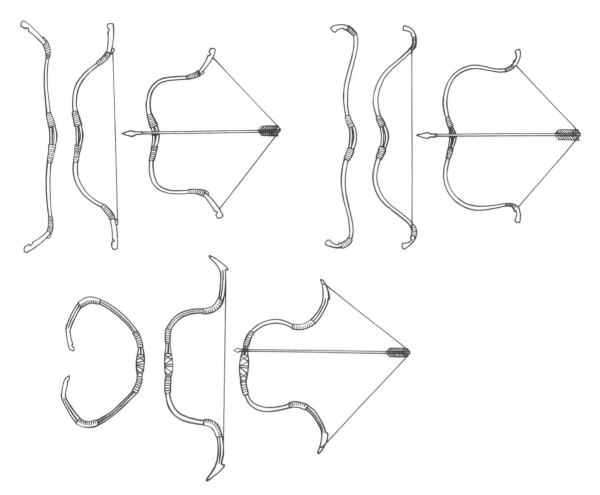

the Huns from their uncle Rua (or Ruga/Rugila, d. AD 434), and he played strong political and military roles among them until his death. Unfortunately, almost all we know about Attila, his life and campaigns, comes from his enemies, who are invariably in awe of the man, seemingly fearful of depicting him as anything less than larger than life. Perhaps this is why contemporary and later Christian chroniclers describe him as 'The Scourge of God'. Better to depict him as the tool of divine punishment rather than suggest that God was powerless to stop someone who cared so little for Christians. Although it is not known how old or militarily experienced Attila and Bleda were at their inheritance, it is thought that they had been raised to take over their uncle's throne, which means that they were probably brought up with all the necessary training in arms and armour, martial strategy and

politics. No doubt they had participated in combat since they were young.

Rua had been actively campaigning on both sides of the Danube and the Rhine Rivers for many decades, fighting at times against the Romans and at other times with them, the latter conflicts principally targeting Burgundians, Visigoths or other Romans. The Huns were ruthless in these wars, as can be seen in a contemporary description of their fighting in Auvergne: 'with raid and fire, and sword and barbarity, and pillage, they were destroying everything in their path, betraying and making void the name of peace.'

Rua died at the outset of a campaign season in AD 434, in which he was planning to invade the Eastern Roman Empire. His death relieved the Romans there, and even the Patriarch of Constantinople, Proclus (d. AD 446 or 447) – along with many other preachers – exulted that God was protecting

Three types of composite bow. Top left, Mongolian bow; top right, Scythian bow; bottom, Turkish composite bow. Most extant recurved composite bows – all dating from the modern period – are shaped like the drawing of the lowest bow here. This would mean that the arms would also bend as depicted here. As this does not match early illustrations of recurved bows, some historians have suggested a less dramatic recurving, as shown in the other two bows, with, however, a consequent loss of power.

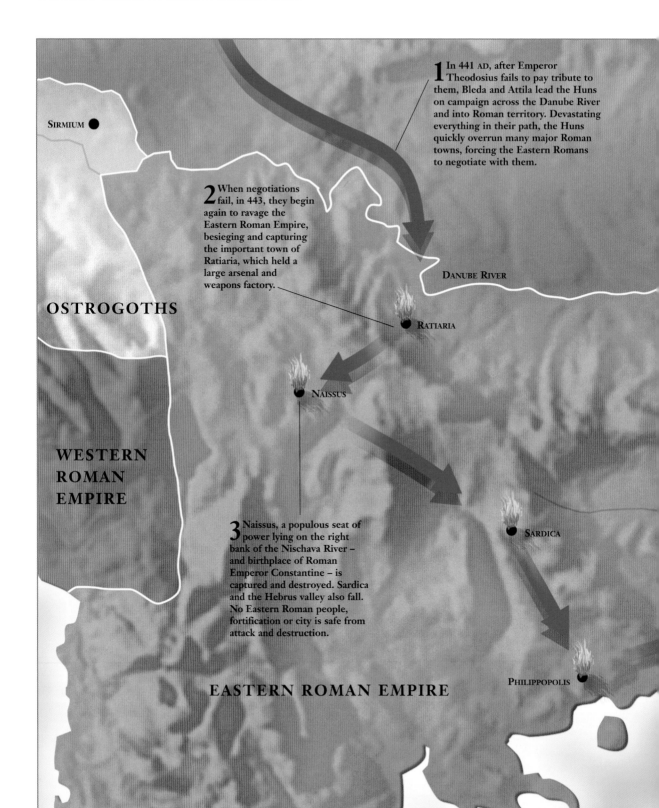

SIRMIUM

1 In 441 AD, after Emperor Theodosius fails to pay tribute to them, Bleda and Attila lead the Huns on campaign across the Danube River and into Roman territory. Devastating everything in their path, the Huns quickly overrun many major Roman towns, forcing the Eastern Romans to negotiate with them.

2 When negotiations fail, in 443, they begin again to ravage the Eastern Roman Empire, besieging and capturing the important town of Ratiaria, which held a large arsenal and weapons factory.

DANUBE RIVER

OSTROGOTHS

RATIARIA

NAISSUS

WESTERN ROMAN EMPIRE

SARDICA

3 Naissus, a populous seat of power lying on the right bank of the Nischava River – and birthplace of Roman Emperor Constantine – is captured and destroyed. Sardica and the Hebrus valley also fall. No Eastern Roman people, fortification or city is safe from attack and destruction.

EASTERN ROMAN EMPIRE

PHILIPPOPOLIS

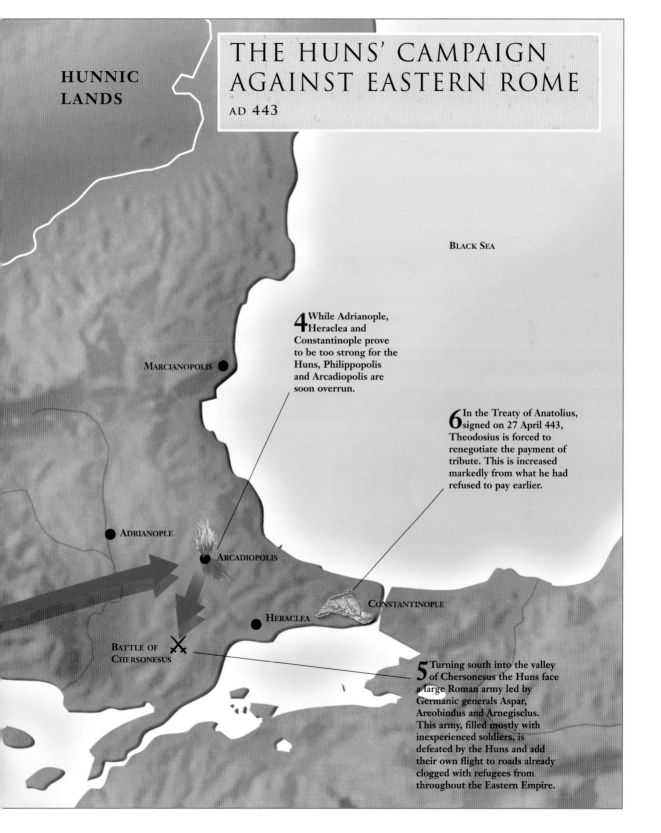

HUNNIC
LANDS

THE HUNS' CAMPAIGN AGAINST EASTERN ROME

AD 443

BLACK SEA

MARCIANOPOLIS

4 While Adrianople, Heraclea and Constantinople prove to be too strong for the Huns, Philippopolis and Arcadiopolis are soon overrun.

6 In the Treaty of Anatolius, signed on 27 April 443, Theodosius is forced to renegotiate the payment of tribute. This is increased markedly from what he had refused to pay earlier.

ADRIANOPLE

ARCADIOPOLIS

CONSTANTINOPLE

HERACLEA

BATTLE OF
CHERSONESUS

5 Turning south into the valley of Chersonesus the Huns face a large Roman army led by Germanic generals Aspar, Areobindus and Arnegisclus. This army, filled mostly with inexperienced soldiers, is defeated by the Huns and add their own flight to roads already clogged with refugees from throughout the Eastern Empire.

A Roman soldier from the fifth century AD was very different from those who had fought with Caesar and Mark Antony. They were not as disciplined or well trained. They were also more poorly armed and armoured. Frequently, as illustrated here, irregular Roman troops – drawn from city militias and the peasantry – were protected only by a rudimentary helmet and wooden shield. They carried spears and short swords, but rarely knew how to use them well.

his own against such a bellicose non-Christian barbarian. But relief was brief, as Attila and Bleda took immediate and unimpeded control of their uncle's forces, with Bleda seemingly the clear leader. He was gregarious and confident, with a particular fondness for a dwarf named Zerco, whom Attila detested. Attila, on the other hand, was serious, unbending and somewhat sullen. Where Bleda was confident, perhaps to excess, Attila was cautious in equal measure.

Nevertheless, together the brothers made extremely effective replacements for Rua and continued his plans to invade the Eastern Empire. Meeting with Constantinopolitan ambassadors outside the walls of Margus in AD 435, Bleda and Attila remained mounted on their horses, forcing their counterparts – who were less used to being on horseback – also to remain painfully mounted. The agreement hatched out also favoured the Huns, with the Eastern Romans agreeing to pay an annual tribute of 700lb (318kg) of gold and to accept a ransom of eight *solidi* for every escaped Roman prisoner the Huns refused to return; at the same time, the Romans were to return all their Hunnic prisoners.

For five years, this peace treaty with the Huns held. Attila and Bleda were not inactive, with campaigns reported against the Scythians and Sorosgi between the Black and Aral Seas, and others as far north as the Baltic Sea. This has allowed some historians to speculate that the Hunnic Empire was much larger than previous thought. Fairly soon after agreeing to the treaty, however, the Eastern Emperor Theodosius (AD 401–450) failed to pay the gold tribute or to return recently captured Hun prisoners. Some have speculated that Theodosius felt more confident after the recent completion (AD 439) of his circuit of walls around Constantinople. Others believe that he found dealing with Hunnic-subjugated tribes nearer his

borders more profitable than the Huns themselves, who were fighting far from the Eastern Roman Empire at the time. Or it may simply be that these and other reasons made Theodosius believe it was safe not to pay such a burdensome tribute.

Additionally, in AD 439, Roman military interests had switched to North Africa, where the Vandals had defeated Carthage, and to Armenia, where the Persians had invaded. Northern Africa was of more concern to the Western Empire, although Theodosius did send men and ships in a vain attempt to help them out there. But Armenia was almost solely the responsibility of the Eastern Empire, and they responded by sending a huge army – including some Hun mercenaries from the Ephthalites or 'White Huns' not associated with Attila or Bleda – thereby so denuding the western borders of troops that Attila and Bleda saw their chance to punish the Romans for failing to keep the Treaty of Margus.

CAMPAIGNS OF AD 441–443

The Hun campaign of AD 441 began with the capture of a Roman fort north of the Danube, which had been used for many years as a trading depot and was previously untouched by the Huns. Not only the fall but the brutality of the attack – made at market-time when the greatest number of civilians were present – was quickly reported to Constantinople. Theodosius naturally protested, claiming this violated provisions of the very Treaty of Margus that he had himself been openly violating. Of course, his protestations went unheeded.

The Huns then crossed the Danube and began attacking Roman fortifications and settlements on the southern bank of the river. Many were devastated, and the major urban centre of Viminacium was completely destroyed, all of its citizens being killed or taken prisoner. Next, Margus, the site of the ineffective AD 435 treaty, was destroyed. The town's bishop, who had overseen the earlier peace negotiations, is said to have opened the gates to the attackers. Other places suffered similar fates: Constantia, Singidunum (modern Belgrade) and Sirmium. Eventually, the campaign year drew to a close, the weather doing what the Romans had not been able to: stop the

Huns. Attila and Bleda's military achievements had been impressive.

In AD 443, the Huns began campaigning once again, AD 442 being a year of unexplained peace. Negotiations between the Romans and Huns had continued in the meantime, but had resulted only in stalling warfare for the year. Attila and Bleda could afford to be patient. At the same time, rather than taking time to recover some of their strength, the Eastern Roman political and military forces dissolved into infighting and jealousy. Indeed, one of the Germanic generals employed by Theodosius, a Vandal known as 'John, the Master of the Soldiers', was murdered by another Germanic general, Arnegisclus, who then replaced him. Morale at all levels naturally suffered, while the idea of effectively countering the Huns faded.

DOWN THE DANUBE

The Huns' campaign of AD 443 started with an eastward drive along the Danube. This initially yielded only a few undermanned fortresses until they came to another important and populous city of Ratiaria, which was besieged and quickly captured. Ratiaria controlled the Roman Danubian fleet and held a large arsenal and weapons factory, both of which fell to Attila and Bleda. The town was looted and destroyed, and its citizens taken away as slaves.

Following Ratiaria, the Huns approached the city of Naissus (Nish today), a populous seat of power lying on the right bank of the Nischava River near the Mediterranean that also held an arms factory. Yet its importance may have been more symbolic than strategic or military, as it was the birthplace of the great Emperor Constantine (c. AD 274–337). Once more, little resistance brought a quick result – total devastation.

Sardica (Sophia today) was also quickly overrun, as was the Hebrus valley (Maritza), Philippopolis and Arcadiopolis. No population, fortification or city seemed safe. Only Adrianople and Heraclea proved too large for conquest – the Huns did not even try, perhaps because they were already overburdened by booty and prisoners, but more probably because they would have

One of the most curious events of Attila's life was his meeting with Pope Leo I 'the Great' at Mincio in 452. Roman historians report that the Pope was able to convince Attila to stop his invasion of Italy. The truth, however, may be that Attila's army was so weakened by illness that the rewards Leo offered him made peace acceptable. In 1514, Raphael celebrated the meeting of Leo and Attila in a fresco for the Papal Palace at the Vatican.

Theodosius' wall at Constantinople protected that great city from conquest. Only twice did it fall, in 1204 to the Fourth Crusaders, and in 1453 to the Ottoman Turks. Even today, its ruins are breath-taking and speak to an age when strong stone walls surrounded all cities and towns, defending their inhabitants from all but the most determined foes.

slowed down their progress, speed being the strategy that Attila and Bleda relied on. Nor was an attack on Constantinople attempted, although the Huns were nearing the city at a pace that must have panicked most of the citizens, if not Emperor Theodosius himself.

So far, too, no Roman army had even tried to counter the Huns' campaign. Finally, outside of Arcadiopolis, an army appeared, led by three barbarian generals, Aspar (an Alan) (c. AD 400–471), Arcobindus (d.506) and Arnegisclus. Several small battles were fought, with the Romans defeated in all of them. Ultimately, using the speed, agility and lethality of their cavalry, the Huns forced their opponents into the Chersonesus valley, cutting off their retreat to Constantinople.

According to contemporary Roman sources, a major battle followed. Beyond that, however, the sources give no detail of what actually occurred on the battlefield, even how long the battle took.

Chersonesus was a significant defeat for the Romans, but it did not determine the fall of Eastern Roman Empire. However, Theodosius was forced into begging for terms before Bleda and Attila turned their forces against Adrianople, Heraclea or Constantinople. The walls of those cities

might have kept them safe for a while, but it is doubtful that any of them, even the imperial capital, would have been able to hold out until help could come from either the Persian theatre, where war also continued, or from the Western Empire, busy with the Vandals in North Africa. Strangely, perhaps, Attila declared terms of surrender: overdue tribute payments – estimated to be 6000lb (2722kg) of gold – were to be paid immediately, with future annual tributes tripled and ransoms increased to 12 *solidi* per Roman prisoner. The Romans were not to accept any Huns as prisoners. The Treaty, called after the city in which it was signed, Anatolius, was agreed on 27 August AD 443. The gold was paid, but the Romans had killed all of the Hun prisoners at the outset of the war, including some relatives of Bleda and Attila. No doubt recognizing that the Romans were hardly going to hold out on such a provision of the treaty, the Huns accepted both the gold and the proffered explanation.

AFTERMATH

Tensions remained high between the Eastern Romans and the Huns for several years following the Treaty of Anatolius. Yet, surprisingly, they never developed into further large-scale warfare. Skirmishes between the Romans and Huns were frequent, but never turned into anything more significant. For a few years, Theodosius and his Eastern Romans hunkered down behind their fortifications and faithfully paid their annual tribute, which must have been particularly burdensome with so little agricultural produce or trade coming in through the northern Imperial lands now controlled by the Huns. Unsurprisingly, in AD 446, the people of Constantinople failed to make their payment.

In AD 444, 445 or 446 – most historians believe it was AD 445 – Attila arranged for Bleda to be murdered and assumed complete control over the Huns. The reasons for this were reported in Priscus's chronicle, but unfortunately that part has been lost. Nor is it known how much disruption the assassination caused to Hunnic unity.

In AD 447, Attila tried to force the Eastern Romans to resume their tribute payments. But it appears they simply had no more to send to the Huns, so Attila again went on campaign, fighting all the way to the walls of Constantinople. As they approached the city, the Huns defeated two large but very inexperienced Roman armies. Yet, despite the walls having been damaged by an earthquake earlier that year, the Huns were unable to gain entrance to the city. Again the Eastern Romans were forced to seek a peace treaty, although it was one they could better afford.

Attila remained at peace with the Eastern Romans for the rest of his life. In spring AD 451, he again started a campaign, this time against the Western Roman Empire. Very little is known about this campaign prior to the Battle of the Catalaunian Plain, as the main sources give no details. They may have captured and sacked Metz and Trier and reached Paris, but there is only slim evidence for this. What is certain is that in June Attila began to besiege Orléans, a rich Roman city. But Orléans, the walls of which may have rivalled those of Constantinople and Rome, held on until a Roman and

Visigothic relief army, led by Roman General Aetius (c. AD 396–454), neared the city. In response, Attila decided to fight a battle on the Catalaunian Plains. This time, the Huns were soundly defeated.

The defeat did not destroy Attila's army, although it seems he was unable to recover completely. He tried to regroup in Hungary but, after turning his army south into Italy on another campaign in AD 452, he found that he no longer retained the same military status. He could not force the Romans to come to battle, and soon his soldiers were succumbing to the same diseases that would so often destroy forces invading Italy in the future. Ultimately, he was offered a way out by Pope Leo the Great (c. AD 390–461) – and took it. He agreed to go no further into Italy, in exchange for the small tribute offered, and left. The following year 'the Scourge of God' died, after an ignominious night of drinking and carousing, according to contemporary sources.

Attila's sons tried to keep their father's empire together, but they lacked both the skill and charisma to do so. Within a few years, the Huns' territory had been considerably reduced in size. Without unity and leadership, they seem to have simply disappeared from the pages of history. Hungary still carries their name and Hungarians still speak a Hunnic language, but there is little more to their legacy – except, that is, for the recurved composite bow. It never disappeared from history, and remained popular, especially among nomadic warrior bands. Even after the advent of gunpowder weapons, some missile troops in the Eastern Mediterranean region still preferred the more accurate power of the weapon that was used by the Huns and which helped to bring down the Roman Empire.

One wonders how the Huns were able to stay on their horses while firing their bows when they did not use stirrups. However, as the stirrup became more widely used, former equestrian techniques were lost, including the secrets of Hunnic cavalry warfare. The fact is, the Huns were superb horsemen who could fire their bows even at full gallop.

AD DECIMUM
13 September, AD 533

THE BATTLE OF AD DECIMUM WAS ONE OF MANY VICTORIES WON BY THE EXTREMELY TALENTED BELISARIUS. THE VANDALS' DEFEAT BY HIS EXPEDITION MARKED THE END OF THEIR ASCENDANCY AND A RENEWAL OF ROMAN GLORY, WITH THE USE OF HEAVILY-ARMOURED CAVALRYMEN, CALLED CATAPHRACTS, PROVING DECISIVE.

WHY DID IT HAPPEN?

WHO An Eastern Roman army numbering about 15,000 under the command of Flavius Belisarius (AD 505–565), opposed by about 11,000 Vandal troops under King Gelimer (AD 480–553).

WHAT The Romans, advancing on the Vandal capital, Carthage, were intercepted by Vandal forces, resulting in a hard-fought battle.

WHERE 16km (10 miles) south of Carthage, North Africa.

WHEN 13 September, AD 533.

WHY Belisarius and his army had been sent against the Vandals as part of the planned reconquest of the Western Roman Empire.

OUTCOME After almost being defeated, Belisarius' force emerged victorious.

The Roman Empire eventually grew too large to be effectively ruled from any one capital. With holdings from Spain to Turkey, to use modern-day divisions, the empire had a vast expanse of frontiers to protect and huge numbers of people to govern. For a time, all was well; victories in the field brought in plunder to swell the economy and kept foreign barbarians on the defensive.

However, there came a time when the frontiers could not be pushed back any further and the loot stopped coming in. Complacency and internal wrangling (often to the point of civil war) weakened the empire, even as its overlords became ever more corrupt.

Growth gave way to stagnation and eventually decline, though there were occasional resurgences as far-sighted or simply fortunate leaders took actions that seemed necessary to preserve the empire or some part of it. One such move was the division of the empire into eastern and western halves, allowing each to be better controlled. The first formal division of the empire came under Emperor Diocletian (AD 245–313), although reunification and redivision took place over the years until east and west separated once and for all on the death of Emperor Theodosius (AD 347–395).

By the time of Eastern Emperor Justin I (AD c. 450–527), the Western Empire was in deep decline. Territory had been given up, Italy had been conquered by Ostrogoths and Rome itself had been sacked. The eastern half was still powerful, however – sufficiently so that some dreamed of a restoration of the empire.

A nineteenth-century illustration of King Theodoric of the Ostrogoths entering Rome around AD 490. Rome's importance had greatly declined by this time, but its fall was a bitter blow all the same.

One man who was particularly enthused by this idea was Flavius Petrus Sabbatius Justinianus, known to history as Emperor Justinian I (AD 483–565). Justinian was a commoner whose uncle was a general in the Imperial Guard. He was adopted by Emperor Justin and educated in all things Roman. He served for a time in the guard and during Justin's nine-year reign was a close friend of the emperor, acting more or less as a regent as Justin became senile in the latter part of his reign.

GENERAL BELISARIUS

Justinian's succession to the throne of the Eastern Empire was a foregone conclusion, and once emperor in name as well as fact he surrounded himself with talented people and set about a mammoth adventure. He had decided to reconquer the West and thus restore the Roman Empire to its former glory.

This was a huge undertaking, and his main instrument was to be General Belisarius. Belisarius had already proven himself loyal and capable in putting down riots and fighting the enemies of the empire. With treaties in place securing peace for the Eastern Empire – at least for the foreseeable future – Belisarius could be spared to go west and begin his great task.

There was no shortage of possible objectives, though a retaking of Rome and Italy would logically feature high on a list of desired outcomes. However, events in North Africa provided an opportunity as well as something of a necessity for intervention.

For many years King Hilderic (d. AD 533) of the Vandals, a Germanic tribe who had established a kingdom in North Africa, had enjoyed good relations with the Eastern Empire, maintaining both political and especially religious links. Now, however, he had been deposed by his cousin Gelimer, who was less friendly. An appeal by Hilderic for aid provided Justinian with a pretext for invasion, and so Belisarius was sent to Africa with an army numbering around 15,000 men, of whom a proportion were allied barbarians and the rest imperial troops.

The troops under Belisarius' command were not the traditional Roman legionaries of times past. The changing circumstances

BYZANTINE CATAPHRACT

The main weapon of the cataphract was his lance, which was often employed in massed charges to smash a hole in enemy formations. Since stirrups were not then in use, the lance was not as effective a shock weapon as it would become later. To offset this, Roman cataphracts used the same saddle that Roman cavalry had used for many years. It had four horns that helped support the rider and keep him in place. Another method of increasing the impact of a cataphract's lance was to secure the weapon to the horse's neck and leg by means of chains, ensuring that the animal's weight was behind the lance when it struck. As back-up to his lance, the cataphract was armed with a sword or sometimes a mace, which he would use in close combat after the charge had smashed home. Some cataphracts were supported by lighter cavalry armed with bows, while some actually employed bows in addition to their other weapons. This permitted a range of combined-arms tactics.

of the empire had led to the adoption of far more cavalry than previously in order to permit marauding barbarians to be met on their own terms. The preponderance of cavalry allowed imperial forces to cover more territory and, overstretched as they were, this was a welcome development.

HEAVY CAVALRY

The main striking arm of Belisarius' army was composed of heavily armoured cavalrymen called cataphracts. These men were professional soldiers rather than noblemen, though in many other ways they resembled the armoured knights of later European history.

The main differences lay in the fact that they were not a social class as such and did not hold political power as a result of their status. They were also much more disciplined and responsive to commands than their feudal counterparts.

A number of variations on the theme of the heavily armoured cavalryman existed at the time, but most were referred to as cataphracts. Some used shields, some did not; armour might be scale mail, lamellar or chain mail, and in some cases was much heavier to the front than the rear.

Their role as mounted shock troops was common to all, however; and in all cases,

LOCATION

Mediterranean Sea

• Rome

Carthage ✛ Ad Decimum

Located on the northern tip of Africa, Carthage was in many ways a parallel of Rome, and had challenged Rome's place as master of the Mediterranean for many hundreds of years.

their horses were armoured to a greater or lesser degree.

Most commonly, the tactic was for the cataphract charge to be supported by archery from bow-armed comrades or specialist horse archers. This would 'crumble' the enemy line before the charge smashed it. The Romans themselves had been on the receiving end of this tactic in times gone by, notably in their wars against the Parthians of Asia, and were impressed by it. Infantry formed up in a mass solid enough to resist the lance charge made an excellent target for arrows, and once their formation had been broken up they became very vulnerable.

COMBINED OPERATIONS

Another cataphract tactic was for part of the formation to draw up with lances facing the enemy, acting as a shelter for their bow-armed comrades, who could then ride out, shoot and retire to reload or if threatened. It was noted that Persian cataphracts shot fast but with little effect while their Roman counterparts were much more deadly.

This evolution – somewhat reminiscent of the 'caracole' of later European history, in which heavy cavalry popped at the enemy with pistols instead of assaulting with their hand weapons – may seem wasteful of the fighting power of the cataphracts.

However, it was a tactic to which an enemy had little means of reply – the waiting lances were a profound deterrent to those thinking they might interfere with the archers' task – and represented a way to soften up and wear down a foe without risking serious losses.

In addition to all this, the Romans also experimented with the use of heavy darts, thrown just before the lance charge hit home. This recalled the way advancing Roman foot legionaries would hurl their *pila* just before impact with the enemy, causing confusion among the ranks, which they then exploited by getting stuck in with hand weapons.

The Western Empire was powerless to prevent the migration of Germanic tribes that pillaged their way across Europe. Here, Vandals are depicted sacking Rome herself.

AD DECIMUM

It was armoured cavalrymen, and not the heavy infantry of a previous era, that represented the main fighting force landed in North Africa by Belisarius. Gelimer must have been dismayed to hear that the Romans were coming for him. Nevertheless, he came out to fight, encountering the Roman army at a mile-marker on the coast, 16km (10 miles) south of Carthage. It was for this 'Ten-Mile Post' (*Ad Decimum*) that the subsequent battle was named.

GELIMER REACTS

Marching to meet the Romans with 11,000 men under his command, Gelimer was outnumbered, but this was not a serious

The ruins of Carthage. Having once been destroyed by Rome in the Punic Wars, Carthage was rebuilt and eventually taken as the capital of the Vandals' North African empire.

The more lightly-armoured Vandal cavalry proved no match for the Roman cataphracts' disciplined movement, despite the formers' numerical superiority.

THE OPPOSED FORCES

BYZANTINE ROMANS
(estimated, including large numbers of cataphracts)

Total:	**15,000**

VANDALS (estimated)

Total:	**11,000**

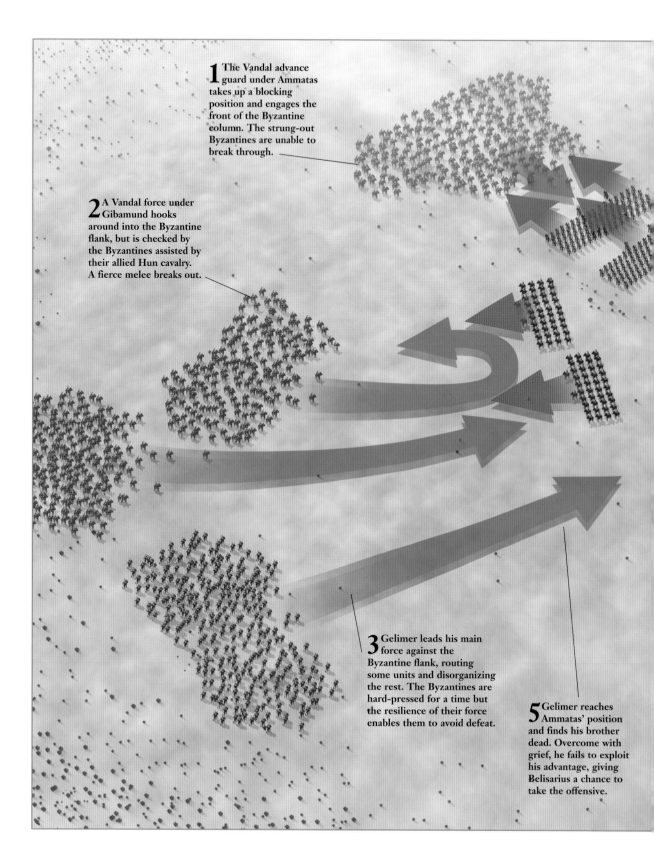

1 The Vandal advance guard under Ammatas takes up a blocking position and engages the front of the Byzantine column. The strung-out Byzantines are unable to break through.

2 A Vandal force under Gibamund hooks around into the Byzantine flank, but is checked by the Byzantines assisted by their allied Hun cavalry. A fierce melee breaks out.

3 Gelimer leads his main force against the Byzantine flank, routing some units and disorganizing the rest. The Byzantines are hard-pressed for a time but the resilience of their force enables them to avoid defeat.

5 Gelimer reaches Ammatas' position and finds his brother dead. Overcome with grief, he fails to exploit his advantage, giving Belisarius a chance to take the offensive.

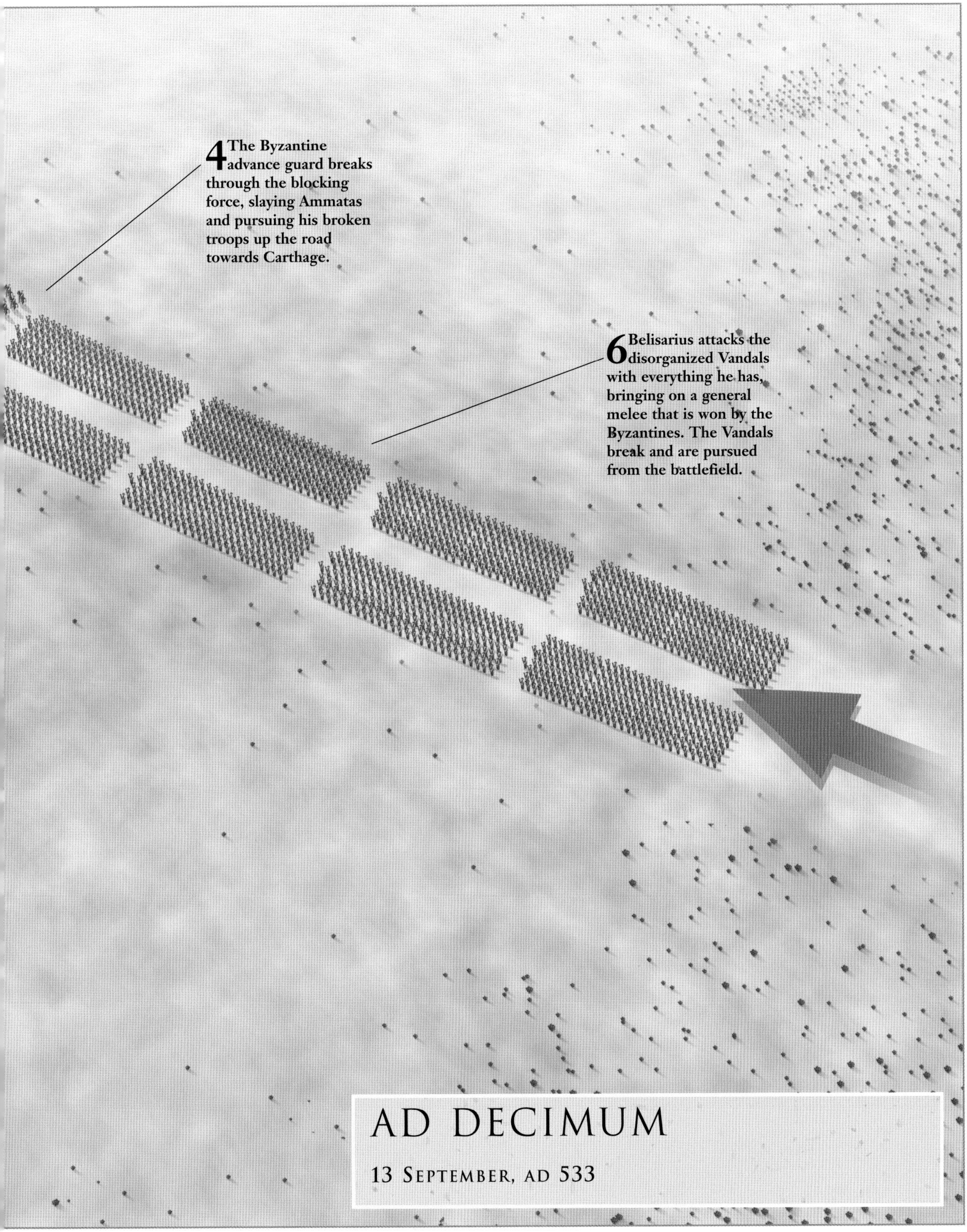

4 The Byzantine advance guard breaks through the blocking force, slaying Ammatas and pursuing his broken troops up the road towards Carthage.

6 Belisarius attacks the disorganized Vandals with everything he has, bringing on a general melee that is won by the Byzantines. The Vandals break and are pursued from the battlefield.

AD DECIMUM

13 SEPTEMBER, AD 533

problem since his troops were a powerful combat force. The best equipped of them wore conical metal helms and long mail coats, with less-well-off men more lightly armoured. They fought with spear and shield from horseback, with a sword as a sidearm. The Vandal force was thus mobile, well protected and capable of delivering a heavy blow.

Gelimer sent an advance guard of about 2000 men under the command of his brother, Ammatas (d. AD 533), to meet the advancing Romans and delay them. The Romans were in marching order, strung out along the road, and so the advance guard would have a local superiority in numbers, at least at first. Ammatas' troops were able

to occupy a strong position near Ten-Mile Post, protected by a steep defile, and should have been able to hold out for a good while. By the time the Romans could deploy and bring greater numbers to bear against the holding force, they would have other problems to face.

Meanwhile, Gelimer had sent another 2000 men under the command of his nephew Gibamund (d. AD 533) to hook around the Roman left flank. Their mission was to launch a flanking attack that would dismay the Romans by threatening their line of retreat. Meanwhile, Gelimer himself waited for his opportunity with 7000 men. He could follow up Gibamund's attack if it went well, or launch an assault of his own.

According to some questionable sources, Belisarius was blinded and reduced to begging after falling from favour. This painting from 1784 is by Jacques Louis David (1748-1825).

MAXIMIANVS

THE BATTLE

The Vandals suffered from many of the vices that beset feudal troops throughout history. With social status at least in part dependent upon performance in battle and with a very macho warrior culture, they were prone to impetuous frontal charges and a general loss of command and control in battle.

This is likely to have contributed to what happened to the holding force under Ammatas. They reached their positions as a disorganized mob, and although the Romans were also disorganized by having to deploy from the march, they were better trained and disciplined.

The action around the Ten-Mile Post was fiercely fought but rapidly turned in favour of the Romans. Ammatas' force was overwhelmed piecemeal and their commander was killed. What remained of the blocking force broke, and was chased up the road towards Carthage.

The flanking attack under Gibamund was not going well, either. After a fierce initial clash, the Vandals were defeated by a mixed force of imperial troops and Hun mercenaries. Gibamund himself was killed and most of his force scattered, though some elements continued to make a nuisance of themselves on the Roman flank.

Gelimer, meanwhile, led his 7000 men straight into the Roman force and met with considerable success. Some imperial units were routed and much of Belisarius' army was thrown into disorder. The Vandals under Gelimer were able to cut their way through the Romans towards Ammatas' position.

Upon arriving there, Gelimer found his brother dead. Overcome with grief, he insisted on burying Ammatas then and there, on the battlefield. Thoughts of victory were gone, and although some elements of the army continued to attack, they were robbed of support and direction while Gelimer was distracted.

BELISARIUS RALLIES

The imperial army was at this point more or less beaten. Elements were strung out up

It is thought that Belisarius may be the bearded figure to the right of Emperor Justinian I (centre, with halo) in this mosaic from the Church of San Vitale, Ravenna, which celebrates the reconquest of Italy by the Byzantine army under the leadership of Belisarius.

the Carthage road, pursuing what remained of Ammatas' forces, and the rest were in chaos, under pressure from repeated Vandal charges. One final coherent effort could have finished off Belisarius' army, but it did not come.

Instead Belisarius was able to regroup some of his forces, and counterattacked the Vandals with everything he could muster. Such command and control as normally existed in the Vandal army was absent; Gelimer did not give any useful commands or even act as a rallying point for his dismayed forces.

The result was growing imperial success, which suddenly became total victory as the Vandals broke and fled the field. Gelimer was unable to scrape together a sufficient

Although technically a 'Roman' soldier, this Byzantine infantryman is very differently equipped. His long spear and sword enable him to tackle the cavalry who had risen to dominate the battlefield.

force to cover Carthage and was forced to abandon his capital.

It was common at the time to put defenders of a conquered city to the sword, but Belisarius had other ideas. He declared that the people of Carthage were Roman citizens oppressed by the Vandals and should be treated with respect.

The citizens of Carthage, for their part, threw open the gates of the city and welcomed Belisarius as a liberator. From the Vandal king's own throne, he declared Carthage restored to the empire and ordered its fortifications improved against an attempt to take the city back.

AFTERMATH

Belisarius inflicted a further defeat on the Vandals at Ticameron the following year and effectively broke their power, restoring the first territories to the empire. He was rewarded with a 'triumph', and this glorious procession through the capital turned out to be the last of its type ever held.

After returning North Africa to the empire, Belisarius was sent to do the same in Italy, where he was again spectacularly successful. Although frequently outnumbered, he was able to use the staying power of his hard-hitting cataphracts to win victory after victory.

Ultimately, however, the reconquest of the empire failed. This was due in part to friction between Belisarius and Justinian, though the first appearance of bubonic plague, which caused untold numbers of deaths, also weakened the ability of the empire to support this ambitious project.

Belisarius had a troubled relationship with Justinian for the rest of his career, in which he defended the empire even after he had ceased adding to it.

The two died within weeks of one another, and with them passed the last

Right: General Belisarius leads his forces against the Goths in this rather romanticised painting. The contrast between 'civilized' Byzantines and 'Barbarian' Goths is obvious from their arms and armour.

chance to renew the glory of Rome. They had increased the holdings of the Eastern Empire by almost 50 per cent, and for a brief time the empire enjoyed the old, glorious days of conquest and power. From now onwards, however, it would know only decline.

The Battle of Ad Decimum marks the beginning of the ascendacy of the heavily-armoured cataphract on battlefields throughout Europe and the Near East, and they remained a much-feared force in their heyday. Cataphracts provided the Byzantine Empire with a motivated and professional force that lasted until the last days of the Empire in the early thirteenth century.

Right: Byzantine troops in Foulkon ('Turtle')
formation. Many armies adopted such close-order
formations, which were excellent for use by
spearmen. The soldiers' shields provided archery
protection while the spears fended off cavalry.

FALKIRK

22 July 1298

BRITISH HISTORY IS REPLETE WITH LEGENDS, AND THOSE OF THE LONGBOW AND WILLIAM WALLACE HAVE BEEN ESPECIALLY POTENT. WALLACE HAS LONG BEEN A HERO TO THE SCOTS AND A POWERFUL ICON OF THEIR STRUGGLE AGAINST THEIR SOUTHERN NEIGHBOURS, AND FREQUENT ENEMIES, THE ENGLISH. THE LONGBOW EVOKES THE SKILL AND ABILITY OF ENGLISH SOLDIERS, OF ALL CLASSES, TO TRIUMPH MILITARILY OVER ENEMIES OF GREATER WEALTH AND STATUS. IN A MOMENT OF GREAT HISTORICAL RESONANCE, THESE TWO LEGENDS CLASHED, AT THE BATTLE OF FALKIRK ON 22 JULY 1298.

Before the end of the thirteenth century, English archers served in English armies in small numbers only. Even in the Assize of Arms of 1242, where archers were named as the second most important class of soldiers after the mounted knight, their numbers were small. This, however, changed in the final quarter of the thirteenth century. Edward I, a king possessed of a strategic and tactical genius that had not been seen since William the Conqueror, began to recruit more and more longbow archers until these had become the most numerous type of soldier in his army. Indeed, sources report that their numbers were greater than 5500 at the Battle of Falkirk – twice the number of cavalry. And in the fourteenth and fifteenth centuries, the numbers of longbow men sometimes reached a ratio of five archers to one man-at-arms, as at the Battle of Agincourt in 1415.

There is still a stone bridge that crosses the Forth River in Stirling near to where the former bridge, the scene of fighting between the Earl of Surrey's English and William Wallace's Scots in 1297, once stood.

The chief advantage of the longbow over other shorter bows was that its string could be drawn to the ear instead of to the chest, allowing for the discharge of a longer arrow. This increased the range of the arrow to almost twice as far, to perhaps as much as 400m (1312ft), and it also delivered an equally increased ballistic impact. Modern tests have also shown that arrows fired from the longbow are capable even of piercing mail armour at a distance of 200m (656ft) and plate at 100m (328ft), a feat impossible at almost any distance by an arrow fired from a short bow.

THE USE OF THE LONGBOW

Some historians have suggested that more important even than the increased range and ballistic force was the tactical use made of longbow archers by Edward I (1239–1307) at Falkirk, and by his successors elsewhere. Edward did not conceive of the English longbowman as a single archer firing his weapon at a single target. Instead, he saw his longbowmen as a unit of archers firing their weapons together at opposing units. The suggestion here is that it did not matter whether longbows were as lethal or 'invincible' as several modern historians believe they were. Some have even doubted the estimates of longbow range and ballistic impact and questioned the findings of modern firing tests. In fact, these historians claim, longbowmen, needing to fire with an extremely steep arc to cover the distance between themselves and the enemy, were thus unable to penetrate their opponents' armour and did little more damage than the killing of a few horses and the wounding of even fewer men.

What did matter is where Edward and his successors placed their longbowmen: along the wings of their lines of infantry and dismounted cavalry. In such a formation, the archers did not need to kill many men; their role was to harass the enemy to such an extent that they broke into a disordered charge, which was narrowed by continual flanking fire as it approached, reached and was stopped by the solid infantry line. It was this then that led to victory – not the longbow archery itself, but the archery-induced disordered charge into the infantry.

THE EARLY LONGBOW

Recent scholarship by Matthew Strickland and Robert Hardy has suggested that the longbow was the 'traditional' bow of the English throughout the Middle Ages. This research certainly makes sense of the numerous illustrations of English archers from the Anglo-Saxon period to the mid-thirteenth century, for example in the Bayeux Tapestry, but it contradicts the previously held thesis that the English first noticed the longbow when it was used in fighting with or against the Welsh sometime during the later thirteenth century. It is believed to have been made of yew, either imported from Spain or grown in England, and shaped in a characteristic D-shaped curve before stringing. It also fired a 'clotharrow' 1m (3ft) long.

WILLIAM WALLACE

Not much is known about the real William Wallace (1270–1305). Most of his story, as depicted in *Braveheart* and recounted by modern biographers, is derived from the romantic *The Actis and Deidis of the Illustere and Vaileand Campioun Schir William Wallace, Knight of Ellerslie* (The Acts and Deeds of the Illustrious and Valiant Champion, Sir William Wallace, Knight of Elderslie) composed by a fifteenth-century minstrel known as Blind Harry (or Hary). There are some discrepancies. For example, the real Braveheart was born sometime in the 1270s into a family of lesser nobles aligned with the Scottish House of Stewart, and was not the peasant of popular myth. He was also reasonably well educated and could read and write in Latin as well as the vernacular languages of the British Isles.

LOCATION

SCOTLAND

Falkirk ✚ • Edinburgh

ENGLAND

The Scottish leaders chose the battlefield of Falkirk, west of Edinburgh, because of what they perceived would be advantageous terrain to fight with large infantry numbers: marshy land in front and a small hill behind their troops.

The Scottish infantry soldier was what we today might call an 'irregular' soldier. He was strong and enthusiastic, but he lacked training or discipline. His arms and armour varied, with most soldiers wielding a spear, sword or axe and being protected by a shield, helmet and sometimes body armour.

It is also impossible to determine why Wallace turned against the English during the last few years of the thirteenth century with such violence and ruthlessness. His father was killed when he was young, although this was not apparently at the hands of the English – it is actually not known how he died. And while he may well have been married to Marion Braidfute of Lamington, it is only Blind Harry who records this and who claims that she met her death at the hands of William Heselrig, the English Sheriff of Lanark. According to Blind Harry, too, Braidfute's death was the spur for Wallace's first attack, in May 1297, against the English, which resulted in Heselrig's own death and dismemberment, and the defeat of his garrison. This was followed by other successful attacks against English soldiers and outposts at Loudoun Hill and Ayr.

Soon, the acclaim of Wallace's raids and attacks increased the numbers who fought with him, even adding members of some of Scotland's most noble families, in particular Sir William Douglas the Hardy. Larger forces were now targeted, such as those at Aberdeen, Perth, Glasgow, Scone and Dundee, all of which were freed from English control. What had begun as one man's vendetta had in only a very short time turned into a widespread Scottish rebellion. Wallace's success also led Andrew Moray to take a large army to Abbey Craig, across the Forth River from the most important and populated English site in Scotland, Stirling Castle, where Wallace's forces joined him in August 1297.

STIRLING BRIDGE

In Stirling Castle, John de Warenne, Earl of Surrey and commander of the English forces in Scotland, felt that it was time to teach the Scottish rebels a lesson. Placing almost his entire army – an estimated 300 cavalry and 6350 infantry – under the command of Hugh de Cressingham, the Treasurer of England, he sent them to meet the Scots. Brash and incautious, Warenne and Cressingham gave no thought to crossing the narrow bridge over the Forth below the castle, even though it is reported that one of the Scottish knights fighting for the English, Richard Lundie, spoke against such a move: 'My lords, if we cross this bridge we are dead men. For we can only go over two by two and the enemy are formed up; their whole army can charge down upon us whenever they will.' He claimed that he could lead the army to a wide ford not far above Stirling, where the soldiers could pass 'sixty at a time'.

However, Cressingham, whose responsibility for the collection of taxes made him hated throughout Scotland, countered that there was no need to fear the rebels: 'It will do us no good, my lord earl, either to go bickering like this or to waste the king's money in vain manoeuvres. So let us cross over right away and do our duty as we are bound to.' Thus ended the discussion, with Warenne agreeing with Cressingham's assessment.

Andrew de Moray and William Wallace could clearly observe the English soldiers marching from the castle, and they must have been delighted to see the strategic failure of using the bridge to cross the river. They hastened their troops – which in number were about the same as the English, an estimated 180 cavalry and 6400 infantry – into position in the woods at the base of Abbey Craig. Allowing about a quarter of the English to cross the bridge, they charged out of the woods in full force, driving this vanguard of troops back against the river. They were quickly defeated, with no quarter given to any who attempted to surrender. Those trapped on the bridge and on other side of the river could do nothing but stare at the slaughter. Soon they found themselves in flight, rushing as fast as they could to the safety of the castle's walls. Only a few made it.

The Scots, flushed with victory, chased down and killed any who lingered or were slow. The banners of Edward I and the Earl of Surrey were captured, but the real prize

The Battle of Stirling Bridge was a great victory for Scotland, but may have been an even greater defeat for the English because it destroyed the notion that the English could not be defeated and added many new recruits to William Wallace's rebellion. This romantic nineteenth-century depiction displays all of the emotion of the battle although it dresses both armies in false armour and has the bridge collapsing.

was the body of Cressingham, who had been killed during the battle.

It was said that Cressingham, previously lampooned for his corpulence, was flayed, and his skin divided among the victorious Scottish soldiers. Wallace, allegedly, made a belt with his portion. Unfortunately for the Scots, Andrew de Moray was mortally wounded and died just a short time after the battle.

THE BATTLE OF FALKIRK

In the months that followed the Battle of Stirling Bridge, William Wallace remained very active. Now the military leader of the rebels, he was knighted by one of the earls of Scotland, possibly Robert Bruce, and named 'Guardian of Scotland and Leader of its armies'. Southern Scotland quickly joined the north in support of the rebellion, and without further opposition Wallace crossed the border into northern England.

This may simply have been to take advantage of the recent defeat at Stirling Bridge, with the singular goal of pillage, although most historians suggest that Wallace's true purpose was to provoke an attack on Scotland by Edward I himself. If so, this strategy would prove to be as brash and incautious as was Cressingham's crossing the Forth by a narrow bridge. Edward was not a military leader to be taken lightly and his armies were larger, well trained and disciplined, and far better armed than the Scots.

The summer of 1298 was greeted in England by the gathering of many soldiers and militia at Roxburgh on the border of Scotland. The defeat at Stirling Bridge and Wallace's raids across the border were well

THE OPPOSED FORCES

ENGLISH (estimated)

Cavalry:	2250
Infantry:	7400
Longbowmen:	5500
Total:	**15,150**

SCOTTISH (estimated)

Cavalry:	500
Infantry:	8000
Longbowmen:	1500
Total:	**10,000**

FALKIRK

22 JULY 1298

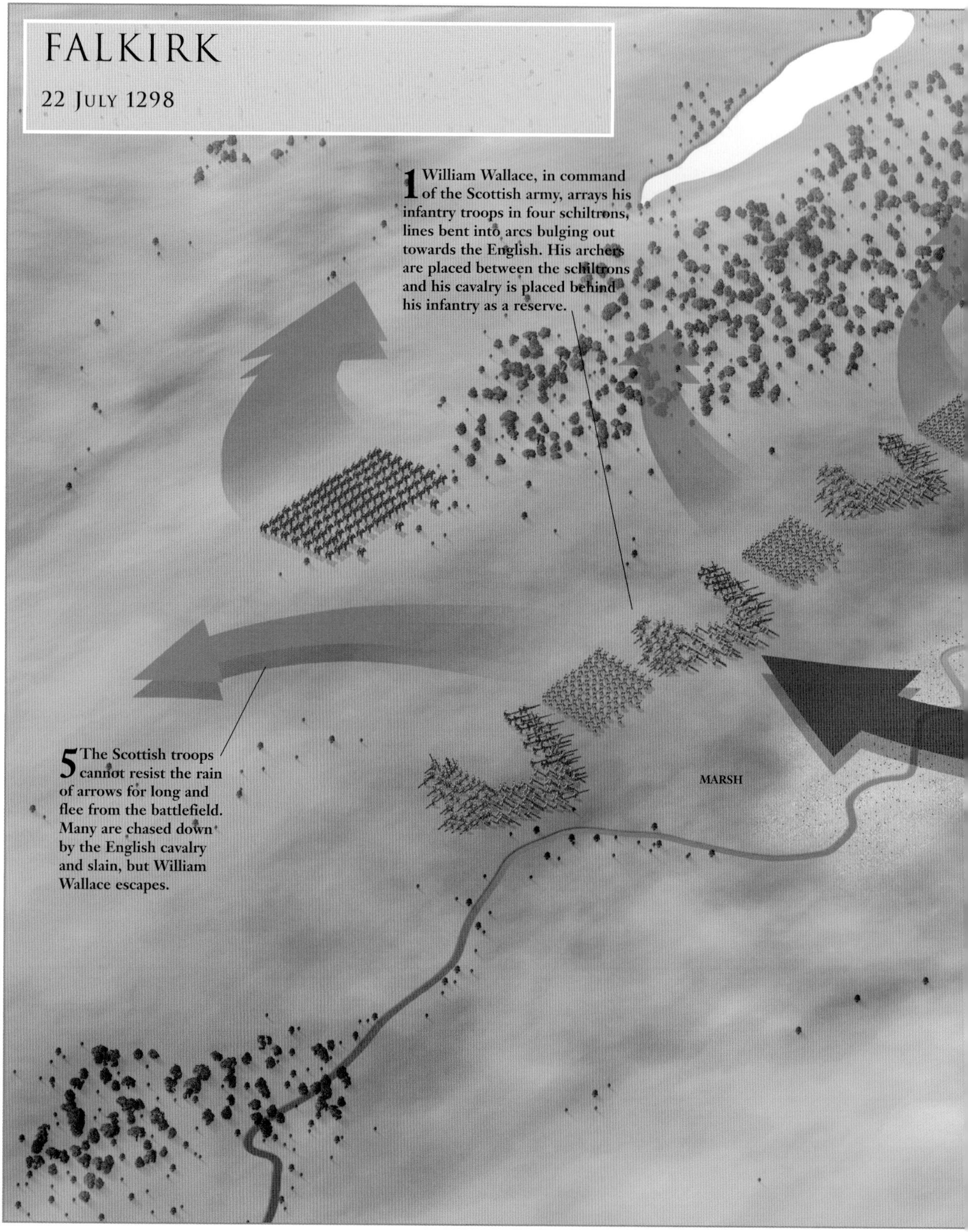

1 William Wallace, in command of the Scottish army, arrays his infantry troops in four schiltrons, lines bent into arcs bulging out towards the English. His archers are placed between the schiltrons and his cavalry is placed behind his infantry as a reserve.

5 The Scottish troops cannot resist the rain of arrows for long and flee from the battlefield. Many are chased down by the English cavalry and slain, but William Wallace escapes.

MARSH

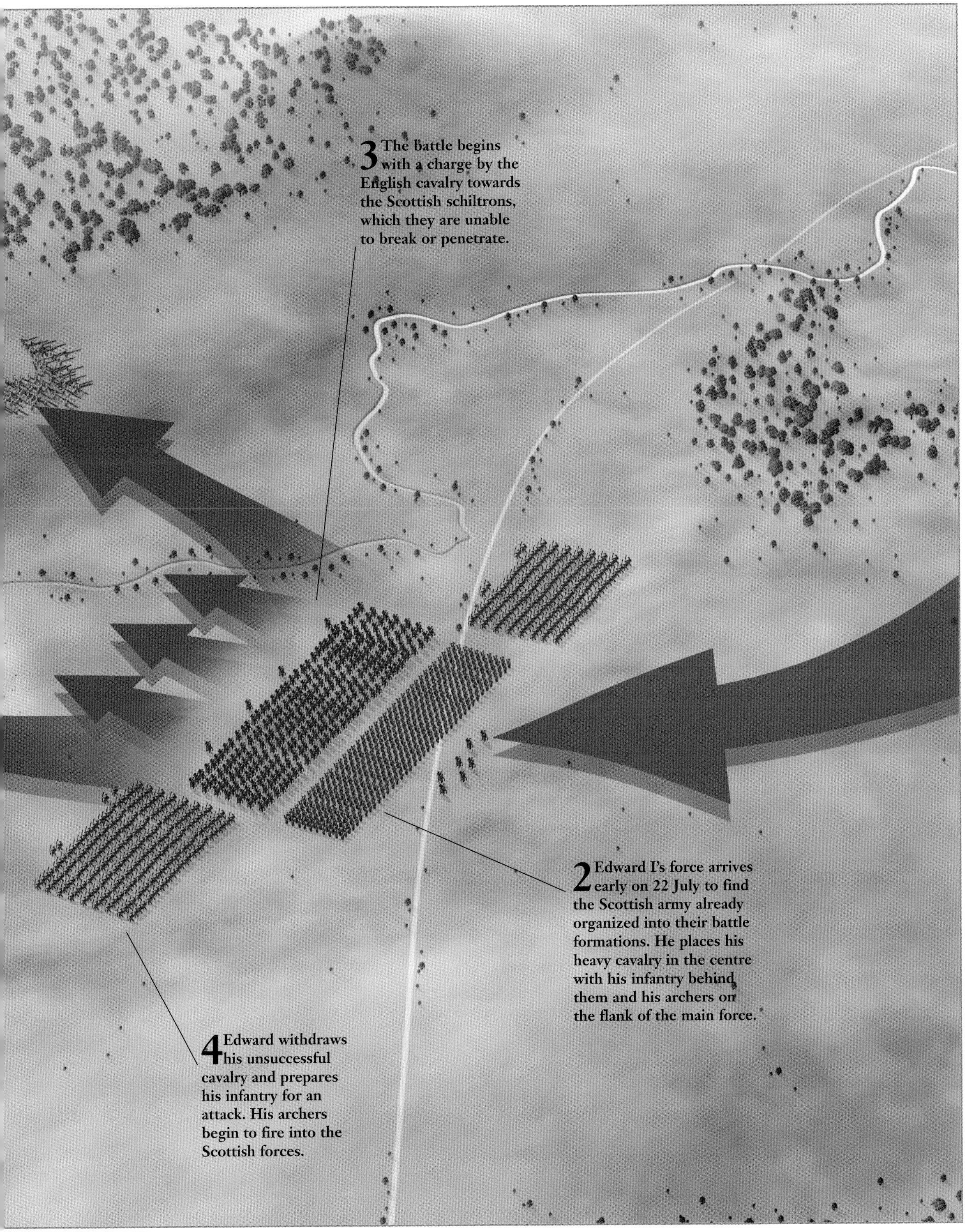

3 The battle begins with a charge by the English cavalry towards the Scottish schiltrons, which they are unable to break or penetrate.

2 Edward I's force arrives early on 22 July to find the Scottish army already organized into their battle formations. He places his heavy cavalry in the centre with his infantry behind them and his archers on the flank of the main force.

4 Edward withdraws his unsuccessful cavalry and prepares his infantry for an attack. His archers begin to fire into the Scottish forces.

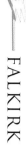

It has been said that William Wallace is 'the Scottish idea of a Scottish hero'. Here, depicted in a Victorian-era portrait (with a ridiculous helmet), Wallace sports a dignified, serious countenance and not the wild-eyed, crazed look that is sometimes given him.

broadcast throughout England, leading many to respond to a call to arms against him. But when the king arrived on 3 July he sent many of these troops home. He reckoned that he could fight a battle against the Scottish rebels with his finest soldiers only. These included an estimated 2250 cavalry and 12,900 infantry. However, among the latter were 5500 longbowmen, the largest force of these troops ever assembled together in a single army and greatly dwarfing the other missile troops, 400 crossbowmen.

(Interestingly, the Scottish army is estimated to have contained 1500 longbowmen, a force almost entirely absent from the Scots at Stirling Bridge, where Moray and Wallace could certainly have used them to attack the English soldiers trapped on the bridge.)

TO BATTLE

Edward moved swiftly against the Scots. On 9 July, his army crossed the border and attacked Lauder; on 10 July, he captured Dalhousie Castle; from 15 to 20 July, he camped outside Temple Liston; on 21 July, he reached Linlithgow; and on 22 July he arrived at the battlefield of Falkirk. The journey had been quick but not without problems, as the English soldiers resented marching with the Welsh archers – who had so recently been their enemy. Perhaps they could also see that the English military was changing, that they were being replaced as the core of the army by new, lower-class soldiers valued for their skill in weapons that killed from a distance and not for their training, discipline or one-on-one fighting abilities. A brawl was even fought between the English and Welsh at Temple Liston, which left 80 Welsh dead. Still, at Falkirk all were to fight together, against their common Scottish enemy.

Before the Battle of Falkirk, William Wallace's forces had been staying out of the way of the English, although this has never been seen as avoidance so much as simply selecting a suitable spot to do battle and gathering as many troops as possible. Indeed, it is thought that almost all the Scots who were willing to fight against the English were at Falkirk, although the army numbered only about two-thirds of the English force – an estimated 500 cavalry and 9500 infantry.

Still, William Wallace had devastated all of the English he had encountered before the Battle of Falkirk, and there was no doubt in his mind, or in any of his soldiers'

The typical English man-at-arms of the late thirteenth century was well armed and armoured, disciplined and trained. He was protected by mail from head to toe, a shield and a helmet. His weapons included both the spear and sword. He was a formidable foe.

Opposite: King Edward I, called Longshanks in contemporary chronicles because of his long legs, dealt ruthlessly with the Scots (and anyone he thought sympathized with them). Devoted to his family, he is shown here in romantic pose holding his son, the first Prince of Wales, who would later succeed his father as Edward II.

FALKIRK

minds, that despite the more numerous English soldiers, the day would be theirs.

THE OPENING PHASES

As dawn broke on 22 July 1298, the English army marched from their camp at Linlithgow to face the Scots. Wallace had awakened his troops early, and by the time the English reached Falkirk the Scots were already arrayed in their battle formation. According to the primary English source of the battle, Walter of Guisborough (who was not an eyewitness), the chief part of this formation were four 'schiltrons' of spearmen, which he took to mean large circles, although some modern historians have suggested that these were closer to lines bent in an arc than to actual circles. Between these schiltrons were the Scottish longbowmen. The few Scottish cavalry seem to have been held in reserve.

Once on the battlefield, Edward and his generals immediately recognized their advantage in cavalry and decided to charge them into the Scottish schiltrons. This was not a bad decision because, when faced by the charge of heavy horsemen, with both men and horses fully armoured, an enemy would often run away. Not so, however, the Scots at Falkirk. They stood solidly in formation, with few believing that they would be defeated.

For more than two centuries, the English longbowman was one of the most feared (and most recruited) soldiers. Longbowmen could turn the tide of a battle even when facing knights or men-at-arms. At Falkirk, they also determined victory against the tightly bunched, poorly armored Scots.

And, at least initially, their faith in their military abilities was confirmed when the charges of the English cavalry, organized into four lines (or 'battles'), were easily turned away. Part of the reason for this was, no doubt, the soggy ground at the base of the hill-slope on which the Scots were arrayed. Although probably not the 'sodden morass' or 'boggy lake' that some historians suggest – Edward would certainly not have chanced a cavalry attack over such terrain – this ground became even more muddy before too many charges had taken place.

FAILED CHARGE

Perhaps the primary reason for the ineffectiveness of the cavalry charges is that the Scottish schiltrons did what they were supposed to: present a formidable formation into which the horses, whose impetus had been slowed by the mud and also by the arrows fired at them by the Scottish archers, could not penetrate. Medieval warhorses, no matter how well trained, would stop, wheel away or drop to the ground rather than skewer themselves on the spears of soldiers formed into lines.

This is what appears to have happened at Falkirk, and the reason why the original sources for the battle insist that some of the English cavalry were unable to land even a single blow. It may also be the reason why contemporary records claim that 111 horses were killed in these charges.

However, Edward I, having led armies for more than 30 years, knew not to rely on a single tactic. He had, in fact, prepared for such a possible outcome. Recalling the cavalry, he moved his infantry into position. But before they could make their own charges, the English longbowmen on the flanks of the other infantry began to fire into the Scottish schiltrons.

While their confidence was no doubt increased by their success against the cavalry, few of Wallace's troops were prepared for the rain of arrows that poured down on them from more than 5000 bows. Most of the Scottish soldiers probably wore little if any armour, with shields and helmets

also insufficient in number to provide much relief against such an onslaught. According to one English chronicle, they began to fall, in large numbers, 'like blossoms in an orchard when the fruit has ripened'.

The devastation was also observed on the English side, with the other infantry soldiers picking up and throwing stones at the Scots so that they, too, could participate in what all could now see as an English triumph, fast approaching.

The schiltrons simply dissolved, although some Scottish soldiers, including William Wallace, were able to get away. (He was not captured until 5 August 1305, when betrayed by a fellow Scottish knight, John de Menteith. Found guilty of treason, Wallace was hanged, emasculated, drawn, beheaded and quartered at Smithfield in London 18 days later.)

AFTERMATH

Following its success at the Battle of Falkirk, the longbow significantly changed English strategy and tactics. With the longbowmen – perhaps, in fact, solely because of them – Edward I had won a significant victory there. And these English victories would continue: against the Scots at Dupplin Moor in 1332, at Halidon Hill in 1333 and at Neville's Cross in 1346; and against the French at the battles of Crécy (1346), Poitiers (1356), Agincourt (1415) and elsewhere during the Hundred Years War.

Thus developed the legend of the 'invincible' longbow and the 'unbeatable' English longbowmen, a legend as potent today as ever. Wallace's legend also remains as vital today as ever. However, when these two legends clashed on the battlefield of Falkirk, it was the longbow that triumphed.

In 1305, William Wallace was captured by the English and taken to London for trial. Despite not recognizing the authority of the English king, he was found guilty of treason against the crown. On 23 August, he was led to Smithfield – as portrayed in this illustration by Wal Paget – and executed. His reputation as a general has risen and fallen, but his reputation as a Scottish hero endures to this day.

CASTILLON
17 July 1453

THE BATTLE OF CASTILLON WAS THE LAST BATTLE FOUGHT BETWEEN THE FRENCH, THE GASCONS AND THE ENGLISH DURING THE HUNDRED YEARS' WAR. WITH THEIR CANNONS, THE FRENCH ARMY DEMONSTRATED THAT VICTORY IN BATTLE WOULD IN FUTURE BE DETERMINED BY GUNPOWDER WEAPONS.

WHY DID IT HAPPEN?

WHO An Anglo-Gascon force under Sir John Talbot, the Earl of Shrewsbury (1390–1453) fought the French forces of Jean Bureau (d. 1463).

WHAT The English cavalry and infantry army attacked the entrenched infantry and cannon of the French forces.

WHERE Castillon, west of the city of Bordeaux, southwest France.

WHEN 17 July 1453.

WHY After the French capture of Bordeaux in 1451, English King Henry VI (1421–1471) sought to re-establish English control of Bordeaux and Gascony by inflicting a decisive victory on French forces in southwest France.

OUTCOME Following the outbreak of the Wars of the Roses, the English were no longer in any position to pursue their claim to the French throne and lost all their land on the continent.

In 1453, guns became recognized as the dominant weapons of war. Gunpowder weapons proved to be significant in three engagements spread across Europe, and the results of these conflicts – and how they were fought – were quickly broadcast throughout the continent.

The most famous of these was the siege and fall of Constantinople to the Ottoman armies of Sultan Mehmed II (1432–81), fought from 2 April to 29 May. Mehmed used his large artillery train, containing all sizes of gunpowder weapons, from huge bombards to medium-sized field cannons and small hand-held guns, to breach the walls of what had once been the most powerful city in the world.

Less well known, though also important as a demonstration of the power of gunpowder weapons, was the final campaign in the Ghent War, begun by Duke Philip the Good of Burgundy (1396–1467) on 18 June. Between then and 23 July, Philip attacked three small

John Talbot, Earl of Shrewsbury, is awarded a sword by King Henry VI. Talbot had fought for the English for more than 40 years. He had served in France on numerous occasions, even opposing and being captured by Joan of Arc in 1429.

EARLY GUNPOWDER WEAPONS

Early gunpowder recipes varied slightly, but all combined saltpetre, sulphur and charcoal in a mixture that, when lit, combusted with a forceful explosion. However, it was not until the early fourteenth century that a weapon was invented in Europe which could use gunpowder to fire missiles: a metal tube enclosed at one end, commonly called a 'cannon' from the French canon, *or 'gun' from the English* gynne. *Over the next 150 years large, medium and small guns were made. Eventually, they also became hand-held. The methods of manufacture also changed, as guns became less frequently made on the forge than at the foundry. Transportation methods, metallurgy and powder chemistry were experimented with and improved. More importantly, gunpowder weaponry led to changes on the battlefield, at sieges and in naval engagements.*

fortifications under the control of rebels from the city of Ghent and elsewhere in Flanders. The castle of Schendelbeke fell on 27 June; Poeke Castle on 2 July; and Gavere Castle on 23 July. Schendelbeke and Poeke were virtually levelled by heavy bombardment from Philip's gunpowder artillery, as numerous and impressive as Mehmed II's. At Gavere, however, with the castle at the point of submission, an army of Ghentenaar rebels showed up. Philip turned his guns on the arriving troops. As the ducal gunfire fell upon the Ghentenaars, the rebels' resolve began to weaken and they became demoralized. Within a very short time, many broke ranks and fled. At Gavere, Philip the Good had proved that the gunpowder weapons which were effective in sieges could be just as effective in battle.

However, the third conflict, the battle of Castillon fought on 17 July 1453, provided the best glimpse of the future of battlefield gunpowder weaponry. In this battle, the final engagement of the Hundred Years War, the French were commanded by Jean Bureau (d. 1463), who had previously served in the army as a gunner and then as master of artillery. He knew the importance of field artillery and hand-held guns, and his victorious plan in the battle was designed around them.

SIEGE WARFARE

The most immediate impact of gunpowder weapons was on siege warfare. Throughout the last two centuries of the Middle Ages, some gunpowder artillery pieces were heavy, large-calibre cannons that fired heavy projectiles. These were ideal for sieges, as the walls of castles could be greatly damaged by the ballistic force of these gunshots. By the middle of the fourteenth century, nearly every siege was accompanied by a gunpowder artillery bombardment. By 1400, cannons were even breaching fortification walls.

Guns had much less impact on late medieval battles. Fourteenth-century battlefield uses of gunpowder weapons were infrequent, and it is in only one battle, at Bevershoutsveld, fought outside the walls of the town of Bruges in 1382, that guns might have decided the outcome. With the adoption of smaller cannons in the early fifteenth century, as well as improved accuracy, gunpowder weapons began to appear more frequently on the battlefield. Hand-held gunpowder weapons also began to appear in greater numbers. These were introduced in the late fourteenth century, and throughout the fifteenth century the influence of these guns, initially called *handgonnes* and *coulevrines à main* and later *haquebuses* or *arquebuses*, greatly increased.

THE HUNDRED YEARS WAR

It would not have been odd for a French soldier at Castillon to wonder why he was fighting the English there. By 1453, everyone, even the leaders of both armies,

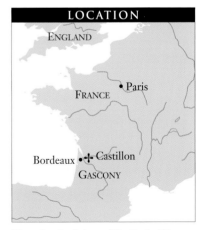

The castle and walled town of Castillon lay 50km (31 miles) away from Bordeaux, the capital of Gascony, where it defended the road and river (Dordogne) access to that city.

In 1453, John Talbot, First Earl of Shrewbury, was one of the few English military leaders who had been victorious in battle. He probably preferred retirement, but when Henry VI summoned him to service he could not turn him down.

THE OPPOSED FORCES

ENGLISH

Infantry (inc. archers):	4500
Mounted knights:	1500
Total:	**6000**

FRENCH

Infantry and men-at-arms:	
	7–10,000
Cannon:	300
Total:	**7–10,000**

advanced on Paris. Even after the Black Prince had captured French King Jean II at the Battle of Poitiers in 1356, the only concern for the English crown was the security of lands – and the payment of a large ransom for Jean's freedom – for which Edward III was willing to give up his claims to the French royal title.

Several years of inaction and peace followed the deaths of the Black Prince in 1376 and Edward III in 1377, during which time the French regained much of the lands they had lost during the war. In 1396, Edward III's successor and the Black Prince's son, Richard II, signed a truce with the French in Paris, dependent on his marriage with Isabella, one of the French King Charles VI's daughters, and a co-equal Anglo–French attendance on a Crusade to the east against the Ottoman Turks. France and England would not 'officially' exchange blows again until 1415.

Nevertheless, the Hundred Years War did continue. Although the English were not involved in France during this period, the military situation seemed to be even more demanding and less easily resolved. Charles VI's mental illness had left an unstable government, with a number of nobles vying for power. Two of these sought control over the ill king: the Dukes of Burgundy and Orléans and their factions – known as the Burgundians and Armagnacs – utilized every means of warfare in their fight against each other, from actual combat to assassination.

Duke Louis of Orléans was killed in Paris in 1407 and Duke John the Fearless of Burgundy on Montereau Bridge in 1419. It was a civil war, one that would infect the French and weaken them to such a point that in 1415, when King Henry V (1387–1422) invaded France, he found instead a divided realm. On one side, the Burgundians were either willing to collaborate with his invasion or to ignore it; and on the other, the Armagnacs could not decide whom they wanted to fight most – the English or the Burgundians.

Henry V's victories at the siege of Harfleur and the battle of Agincourt in 1415, and the conquest of Normandy and Maine in 1417–20, placed England once again in control of large parts of France.

may well have forgotten why the Hundred Years War had broken out – 116 years earlier in fact. When the English King Edward III (1312–1377) launched his first invasion of France in 1337, it was seemingly to recover his crown as king of France, a crown that in his view had been 'stolen' from him in 1328 when, despite being the closest heir to the dead king, Charles IV, he was declared ineligible to inherit because his royal descent was gained through a woman. The throne instead was given to his cousin Philip of Valois, who was crowned King Philip VI (1293–1350) of France.

However, in the intervening years, English justification for continually taking armies across the sea to France had changed. Edward III and his son Edward the Black Prince won several major battles during the first phase of the war, but never

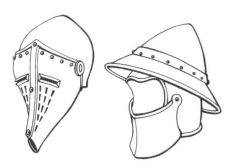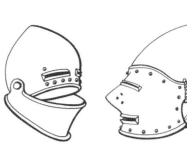

Late medieval cavalry helmets varied in style with the wearer's preference. They generally fitted more tightly to the face and neck. Still, some soldiers and leaders felt that they limited vision and communication too much. Therefore, they chose to raise their visors or fight without them.

More importantly, the Treaty of Troyes, agreed to by Charles VI after all of the English victories, was sealed between the two crowns with the marriage of Henry and Charles's daughter, Catherine of Valois, and the promise that their eldest son would gain clear title to the two kingdoms upon the deaths of the sitting kings. There seemed little chance that Henry would not soon gain control of France, as Charles was an ill old man, and he was much younger.

JOAN OF ARC

However, when an illness caught at the siege of Meaux meant that the English king predeceased his French equal by two months, leaving a son, Henry VI, less than a year old, the issue of inheritance was once again raised. Charles VI's last living son, Charles, was not willing to accept his disinheritance without a fight, so, supported by Armagnac nobles and armies, he pushed forward his own claim to the throne. For the first few years, his fight did not go well; in fact, the Armagnacs actually lost more land than they gained. That changed in 1429, however, with the rise of a young peasant girl, Joan of Arc, who had visions of a France without Englishmen. What followed was a story too preposterous for a work of fiction, yet true. In a little less than two years, thanks to this peasant girl, the armies of France, once pinned down behind the Loire River, had freed all besieged and captured cities and witnessed, on 17 July 1429, the crowning of Charles as King Charles VII (1403–1461) in Rheims, which had previously been deep in Burgundian territory. Joan of Arc was captured at Compiègne in May 1430 and burned as a witch in Rouen on 30 May 1431.

From the time of Joan's victories to the end of the Hundred Years War, there were few military setbacks for the French. Within five years, a peace conference was held at Arras. This failed to stop the war between England and France, but it did force the Burgundian Duke, now Philip the Good, to 'switch sides', withdrawing any active support for England, while not allying himself completely with Charles VII. The English and their war effort in France never recovered. It took another 17 years but eventually they lost all of their lands in France, except for Calais. Paris was retaken in 1437; the rest of the Ile-de-France by 1440; Maine in 1449; Normandy in 1450; and Gascony in 1453.

GASCONY

That Gascony was the last holdout of English France in the fifteenth century should surprise no one. Brought to English royal ownership by Eleanor of Aquitaine at her marriage on 18 May 1152 to Count Henry Plantagenet, later King Henry II,

Full plate armour appeared only in the middle of the fifteenth century. It was cumbersome, heavy and expensive, but offered better protection. Although it cannot be known for certain, it is likely that John Talbot's son, the Lord Lisle, and several other nobles and knights at Castillon wore plate armour, but Talbot himself promised that he would not don armour against the King of France.

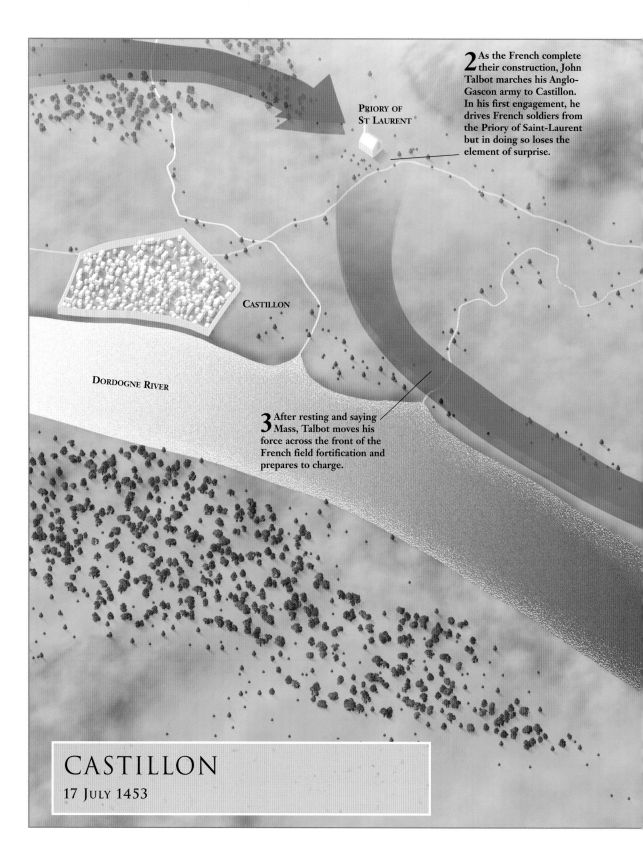

2 As the French complete their construction, John Talbot marches his Anglo-Gascon army to Castillon. In his first engagement, he drives French soldiers from the Priory of Saint-Laurent but in doing so loses the element of surprise.

PRIORY OF
ST LAURENT

CASTILLON

DORDOGNE RIVER

3 After resting and saying Mass, Talbot moves his force across the front of the French field fortification and prepares to charge.

CASTILLON
17 JULY 1453

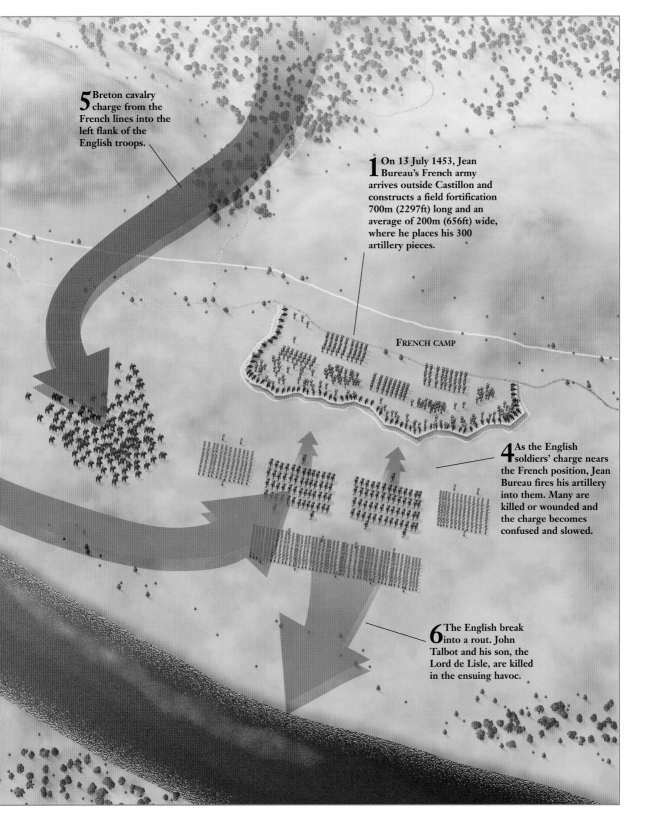

5 Breton cavalry charge from the French lines into the left flank of the English troops.

1 On 13 July 1453, Jean Bureau's French army arrives outside Castillon and constructs a field fortification 700m (2297ft) long and an average of 200m (656ft) wide, where he places his 300 artillery pieces.

FRENCH CAMP

4 As the English soldiers' charge nears the French position, Jean Bureau fires his artillery into them. Many are killed or wounded and the charge becomes confused and slowed.

6 The English break into a rout. John Talbot and his son, the Lord de Lisle, are killed in the ensuing havoc.

This nineteenth-century painting depicts the moment when the Earl of Shrewsbury's horse falls from under him. From the Galerie des batailles *(Gallery of Battles), Château de Versailles, France.*

Gascony became part of Richard the Lionheart's inheritance. Nor did it fall out of that control after the French King Philip Augustus won the Battle of Bouvines in 1214, unlike almost all the other English lands in France.

Indeed, English kings and armies had always fought to hold the rights to Gascony, its retention being the core of almost all agreements between France and England from the thirteenth to the fifteenth century. The Gascons saw themselves as English, and their economy – driven mostly by the wine trade – and politics were dependent on their ties to that island kingdom far to their north, which almost always had to be reached by sea.

With things going badly for England in the late 1440s and early 1450s, and with no English soldiers to protect them or money to sustain them, the Gascons reluctantly surrendered to the French, with the armies of the Count of Dunois, whose leadership stretched back to the time of Joan of Arc, entering the capital, Bordeaux, on 30 June 1451. Less than a year later, however, the situation was still not settled, and a group of the leading burghers sailed to England and asked Henry VI to send a force to free them from what they saw as an occupation by 'foreigners'.

THE BATTLE OF CASTILLON

Yet, in 1452, there were few English interested in returning to the continent for any reason, and hardly any generals of experience wishing to risk their already weak military reputations on such an expedition. As a consequence, Henry was forced to seek out John Talbot, Earl of Shrewsbury, whose career as a soldier stretched to the very early years of the fifteenth century (1404–13), when he fought in Wales against the rebellion of Owain Glyndër.

Talbot had served in France from 1420 to 1424, in Ireland in 1425, and again in France from 1427 to 1429. He, too, knew Joan of Arc, as an opposing leader and then as her captive when he was taken at the Battle of Patay (18 June 1429) and released only after four years of imprisonment in exchange for French General Jean Ponton de Xantrailles. From then until 1449, he continued fighting in the Hundred Years War, until captured once again at the fall of Rouen.

By this time, he had been named Constable of England, awarded the Earldom of Shrewsbury and been given the nickname 'the English Achilles' by the numerous French writers who chronicled his military history. His had been a valiant effort, one that brought several small victories and great honour, but one, too, that had not ultimately prevented the French defeating the English. Now,

however, there was to be a conclusion to this very long conflict and John Talbot, aged somewhere between 63 and 69 (contemporary writers are uncertain, while modern authors place his age as high as a very exaggerated 80), was to see the fate of Gascony decided.

DISPOSITIONS

Unfortunately for Talbot, the numbers of English soldiers who responded to the recruitment call were not high, with no more than 3000 in total sailing with him to Gascony in October 1452. Later reinforcements brought over from England by his son, John Talbot, the Lord de Lisle, boosted that number to around probably 5500, with Gascons also adding some more.

Still, there were no more than 6000 Anglo–Gascons in his army, and although many were certainly experienced veterans, it seems far too small a force to retake Gascony, never mind make any other progress against the French.

Talbot's opponent, Jean Bureau, was equally as experienced in battle, and although he carried few of Talbot's lofty titles, he had been knighted in 1461. But while Talbot had almost always fought from a leadership position, as a cavalry man-at-arms, Bureau had always been a gunner. This meant that he had entered French military service, together with his brother Gaspard (sometime in the 1430s, nothing more specific is known), as a specialist trained in fighting with the relatively new gunpowder weapons. He had thus started at the very bottom of the military hierarchy, but as the numbers of gunners grew and more leaders were required, Bureau was given more and more responsibility.

By 1439, he had been named master of artillery by Charles VII and led his gunners

from that position at the successful sieges of Pontoise, Harfleur, Bayeux, Caen and Bergerac, cities whose capitulation eventually led to the fall of Normandy in 1450. He had also captured the castles of Montguyon, Blaye and Libourne in Gascony. So, while it may appear to modern historians that his was an odd choice to lead the French armies at Castillon, for a king who owed his very crown to the acceptance of Joan of Arc's non-noble leadership, Bureau's experience made him the ideal general to oppose John Talbot.

By the summer of 1453, Talbot had decided that, rather than waiting for the inevitable, prolonged and taxing French siege of Bordeaux that was sure to come that year, he would venture out with his own forces to attack French holdings surrounding the city. His strategy was simple: if he forced the French to have to conquer more sites, the chances of further English reinforcements arriving would increase. He might even be able to force the French into some sort of conditional surrender that would ensure Gascony remained English.

On his arrival in Gascony, Talbot had sent English troops to occupy all the fortifications within a short distance from Bordeaux. There were several of these and the few soldiers available meant that his army was spread quite thin; but it would be worth it, if he could postpone an attack on Bordeaux itself. One of these sites was the castle and walled town at the aptly named Castillon, some 50km (31 miles) away. There is no doubt that this distance, and the fact that it had both road and river access to Bordeaux, led Castillon to become the target of Jean Bureau and the French.

THE FRENCH DIG IN

Bureau's army was substantially larger than Talbot's, perhaps as much as twice the size. It was filled not only with men-at-arms and archers, but also 300 cannons and an even larger number of *couleuvrines à main* and *hacquebuses*. Talbot had some gunpowder weapons, but not anywhere near the number in the French army. More important, though, than the number of gunpowder weapons Bureau had was how he decided to use them. Rather than setting up the traditional siege lines around the town and castle, which would have spread out both his gunpowder weapons and soldiers, the experienced French general decided to build an entrenched camp in the

likely direction of the English approach, where he placed most of his army. To protect this position, he constructed an earth-and-wood rampart around the entire camp and set his cannons on top of it.

It is recorded that for four days, 13–16 July, Bureau's soldiers, engineers and pioneers built this camp. No one was exempt from pitching in. At the end, he had a well-protected field fortification 700m (2297ft) long and an average of 200m (656ft) across, which on one side butted against the small but impassable River Lidoire. Its remains can still be viewed in the farmers' fields today. Bureau also seems to have taken into account all of the more recent experiments in artillery fortifications, with a shape to provide some oblique and enfilading fire to cover the most vulnerable spots. Clearly, he had not forgotten his many years of service as a gunner.

About the time that this field fortification was being completed, Talbot decided to march his troops out of Bordeaux to face the French. He marched them through the night, perhaps hoping that the darkness might conceal their progress or, more likely, simply to avoid the heat of the day. At dawn, he attacked and destroyed an outpost of French archers at the Priory of Saint-Laurent. This victory was short-lived, however, as it allowed the main French force to prepare for the ensuing English assault. If surprise had been the advantage

that the English had hoped to exploit, it was now lost. Talbot decided to halt his march and wait for his entire army to arrive at the battlefield.

In the intervening time, the English ate, rested and held mass. Talbot himself took part in these activities, before donning a rich robe and a purple velvet cap, for he wore no armour, having stipulated that he would not fight in armour against the King of France as part of the negotiations for freedom following his capture at Rouen. He was not about to break that oath, although he must surely have known that it might lead to his death should he encounter any French soldiers. Perhaps he counted on his worth for ransom, the richness of his robe and cap denoting to all that a rich pay-day would result from his capture, not his death.

TALBOT ATTACKS

After studying the French position for a while, Talbot decided to attack from the south. Why he did so is not recorded, nor does it seem to have been a logical tactic, as this meant that the English army would line up, thinly, opposite the strongest part of the French position, well within range of Bureau's guns. Some have suggested that this manoeuvre was meant to exploit a weak position or perhaps to intimidate the French by demonstrating the size of the English army, although the latter seems highly unlikely. Most do not believe that

Larger gunpowder weapons necessitated a crew to operate them. Before the cannon could be fired, they needed to be cleaned and washed out. Projectiles and gunpowder had to be loaded and tamped down, usually with a tampion to serve as wadding in front of them. Many cannons also had removable chambers, filled with gunpowder, which had to be wedged tightly into place. Finally, one of the gunners was needed to raise the mantlet and another to light the gunpowder by pushing a match through the cannons' touch-holes.

Defeat at the Battle of Castillon meant an end to the 300-year English occupation of Gascony. This illumination of the battle, from the Chroniques de Enguerrand de Monstrelet, *incorrectly depicts both cavalry forces in full armour.*

Talbot would knowingly have made such a poor decision. Still, the question remains: had Bureau done something to lure Talbot into such a tactic, perhaps hiding his guns from view or making it seem as if his southern ramparts were weaker? Unfortunately, neither historical nor archaeological sources have ever clarified the matter.

Bureau allowed the English to complete their manoeuvre and to dismount their cavalry, as was traditional at the time. He also allowed them to begin their charge, which they did, shouting 'Talbot!' and 'St George'. Then, however, he let them have it, turning the full force of his cannons and handguns against them. Few made it far, mowed down by the bombardment. Some were killed outright by iron and stone gunshots; others simply ran forwards, without order or impetus. Within seconds, the charge became confused and slowed. No doubt, the smoke and noise emanating from the guns also hindered its progress.

It was then that Bureau delivered the *coup-de-grâce* by sending a contingent of Breton men-at-arms out from the eastern side of his camp and into the right flank of the English. Whatever order was left in their line dissolved, as this flank folded onto the centre. Everyone turned and fled. Some were drowned as they tried to cross the Dordogne River behind them; others were hunted down and slaughtered. The battle itself had probably not lasted for more than a few minutes; the slaughter of fleeing soldiers took the better part of the day. Hardly a Frenchman had been killed or wounded.

Talbot also tried to flee with his troops. Accompanied by his son, it appears that he attempted to ride to a nearby ford to cross the Dordogne. But, before he even made it to the banks of the river, a cannonball killed his horse and pinned him to the ground beneath it, where a French soldier, Michel Peunim, eschewing the possibility of a rich ransom, killed the unarmoured general with his axe. The Lord de Lisle was found near his father, also dead.

AFTERMATH

The Bordelais tried to hold out until more soldiers from England could arrive to aid their cause. But none came, and on 10 October 1453 they opened their gates to Jean Bureau and the victorious French. Those who had requested and supported Talbot's expedition the year before – at least, those without the means now to flee to England – were summarily executed along with their families.

Interestingly, there is a fascinating and much later postscript to the Battle of Castillon. In the 1970s, a cache of swords was dredged up from the Dordogne River near the battlefield. With many in excellent condition (they are now to be found in arms and armour museums around the world), it has been suggested that these swords were gathered from among the dead English soldiers at the battle and placed together, in a barrel or chest that fell overboard as it was being shipped to a nearby arsenal. These swords remain a fitting tribute to the last English soldiers to die in the Hundred Years War, but they also stand as a symbol of the medieval arms that were so dramatically superseded, as at Castillon, by gunpowder weapons.

NOVARA
6 JUNE 1513

SINCE THE BEGINNING OF TIME, SOLDIERS WHO FOUGHT FOR MONEY SUPPLEMENTED THE MILITARY FORCES OF THOSE WHO COULD PAY FOR THEIR SERVICES. BY THE END OF THE MIDDLE AGES, THE PROSPERITY OF ITALIAN CITY-STATES LED TO THE EMPLOYMENT OF LARGE NUMBERS OF MERCENARIES, AS THESE TOWNS CONSTANTLY FOUGHT AGAINST EACH OTHER. PIKE-ARMED MERCENARIES FROM SWITZERLAND BECAME ESPECIALLY VALUED IN THESE CONFLICTS, AND THE SWISS WAY OF WAR WAS BORN.

WHY DID IT HAPPEN?

WHO French general Louis de la Trémoille (1460–1525) against Milanese leader, Maximilian Sforza (1493–1530), and his mercenary Swiss soldiers.

WHAT The French army of 10,000 were besieging Novara, a Milanese city, when attacked by a relief force largely composed of Swiss mercenaries employed by the Duke of Milan.

WHERE Near Novara, northern Italy.

WHEN 6 June 1513

WHY The French had been victorious at Ravenna the previous year. Nevertheless, the French under King Louis XII were driven out of the city of Milan the following month by the Holy League.

OUTCOME The French defeat by the Swiss pikemen forced Louis XII (1462–1515) to withdraw from Milan and Italy in general.

Medieval battles before the fourteenth century were infrequent. Large battles were fought mostly in desperation, only when an army was invading or trying to stem an invasion – for example, Poitiers, Edington, the Dyle, Lechfeld, Stamford Bridge, Hastings, Manzikert, Northallerton, Arsuf and Falkirk; or when leading or encountering feudal rebellions – for example, Cassel, the Elster, Brémule, Bourgthérolde, Lincoln, Legnano, Parma, Benevento, Tagliacozzo, Lewes, Evesham and Bouvines. Only on very rare occasions would a leader fight more than one large battle – for example, the kings William the Conqueror and Henry I, and the emperors Henry IV and Frederick II – and then, it seems, only when their self-confidence exceeded their wisdom. As often as not, a leader flushed with victory in one battle, would meet defeat in an ensuing engagement – for example, Harold Godwinson, Simon de Montfort and William Wallace. Even the renowned warrior, Richard the Lionheart, was involved in only three pitched battles

In a sixteenth-century woodcut, the town of Novara is depicted with the 1513 battle raging outside it. Battle illustrations were popular in this century and as an art form they are quite interesting, although they tend not to be very historically accurate.

during his career, including those fought during the Third Crusade.

For capturing land, the siege was almost always far more important and profitable for medieval leaders. For example, a military leader as astute as King Philip II (Augustus) fought only one major battle during his lengthy reign over France (1180–1223): the Battle of Bouvines, in 1214, which could be said to have profited him very little in terms of actual land gains. Yet his sieges of notable fortifications and towns throughout Anjou, Normandy and Aquitaine brought him nearly all of the 'English' lands in France, except for Gascony.

THE RISE OF INFANTRY

In medieval battles, the numbers of cavalry soldiers on the field never exceeded those of the infantry. Even so, sometime after the rise of the Carolingians, they began to dictate what occurred in military engagements, and their deaths became less frequent. The ransoming of 'knights' and other cavalry soldiers became more lucrative than killing them. However, the medieval tradition of few battles without large numbers of casualties seemed to cease at the beginning of the fourteenth century. Battles fought between then and 1529 grew ever more numerous. For example: between 1302 and 1347, no fewer than 19 major battles were fought in Europe; battles at Formigny in 1450 and Castillon in 1453 ultimately drove the

English from Normandy and Gascony in the Hundred Years War; three battles, at Grandson, Murten, and Nancy, fought in 1476–77, decided the fate of the Swiss–Burgundian Wars in favour of the Swiss and Lorrainers; the Wars of the Roses had no fewer than 15 major battles during its 32-year span; and, finally, the wars between the Holy Roman Empire/Spain and France (and their allies), mostly fought in Italy during the late fifteenth and early sixteenth centuries, are characterized more by their battlefield engagements – at Seminara in 1494, Fornovo in 1495, Cerignola in 1503, Garigliano (two battles) in 1503, Agnadello in 1509, Ravenna in 1512, Novara in 1513, Marignano in 1515, Bicocca in 1522, Pavia in 1525 and Landriano in 1529 – than by any other military activity.

Death rates also increased noticeably in these battles, even among noble and upper-class soldiers who could bring the highest ransoms. Examples in the early fourteenth century include Courtrai, in 1302, where between 40 and 50 per cent of the French cavalry were killed; Bannockburn in 1314, where between 154 and 700 English nobles were killed; Mons-en-Pévèle in 1304, where both the French and the Flemings lost upwards of 4000 each; Neville's Cross in 1347, where the lowest estimate of Scots killed is 2000; Crécy in 1346, where nine French princes, more than 1200 knights and between 15,000 and 16,000 others died; and Kephissos in 1311, where nearly the whole Athenian Frankish force disappeared.

Novara is located west of Milan in Piedmont. Faithful to the Milanese duke, the French felt that if they conquered Novara they might again force the Milanese under their control.

ARMOURED PIKEMAN

This figure represents a well-armoured Swiss pikeman from the early sixteenth century. On his head, he wears a sallet, while his body is protected both by mail and plate armour. Only the legs are lightly armoured to allow a greater freedom of movement. Although the Swiss are traditionally associated with the pike, they frequently fought with other staff weapons, such as the halberd. By the end of the fifteenth century, pike/halberd units became mixed with arquebus units, the origin of the pike-and-shot tactical organization of the early modern period.

In 1500, Maximilian Sforza was only seven years old when he became Duke of Milan following the death of his father, Ludovico 'il Moro' (the Moor). Historically he was an ally of the Holy Roman Empire, with this early sixteenth-century illumination showing the young duke doing homage to Emperor Maximilian I. Thus Milan became the frequent target of French conquest during his reign.

THE OPPOSED FORCES

FRENCH

Total:	**10,000**

SWISS/MILANESE

Cavalry	200
Infantry	8–9000
Total:	**8–9200**

the charge did come, it quickly became disordered and confused. The impetus was lost, and the soldiers, cavalry or infantry hit their target with little force. Horses were stopped in front of the infantry lines, and infantry could not penetrate them. Cavalry soldiers were pulled from their horses and infantrymen were knocked down. There they became vulnerable to attacks from their opponents' weapons – lances, spears, swords, axes, polearms, 'goededags' – and other short-range weapons that proved effective against all whom they faced, no matter who they were or how well they were armoured. Eventually, these weapons and those used by other infantry forces were supplemented by hand-held gunpowder weapons, which would become prominent on the battlefields of continental Europe by the 1440s. Consequently, the number of dead rose and was always impressive to contemporary writers.

THE SWISS WAY OF WAR

Centralized authority in the medieval Holy Roman Empire was never very stable and, by the thirteenth century, had almost completely disappeared. With this disintegration came a desire for those living on the borders of the Empire to seek sovereignty. No doubt the most obvious of these 'rebellions' to modern historians were those fought by the city-states of northern Italy. By the end of the thirteenth century, Venice, Milan, Florence, Lucca, Pisa and Genoa, to name only the most prominent of these independence-seeking states, had shed their German political rulership and begun the process of self-government.

The separate cantons of Switzerland, though much smaller in population, desired sovereignty just as much. Associated with the rest of the Holy Roman Empire since the time of Charlemagne, but different in language, culture, society and economy, the medieval Swiss were faithful to the emperors during times of Imperial solidarity. In times of instability, however, they were ignored. Consequently, the Swiss towns, far smaller than German or Italian cities, learned to be quite self-sufficient. To survive, they also often connected with neighbouring towns and rural enclaves to form independent political organizations,

A reason for the increased numbers of battles and the higher casualty rates between 1302 and 1529 was that infantry had begun to dominate the battlefield. Although several previous battles during the Middle Ages had been fought using primarily infantry troops, and in some instances these troops had been victorious, the myth of cavalry superiority prevailed. This would change in the early fourteenth century, when Flemish, Scottish, Swiss, Frisian and Liégeois infantry soldiers all began to gain victories over largely cavalry-based French, English, Austrian and German armies.

Tactics used by these forces for victory quickly caught on: after choosing a suitable site for a battle and/or preparing the battlefield by digging ditches, constructing wagon-fortresses or flooding already marshy ground, which ensure that their opponents had only one course of attack (the frontal assault), the infantry were ordered into a defensive formation in one or more solid lines, to await a charge. When

Confident mercenary arquebusiers of the earlier sixteenth century sometimes felt it was better to be fashionable than well-protected. A favourite attire was the slash-sleeve coat that these two men are wearing. However, because of their slow rate of fire, the arquebusiers needed the protection of the pikemen.

Sempach (1386), both victories over the Austrians; the Battles of Grandson (1476), Murten (1476) and Nancy (1477), victories over the Burgundians; the Battles of Giocorno (1478) and Crevola (1487), victories against the Milanese; the Battles of Hard, Bruderholz, Schwaderloh, Frastanz and Calven, all fought in 1499; and all victories against the Holy Roman Empire. However, at times, these military alliances also turned against each other, as at the Battle of Laupen in 1339 and in the Old Zurich War (1440–46).

It is difficult to know exactly when among these numerous late medieval battles and wars that the reputation of the Swiss as superb, somewhat unique soldiers was formed. Machiavelli had certainly recognized it by the time he wrote his famous works, *The Prince* and *The Art of War*, in the second decade of the sixteenth century. He identified the Swiss 'way of war' as one in which infantry militias armed with pikes and polearms were able to face and defeat more traditional, medieval cavalry-based forces. He likened the Swiss troops to the Ancient Greeks and Romans, who had dominated their opponents not by fighting on horse, but by fighting in large, organized and disciplined infantry masses. Machiavelli, though, was simply taking his lead from the military leaders of his time, who had by then been hiring Swiss mercenaries for at least two generations.

Indeed, the Swiss way of war was being reported outside of Switzerland as early as the victory over the Austrians at Mortgarten in 1315. But it was undoubtedly the Swiss and Burgundian War, fought from the summer of 1476 to early in 1477, which did the most good for the reputation of the Swiss soldiers. In three

Armour was still quite expensive, and mercenary Swiss soldiers most often acquired theirs as war booty from enemy soldiers or from fallen companions. At the outset of their careers, many wore no armour at all. As gunpowder weapons became more powerful in the sixteenth century, the need for armour also became less important.

known as cantons. In 1291, three of these cantons – Uri, Schwyz and Unterwalden – allied to form a political and military union, the first Swiss Confederation.

During the fourteenth and fifteenth centuries, more political–military unions and 'Swiss Confederations' followed. Ostensibly, these were formed, like the first in 1291, as defensive alliances against incursions from outside military forces. The Holy Roman Empire and its various parts – especially Habsburg Austria, the traditional rulers of Switzerland – always posed a threat, as did the Kingdom of France, Duchy of Burgundy and Duchy of Milan. Surprisingly, in almost all of these engagements, Swiss armies of generally smaller size defeated these foreign forces, as at: the Battles of Morgarten (1315) and

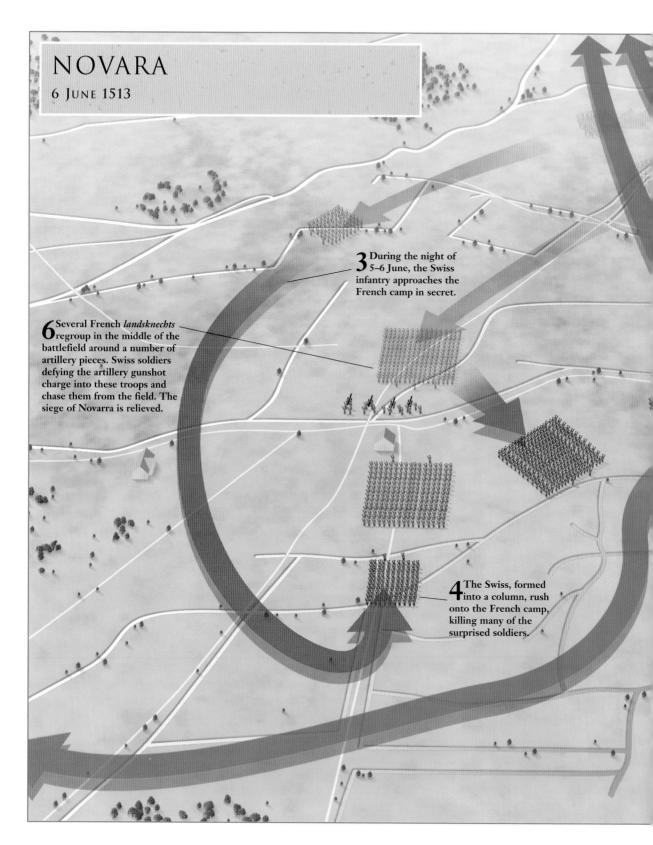

NOVARA
6 June 1513

3 During the night of 5–6 June, the Swiss infantry approaches the French camp in secret.

6 Several French *landsknechts* regroup in the middle of the battlefield around a number of artillery pieces. Swiss soldiers defying the artillery gunshot charge into these troops and chase them from the field. The siege of Novarra is relieved.

4 The Swiss, formed into a column, rush onto the French camp, killing many of the surprised soldiers.

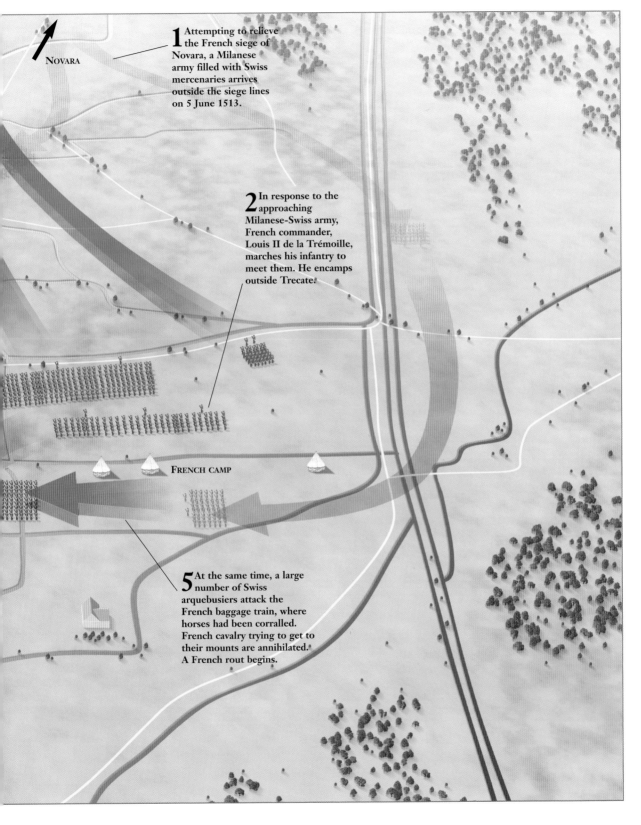

NOVARA

1 Attempting to relieve the French siege of Novara, a Milanese army filled with Swiss mercenaries arrives outside the siege lines on 5 June 1513.

2 In response to the approaching Milanese-Swiss army, French commander, Louis II de la Trémoille, marches his infantry to meet them. He encamps outside Trecate.

FRENCH CAMP

5 At the same time, a large number of Swiss arquebusiers attack the French baggage train, where horses had been corralled. French cavalry trying to get to their mounts are annihilated. A French rout begins.

battles – Grandson, Murten and Nancy – the Swiss so outfought the vaunted Burgundian forces of Duke Charles the Bold (1433–1477) that by the end of the war Charles was dead and virtually the entire Burgundian Army had disappeared. Among the Swiss, however, there had been very few casualties. They had also faced and defeated perhaps the best gunpowder artillery train in the world. All this had been done while fighting on foot, with pikes, polearms and hand-held guns. Swiss tactical movements had been especially impressive, as they manoeuvred their thick columns of troops through woods and across fields with a fluidity and discipline – a 'professionalism', to use a modern term – unseen in other armies of their time. And the reputation of their ruthlessness, love of war and refusal to take prisoners – defying the 'chivalric' rules of medieval warfare – became celebrated.

Soon it became fashionable for military leaders to try to hire as many Swiss soldiers to fight for them as possible. These mercenaries quickly became expensive, so it was not uncommon to find soldiers of other nationalities, but able to speak French or German, claiming that they, too, were Swiss. These Swiss mercenaries came not as single soldiers but as units, able to fight with the same weapons and to deliver the same manoeuvres on the battlefield as were seen in the Swiss and Burgundian War. By the

start of the Italian Wars, almost every army contained a contingent of Swiss mercenaries, although at the time of the Battle of Novara they fought almost solely for the Holy Roman Empire and its allies.

THE ITALIAN WARS

In 1494, King Charles VIII (1470–1498) of France marched his army south into and through Italy in an effort to exert a French claim to the throne of Naples. The expedition turned out to be relatively fruitless, with most of Charles' men dying of disease or at the battle of Fornovo (6 July 1495). Nevertheless, it opened floodgates of European conflict in the peninsula, which would not be closed until the middle of the sixteenth century. It seems this began because none of the Italian city-states felt that they could face a force as large as the French Army in battle. In fact, some of the larger city-states – Milan, Florence and the Papal States – chose to ally with the French, not only to allow them free access through their lands, but also to supply them, while others – Venice and Naples – chose to oppose them. Of course, for the previous two centuries, these Italian principalities had continuously fought against each other, so there is little reason to believe that they might have united at this time.

In 1495, Charles VIII withdrew to France, leaving his former allies to fare as

best they could. Spanish forces under the famous General Gonzalo Fernández de Córdoba (1453–1515) entered Naples and threw out the small French garrison there. The Milanese, led by Duke Ludovico Sforza (1452–1508), feeling abandoned by the French, quickly sought peace and an alliance of its own with the Spanish and Imperial forces.

Once again, however, the tide turned. Louis XII (1462–1515), who as Duke of Orléans and cousin to the king had assumed the French throne on Charles VIII's death in 1498, marched into Italy the following year, targeting and defeating Milan and then once again taking his army to Naples. But after a tenuous peace with Fernández de Cordoba fell through in 1503, the French were defeated at the Battles of Cerignola and Garigliano and retreated to France once more.

Left once more on their own, the previous allies of France soon made peace with the Spanish, who seemed satisfied for the moment with control of Naples, and determined to turn their bellicose animosity against Venice, which up to this time had

---

The strength of Swiss mercenaries was their tactical unity. Initially this was based on community (or canton) similarity, but later it was more likely to come from unit discipline, honour and survival.

stayed largely out of the fray. In 1508, Pope Julius II (1443–1513), himself a general who thought nothing of changing from his papal robes and mitre to armour, formed the League of Cambrai – taking the name of the French town where the agreement had been signed. This was an alliance of France, the Papacy, Spain and the Holy Roman Empire designed to hold back the Venetians. With such a large number of members, it would seem that the Venetians had little chance of success, a judgement initially confirmed by their defeat at the Battle of Agnadelo in 1509. However, the League could not take Padua in 1510 and, in a strange move, this prompted Julius II to leave the alliance he had founded and join with Venice.

The pope's animosity had turned against France and soon, despite a number of defeats in 1511, other nations had joined with him in a Holy League against Louis XII, including Spain, the Holy Roman Empire and, a newcomer, England. Still, the French Army, led by Gaston de Foix (d.1500), responded with a victory at the

Battle of Ravenna the following year. Having lost de Foix in the battle, however, it withdrew to France shortly thereafter.

THE BATTLE OF NOVARA

As France was retreating, the Swiss were invading. They had been hired by Emperor Maximilian I (1459–1519) to restore his ally, a Sforza duke, also named Maximilian, to the Milanese throne. The French having left Italy, the Swiss conquered the city easily. Although they showed no inclination to expand beyond Milan, the Venetians regarded this as a threat and – despite the Holy Roman Empire being allied with them – changed sides, petitioning France to return to the conflict. Louis responded in 1513 by sending back into Italy an army of around 10,000–12,000 (including a large contingent of *landsknechts*, mercenary soldiers who imitated the Swiss method of fighting).

Louis II de la Trémoille (1460–1525) now led the French, and he was an entirely different leader from his predecessor. Where Gaston de Foix was young,

This romantic illustration depicts the ride of one of the French leaders, Robert de la Marck, Duke of Bouillon, to save his sons, Florange – who had been badly wounded – and Jamets.

egotistical and brash on the battlefield – traits that had undoubtedly enabled his victory at Ravenna but which may also have led to his death in the waning moments of the battle – La Trémoille was older and much more cautious. While de Foix had pushed for battle, La Trémoille decided to pursue the more cautious strategy of the siege – and not even the siege of Milan itself, but of the smaller Milanese town of Novara, 40km (25 miles) west of Milan. Apologists for the French general suggest that either he believed that his army was too small to face the Swiss and Milanese forces or that he chose Novara as his desired battlefield, reckoning that the Swiss would respond to his invasion with a battle, and that it was better for him to select the terrain rather than them.

Despite their grisly occupations, most soldiers in the sixteenth century strongly believed in God and sought justification for the wars they were involved in, even if they were being paid to fight. Before battle, they would pray and attend Mass, as depicted in this nineteenth-century illustration.

not to wait until morning, or even to wait until their entire army had arrived, but to surprise the French with a night attack, hoping to catch many of the French asleep or at least unprepared to fight a battle.

DISPOSITIONS

The Swiss Army was almost entirely made up of infantry soldiers, pikemen, polearmers and arquebusiers. Of the 8000–9000 troops, only about 200 were Milanese cavalry, accompanied by only eight falconets, light field artillery pieces. The infantry was divided into three sections: two of around 1000 men each were to watch the flanks from cavalry attacks, and a third section of 6000–7000 soldiers was to attack the infantry camp and artillery park. The units marched quietly to the battlefield, trying not to arouse any French scouts or pickets.

The result was just as the Swiss captains had planned. Arriving outside the camp without any alarm being sounded and without breaking formation, the infantry rushed onto the sleeping Frenchmen. La Trémoille's army was entirely surprised. In fact, so complete was the surprise that neither of the flanking columns was directly engaged, despite expecting the customary French flanking cavalry manoeuvre. On the left, the Swiss were able to sweep around the camp and the town of Trecate to fall onto the virtually unprotected French baggage train. The right column came out of the woods, which they were using to hide their movement, and set upon the French cavalry, who were confused and unable to mount any resistance. The arquebusiers in this contingent simply fired round after round of gunshot into the cavalry until they were killed or had fled. The remaining soldiers in this column performed their own flanking attack, joining their middle column in an assault on the French camp.

However, it was the large centre column of the Swiss that did the most damage to the French, whose tents were quickly overrun. Many French soldiers immediately fled in rout. But a large number of *landsknechts* regrouped in a defensive line near Trecate, their artillery – which seems largely to have survived the initial attacks – positioned in front of them. The Swiss, too, had regrouped into their columns and, defying

Perhaps these were La Trémoille's thoughts, for the Swiss immediately responded to the French siege of Novara, arriving at the city on 5 June. La Trémoille then left his siege lines and marched to a field 4km (2.5 miles) away, close to the small town of Trecate, which he had obviously scouted out as the most tactically advantageous site for a battle. There he encamped for the night, expecting the Swiss to do battle with him the following morning. The Swiss, however, were not accustomed to do the 'expected' in warfare. That, indeed, was their reputation and La Trémoille should have known this. The Swiss leaders – who seem to have had a central command committee of captains rather than a single commander – decided

the artillery barrage, charged. Contemporary reports, including one written by Florange de la Marck, the commander of the French *landsknechts*, claim that a volley of cannonballs fiercely mowed through the Swiss. It did not stop them and, before a second volley could be fired, they were upon the *landsknechts*, killing and wounding with a ruthlessness fitting their reputation. It was over quickly. Florange writes: 'To put it shortly, we lost the battle, and the *landsknechts* got no help: for of the French infantry not a man stood to fight when they saw the other French column coming down upon them, so my *landsknechts* were broken and routed, and all the artillery was taken.' Florange himself was saved only when his father, Robert de la Marck, Duke of Bouillon, rode into the midst of the battle and rescued him – 'with 46 cuts upon me,' he alleges – and his brother, Jamets.

Where was La Trémoille? It seems he had fled from his Trecate headquarters at the initial Swiss attack. Most historians have thus branded him a coward, although his supporters claim that he was merely trying to set up a cavalry counterattack. If so, it never materialized; in fact, most of his cavalry fled with him. Cowardice therefore seems a justifiable conclusion. Almost all of the French cavalry got away, with only about 40 losing their lives while more than 5000 infantry lay dead or dying on the battlefield.

AFTERMATH

The Swiss death toll was also large, with as many as 1300 being killed, 700 of them from the single artillery bombardment at the beginning of their final charge. Perhaps this is why the Battle of Novara, so decisive in its vindication of the Swiss way of war, was also the last great Swiss victory. The methods used by them were bound to be costly. As shown by the slaughter caused by the French artillery in a single barrage, the reckless 'berserker' tactics of the Swiss infantry could not be sustained. At Novara, it was the surprise as much as – or indeed more than – the infantry columns that brought them victory.

The future for warfare lay not in the Swiss way of war, but in the pike-and-shot formations that would become more prevalent in the next century of warfare. Pikemen would dominate the battlefield for the next 150 years.

This painting from the early sixteenth century shows the Swiss fighting for Louis XII against Imperial troops at Geneva in 1507. The artist may not have been at the battle, but his accuracy of the Swiss arms, armour, clothing and heraldry indicates that these troops were well known to him.

NAGASHINO

28 June 1575

THE BATTLE OF NAGASHINO WAS A CLASH OF OLD AND NEW TECHNOLOGIES. THE TRADITIONAL JAPANESE 'WAY OF THE SWORD' CONFRONTED THE REALITY OF EARLY FIREARMS, WITH DECISIVE RESULTS THAT WERE TO CHANGE THE WAY BATTLES WERE FOUGHT IN JAPAN.

WHY DID IT HAPPEN?

WHO The *daimyo* (feudal lord) Takeda Katsuyori (1546–82) fought the combined forces of Oda Nobunaga (1534–82) and Tokugawa Ieyasu (1543–1616).

WHAT Takeda besieged Nagashino Castle, to which Oda and Tokugawa sent a massive relief army that was heavily armed with arquebus gunners.

WHERE The area around Nagashino Castle, in Totomi Province, central Japan.

WHEN 28 June 1575.

WHY Takeda had wider territorial ambitions for central Japan and was aiming to defeat the Tokugawa armies and advance against Kyoto.

OUTCOME An eight-hour battle saw the almost complete destruction of Takeda's army, with devastating casualties caused by volley fire from enemy arquebusiers.

The Battle of Nagashino was born out of a time of great social turmoil in Japan. The decline of the Ashikaga shogunate (1336–1573), previously a unifying presence within Japan, in the second half of the fifteenth century led to the country's splitting into numerous different fiefdoms, each ruled by *daimyo* leaders and their own personal armies. The *daimyo* fought amongst themselves for the next century, trying to gain control over greater territories and over the still symbolically powerful figure of the shogun, the emperor's military commander-in-chief and effectively ruler of Japan. By the end of the 1560s, one of the big winners in the struggle was Oda Nobunaga. Oda was a great and ruthless samurai general, who from 1568 took the Japanese capital, Kyoto, installed a puppet shogun and controlled a large swathe of territory in central Japan.

Oda's enemies, however, were not far away. One of the greatest threats lay in the eastern provinces controlled by the *daimyo* Takeda Shingen (1521–73), who also had his eyes set on Kyoto. The chief obstacles to Takeda's ambition were the territories of the Tokugawa family (Totomi and Mikawa Provinces), which along the Pacific coast separated Takeda's provinces from those of Oda. In 1572, Takeda went for broke, pushing into Tokugawa territory and besieging the castle of Noda, seat of the Tokugawa leader and general Tokugawa

Okazaki Castle, Tokushima, Shikoku, Japan. It was here that the great Tokugawa Ieyasu was born in 1542. Ieyasu proved himself a brilliant politician and soldier, and became Shogun in 1603.

ARQUEBUS-ARMED SAMURAI

A sixteenth-century Japanese arquebusier takes aim with his matchlock weapon. His uniform is relatively simple – he wears a cone-shaped helmet, a light armoured cuirass and protective leggings. Footwear is a pair of straw sandals known as waraji. *The bundles hung over his shoulder contain portions of rice, while the bags on the belt hold powder and shot. Two swords are stuck into the belt on his opposite hip; the pair are called* daisho, *and consist of a longer* katana *and a shorter* wakizashi. *Note that the arquebus has nothing in the way of sights on it. Because of its poor accuracy, the weapon would simply be pointed in the direction of the enemy rather than aimed with any precision.*

Ieyasu (1542–1616). There his ambitions were thwarted – Takeda was killed by a sniper's musket ball.

Takeda's son Takeda Katsuyori, however, kept the candle of expansionism burning. In 1575, he invaded Tokugawa territory, but quickly found himself in difficulties. An attempt to take Okazaki Castle in western Mikawa Province was abandoned when Takeda's man on the inside, who was to open the castle gates for the invaders, was unmasked in advance and executed. A subsequent onslaught against Yoshida Castle, further to the south on Mikawa Bay, was stopped militarily, the Tokugawa having brought the garrison up to a strength of 6000 men. Yet Takeda soon found another target – the castle of Nagashino, further north along the Toyokawa River.

SIEGE CONDITIONS

Nagashino Castle sat between the forks created by the Takigawa (west) and Onogawa (east) rivers, where they joined to form the Toyokawa. The banks of the rivers towered up to 50m (164ft) high, hence placing the castle in a strong defensive position. The castle itself consisted of a series of wooden dwellings contained within the stone walls of the *hon-maru* (inner bailey) and protected by two more ranks of outer defences, the *ni-no-maru* (second bailey) and *san-no-maru* (third bailey). Four gates punctuated the outer walls; holding these would be critical to the defence. Though physically well protected, the castle contained a military garrison of only some 500 men against the 15,000 troops that began to surround the fortification in mid-June 1575. Between 17 and 27 June, Takeda threw his army against Nagashino Castle in several major attacks. Remarkably, all were battered off by stubborn defence. Takeda therefore decided to place the castle under siege and starve the defenders out.

Yet by this time Takeda had a larger problem than Nagashino Castle looming. An enemy relief force was on its way. On 24 June, Oda Nobunaga and Tokugawa Ieyasu, both at Okazaki, were informed of the situation at Nagashino and, motivated by reports that the garrison had only three more days of supplies, quickly moved to raise a relief force. A total of 38,000 troops was assembled (Oda 30,000 and Tokugawa 8000) and marched for Nagashino.

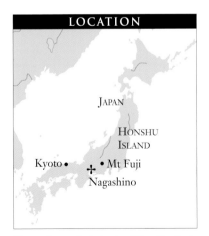

LOCATION

JAPAN

HONSHU ISLAND

Kyoto •

✛ • Mt Fuji

Nagashino

The cross here marks the location of Nagashino Castle. The struggle for political power in sixteenth- and seventeeth-century Japan focused upon central Honshu, which contained the capital Kyoto.

NAGASHINO

A member of a reenactment society displays traditional samurai armour, with bow and horned helmet, at the Nara Festival, Japan. Archers provided more accurate fire than arquebusiers, but required much more training to bring to any level of competence.

THE OPPOSED FORCES

ODA/TOKUGAWA (estimated)

Total:	**38,000**

TAKEDA (estimated)

Total:	**15,000**

ARMIES AND ARQUEBUSES

The Japanese armies of the sixteenth century were basically split into two different orders. Occupying leadership and warrior roles were the samurai, highly trained armoured troops who traditionally fought mounted, although economic conditions in the late 1500s forced many to operate on foot. The classic samurai weapons were the sword, bow and, most tactically important, the *mochi-yari* spear, a stabbing and slashing weapon some 3.5–4m (11.5–13.1ft) long. The samurai cavalry were a true elite, and were used to smash or outmanoeuvre enemy lines in close-quarter combat.

Beneath the samurai – but critical in forming the bulk of an army – were the *ashigaru* footsoldiers. The *ashigaru* were more lightly armoured than the samurai, and as combatants they were principally armed with spears, bows and arquebus firearms, although around 25 per cent of

ashigaru were non-combat support troops. Dedicated spear units armed with weapons up to 6m (19.7ft) long would make up the largest combatant portion of the *ashigaru*. By contrast, the smallest portion consisted of the archers, their numbers restricted by the skill and time-demanding training required of their profession. The great advantage of the archers was their accuracy over a 400m (437-yard) range and their rate of fire – an arrow could be unleashed every five to six seconds.

The third type of armed *ashigaru* were those equipped with the arquebus. First introduced into Japan by the Portuguese in 1543, the arquebus was a simple muzzle-loaded matchlock firearm, light enough to

Opposite: A gentle depiction of a samurai warrior of the Ashikaga period, seated beside his bow, fanning himself. Composite bows such as this one would have a range of up to 400m (437 yards).

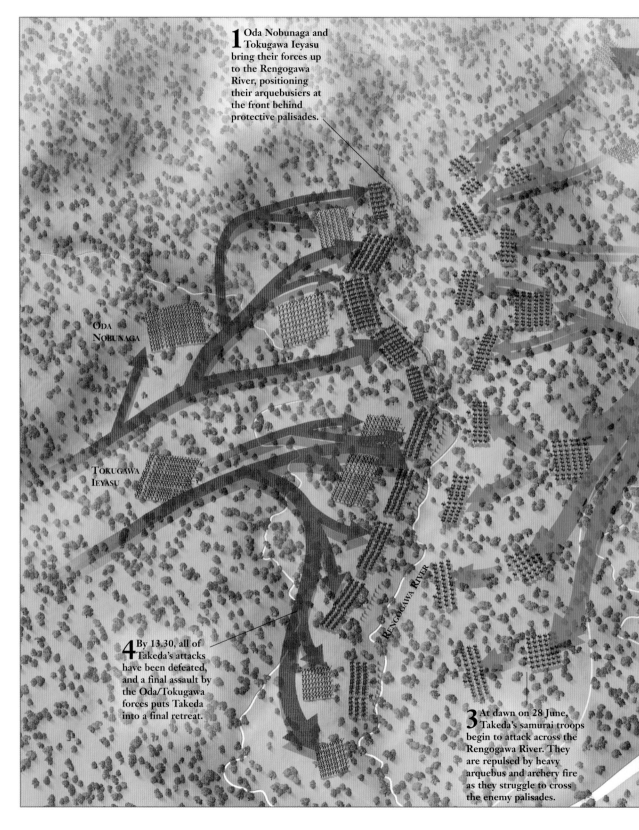

1 Oda Nobunaga and Tokugawa Ieyasu bring their forces up to the Rengogawa River, positioning their arquebusiers at the front behind protective palisades.

ODA NOBUNAGA

TOKUGAWA IEYASU

RENGOGAWA RIVER

4 By 13.30, all of Takeda's attacks have been defeated, and a final assault by the Oda/Tokugawa forces puts Takeda into a final retreat.

3 At dawn on 28 June, Takeda's samurai troops begin to attack across the Rengogawa River. They are repulsed by heavy arquebus and archery fire as they struggle to cross the enemy palisades.

NAGASHINO
CASTLE

5 Later, Takeda's siege
lines on Tobigasu Hill
are breached by a 3000-
strong raiding party from
Oda's army, bringing the
siege to an end.

TAKEDA
KATSUYORI

2 Leaving behind a 2000-
strong siege force at
Nagashino Castle, Takeda
Katsuyori pulls the bulk
of his troops away to face
the combined
Oda/Tokugawa army.

NAGASHINO

28 JUNE 1575

NAGASHINO

be fired from the shoulder, although heavy versions that required a support were also used. The capabilities of individual arquebuses were extremely limited. Accuracy was very poor; range was limited to just a few hundred metres, although the effective range against armour plate was little more than 50m/55 yards; misfires were common; and a laborious loading procedure meant that the maximum rate of fire was some three rounds per minute, and often much slower if the gun was in inexperienced hands or was fouled. The true advantage of the arquebus, however, emerged when the weapon was used in volley. Oda had learned this lesson himself when fighting against Buddhist Ikko-Ikki rebels around Ishiyama Hongan-ji in 1570 – volleys from some

3000 arquebusiers had a lethal impact upon his army's ranks. Furthermore, handling an arquebus required a fraction of the skill demanded of a bowman; therefore an army could more rapidly increase its firepower.

Both sides in the Battle of Nagashino had enthusiastically embraced firearms, but it was Oda, drawing on his brutal experience, who best understood the tactical applications of such weapons. Oda took 3000 arquebusiers with him to the Nagashino battlefield, and had trained them in the application of disciplined volley tactics. During the lulls in reloading, the archers would take over to maintain a constant rain of direct fire on the enemy. Takeda also had arquebus-armed troops, but at the time of Nagashino he still relied on cavalry dash.

THE BATTLE

By 27 June, the Nagashino relief forces were assembling on the battlefield. This was not the immediate surrounds of the castle; instead the Oda–Tokugawa troops gathered on the plain of Shidarahara, some 5km (3.1 miles) from the castle, behind the banks of the Rengogawa River. The river was actually little more than a shallow stream, but sitting 100m (109 yards) in front of the relief force's lines it provided a soggy obstacle to cavalry. A three-tiered palisade of wooden stakes just high enough to prevent a horse jumping over it was also built a short distance behind the river, which served to further break up Takeda's cavalry. The wooden structure, with gaps to enable counterattack movement, also provided cover for Oda's arquebusiers, who were sited forward. Protecting the Oda–Tokugawa right flank was the Toyokawa, which bent around beneath the army to the west, while on the left flank there was forested and hilly ground.

The relief troops acted as a carrot for Takeda, despite commanders such as Baba Nobuharu (1514–75) urging that the castle be taken first. Baba wisely argued that it would be make better sense to fight Oda from defensive positions within the castle rather than to take heavy casualties from ball and arrow while charging across open ground. Nevertheless Takeda, tempted by prospects of glory, ordered all but 2000

Mounted samurai with banners here make a ferocious charge. These soldiers are obviously wealthier samurai, since by the time of the Nagashino battle many samurai did not have the financial means for horses.

A dismounted samurai soldier, providing a good view of the typical body armour of the time. The jingasa *helmet gave protection to both the skull and the back of the neck, and the armour was often formed out of plates of lacquered iron.*

troops to leave the castle siege and head out for the confrontation. The 12,000 men going into battle would be arranged in four divisions, each consisting of some 3000 troops and together forming right, centre and left wings plus a headquarters reserve. In addition, a further 1000 men were based in wooden forts near the castle, on Tobigasu Hill to the east.

FRONTAL ATTACK

A frontal attack seemed the most judicious plan, since from woodland at the east of the plain to the nearest point of Oda's lines was a distance of little more than 200m (219 yards). Although open to enemy fire, this could theoretically be covered at speed. Takeda also surmised that many of the enemy arquebuses would prove useless because of wet weather. As it happened, the arquebusiers' powder had been kept dry, and the principal effect of the rain was to create soggy ground that was ill-suited to a fast cavalry charge.

The battle began on 28 June at 0600, as Takeda's cavalry emerged onto the plain and began a thunderous, drum-motivated charge towards the enemy lines. The charge was initially uncontested, except by the Rengogawa River, which slowed the cavalry in its crossing. However, as the horsemen emerged up the far bank, a withering fusillade of fire rippled out from the 3000 matchlockmen, arranged behind the palisade in three ranks, each rank firing in turn. Some 9000 rounds were fired in the first three rapid volleys alone, and cavalrymen and horses dropped in horrifying numbers as shot hit home from around 50m (55 yards). Oda had placed some of his best commanders in charge of the arquebusiers; Takeda had done likewise with his cavalry, meaning that with each volley he lost some of his most important leaders, while Oda's finest remained behind the protective wooden shield. Those cavalrymen who survived the gunfire found themselves pressed up against the palisade. Here they were easy prey for *ashigaru*

Katsutaka (below right), besieged in Nagashino castle, broke out and sought help from Tokugawa Ieyasu. He was captured when he tried to return, but in an act of heroism he shouted to the castle garrison that they would soon be relieved. He was immediately killed.

Right: A statue of Tokugawa Ieyasu. As a military commander, Tokugawa was known for his personal bravery, a man who would endure physical injuries to prosecute an attack. He held the position of Shogun from 1603 to 1605.

Below: An extensive set of samurai body armour, as would have clad the more affluent warrior. Such armour could be time-consuming to put on. One method for speeding up the entire process was to hang the set of armour from cords, then stand up into it.

spearmen, who simply drove their long spears up through the defences to pierce horse or rider. Other cavalrymen who found themselves channelled through the gaps in the palisade were attacked by further Oda–Tokugawa *ashigaru* and the dismounted samurai.

Successive waves of attackers were soon throwing themselves against the palisade, with similar results. Meanwhile, the battle was widening. Oda had sent the Tokugawa officer Sakai Tadatsugu (1527–96) with a raiding party of several thousand troops – including 500 matchlockmen – to attack the Takeda siege lines around Nagashino Castle, focusing on the four forts commanded by Takeda Nobuzane (d. 1575). The attack went in at 0800, and such was its success that defenders from Nagashino Castle itself entered the battle. Takeda Nobuzane was killed, along with 200 of his men. The battle was beginning to tip in favour of the Oda–Tokugawa army.

FINISHING THE FIGHT

On the Shidarahara Plain, the efforts of Takeda's army to break the Oda–Tokugawa lines were steadily failing. Throughout the morning, the cavalry and other troops threw themselves in vain against the palisade defences, while taking constant losses from arquebus fire, arrows and spears. Dozens of Takeda's top commanders fell. Flanking attacks over on the left wing of the battlefield had proved to be futile and had more than justified Oda's choice of battleground. Over on the right wing, however, the battle was going somewhat differently, principally because here the Oda–Tokugawa troops under Okubo Tadayo (1531–93) had no protective barrier in front of them. Here the enemy soldiers of Yamagata Masakage (1524–75) made a powerful assault that resulted in bloody hand-to-hand combat, with the samurai of both sides given the opportunity to show their courage in action and their skill with sword and spear. One notable victim of the clash was Yamagata himself. Fighting from horseback, supported by three samurai, he was finally killed by a fusillade of arquebus fire. In traditional samurai style, his head was cut from his body as a battle trophy.

FINAL ASSAULT

While Yamagata was fighting his last battle, Takeda had also launched his forces in a final all-out attack, pulling in his reserves for the fight. Close-quarter combat raged up and down the line for several hours until, at around 1300, Oda gave the signal for disengagement and a withdrawal to fall-back positions. However, this order was quickly reversed into an attack command when it became apparent that Takeda's forces themselves were in retreat. Now the Oda–Tokugawa mounted samurai could have their day. They charged the fleeing enemy, killing hundreds of men and adding to the toll of commanders who were left on the battlefield.

Some eight hours after the fighting had first begun, the battle was over. The Oda–Tokugawa army was victorious, having killed 10,000 of Takeda's 15,000 men, including more than 50 per cent of his samurai commanders. The siege of Nagashino was broken, and Takeda Katsuyori, who survived the battle, retreated back to Kai and Shinano Provinces, where he fought on the defensive for the next seven years. Steadily his allies deserted, and then turned on him, giving the opening, in 1582, for the Oda and Tokugawa to deal the finishing blow. Takeda committed suicide at Toriibata, only 300 soldiers remaining by his side.

Historical studies of the Battle of Nagashino have frequently overplayed the contribution of the arquebus to its outcome. That the battle lasted eight hours suggests that the bow, sword and spear must also have played their part in the Oda–Tokugawa victory. Nevertheless, it is certain that the arquebus was central to the battle's outcome, its correct application as a volley-firing weapon, combined with an excellent defensive arrangement, causing a high level of casualties and dealing a crushing blow to a force that was employing traditional methods of warfare.

The samurai were meant to embody the essence of martial ferocity. Here, in a picture from the nineteenth-century artist Yoshitoshi, a mounted samurai smashes through a foot soldier, splitting his opponent's sword in half in the process.

SACHEON
29 May 1592

BY NEGLECTING THE DEVELOPMENT OF AN EFFECTIVE NAVY, JAPAN WAS COURTING DISASTER IN ITS INVASION OF KOREA IN 1592. AT SACHEON THE KOREAN NAVY, COMMANDED BY ADMIRAL YI SUN-SHIN AND ARMED WITH GROUND-BREAKING 'TURTLE SHIPS', UNDERMINED THE ENTIRE JAPANESE ENTERPRISE.

WHY DID IT HAPPEN?

WHO Japanese naval forces, under ultimate command of Toyotomi Hideyoshi (1536–98), were confronted by the smaller but more modern Korean fleet under Admiral Yi Sun-shin (1545–98).

WHAT Admiral Yi attacked a Japanese naval squadron anchored at Sacheon, drawing it out to sea, where he had the advantage of manoeuvrability and superior naval gunnery.

WHERE Sacheon, on the southern coast of the Korean Peninsula.

WHEN 29 May 1592.

WHY With Korean land forces being routed by the Japanese, Admiral Yi chose a strategy of interdicting the Japanese maritime supply routes.

OUTCOME Up to 40 Japanese ships lost for no Korean vessels, and the beginning of Korean naval supremacy in the Imjin War (1592–98).

The origins of the Battle of Sacheon lay in the territorial ambitions of Toyotomi Hideyoshi, the Japanese *daimyo* (feudal lord) who held together a fractious nation. By the late 1580s, Hideyoshi was developing plans for a Japanese invasion of Ming dynasty China, plans fuelled by the need to cement his samurais' loyalty with material gain and a desire to fulfil the similar dreams of his predecessor Oda Nobunaga (1534–82). Korea, however, stood as the geographical wedge between Japan and the Chinese hinterlands.

WEAK AGAINST STRONG

At this point in its history, under the leadership of King Seonjo (1552–1608), Korea was acutely vulnerable. Its principal alliance was with China, with whom Korea had built decent trading connections since the late fourteenth century. Korea's good relations with its neighbour, however, had bred military complacency by the second half of the sixteenth century. The army in particular was critically weakened. It had been repeatedly downsized, despite protestations to the court from influential officials such as Yu Seong-ryong (1542–1607), who later advocated a strong policy of conscription to counter growing Japanese power. Coastal fortifications were allowed to crumble and were inadequately garrisoned, and the weaponry of footsoldiers was beginning to date.

Seoul, South Korea – South Korean students look at a miniature replica of the 'turtle' ship of Admiral Yi Sun-shin. Note the dragon's head at the bow; another carved war-face sat just below this on the waterline.

TURTLE SHIP

The kobukson *turtle ship, showing its fearsome spiked metal armour on the top deck. This armour prevented the enemy using boarding tactics, while it also gave protection to the crew beneath, who were able to focus all their efforts on bringing the cannon to bear. The new vessel's design was generally attributed to Admiral Yi, and had much in common with the* panokson *– it was flat-bottomed, of pine construction and had two masts supplemented by oar power; but it had some defining differences. The upper deck of the ship was entirely covered in spiked boards or plates – hence the nickname of 'turtle ship'. The layout not only protected the crew from enemy fire beneath a closed deck, but the spikes also prevented the enemy from easily boarding the vessel without suffering injury. Although many argue that the deck plates were metal and hence the* kobukson *constituted the first 'ironclad' warship, the sources are far from conclusive on the matter. The protective deck may well have been simply wooden, the iron spikes driven through the wood; although some Japanese battle reports do suggest an overall metal construction.*

The issue of weaponry was critical. The Japanese had invested heavily in arquebus matchlock firearms since their introduction into Japan in 1543 by the Portuguese. The Koreans, by contrast, had rejected the early firearms out of hand and ignored Yu Seong-ryong's advocacy of them, preferring instead to rely on long-range composite bows as their direct-fire weapons.

It was an unfortunate decision. Although arquebus weapons were individually inaccurate, they required a fraction of the training time necessary to produce a competent archer and were devastating when fired in volley – an advantage despite the fact that the bow could be fired more quickly.

Since Japan's production of arquebus firearms was running at around 3000 by 1590, the Japanese army quickly outstripped Korea in terms of firepower, especially as it was expanding its ranks and also had an excellent body of archers. In most other

regards, the Japanese army overshadowed its Korean counterpart, too.

While most Korean footsoldiers went into battle without substantial body armour (the use of mail was no longer widespread by the mid-sixteenth century), Japanese soldiers retained mail and plate armour, which gave a reasonable degree of protection to the torso, arms and legs. Even though Korean mounted troops and officers generally wore armour, arquebus balls could penetrate substantial plate at ranges of over 50m (55 yards).

The military inequalities between Korea and Japan became critically relevant in the early 1590s. Hideyoshi informed King Seonjo of his intention to invade China, and requested that his army be granted free passage through Korea.

Whether he underestimated the Japanese threat or placed greater store in his alliance

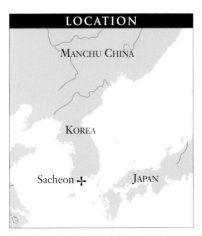

LOCATION

MANCHU CHINA

KOREA

Sacheon ✚   JAPAN

It was almost inevitable that Sacheon would become an invasion battleground. If Japan could consolidate the southern Korean ports, its navy would be able to support the landward drive north to China.

Opposite: The Kabuki actor Ichikawa Danjuro IX in the role of Kato Kiyomasa, the sixteenth-century general, his eyes unfocused to signify deep emotion in this 1876 painting. The codes of Bushido – the 'way of the warrior' – influenced all services of the Japanese military, including the Japanese navy.

THE OPPOSED FORCES

KOREAN NAVY (estimated)
   26 warships
   1 kobukson (turtle ship)

Total: **27 ships**

JAPANESE NAVY (estimated)

Total: **70 ships**

The Atakebune *ship was the largest of the Japanese fighting vessels, as this illustration here suggests. It was a boxlike multi-deck vessel with up to 100 crew and fighters aboard. Note the loopholes along the side of the vessel, through which matchblockmen, crossbowmen and archers were able to fire.*

with China, King Seonjo rejected the request. Hideyoshi responded quickly – on 23 May 1592, a force of some 150,000 Japanese soldiers made an amphibious landing on Korea's southern coastline at Busan and Dadaejin.

The Japanese invasion, made by the 1st and 2nd Divisions under Kato Kiyomasa (1562–1611) and Konishi Yukinaga (1555–1600) respectively, began a complete, catastrophic rout of the Korean land forces. Having consolidated the southern ports, the Japanese began a seemingly relentless march to the north.

Korea did attempt to respond to this threat, and the prophetic Yu Seong-ryong became overall military leader. However, fortresses and cities fell in quick succession, including Sangju, Chungju, Gyeongju and Hanseong (modern Seoul), until the Korean Government itself was forced to take flight.

It initially fled north to Pyongyang, but by early 1593 that city had also fallen, and the Japanese drove up to the Yalu and Tumen Rivers on the border with China. By this time, however, the tide was turning against the Japanese in Korea.

NAVAL POWER

While the Korean army had suffered from careless underinvestment during the second half of the sixteenth century, the same was not true of the Korean navy. Partly because of the need to protect its coastal trade lines (Korea had suffered the depredations of Japanese pirates for much of the 1500s), and partly because of the efforts of Admiral Yi Sun-shin, who recognized the Japanese threat, the Korean navy had maintained a respectable strength and had even invested in new technology. The Japanese, by contrast, had to conduct a major shipbuilding exercise at breakneck pace to

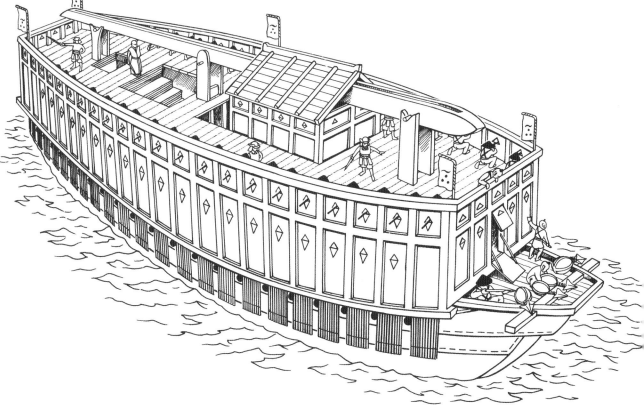

SACHEON

29 May 1592

2 The Korean naval leader Admiral Yi-Sun-shin receives reports of the Japanese deployment, and deploys a force of 27 fighting vessels from his headquarters at Yeosu to the west.

5 The *kobukson* turtle ship gets in amongst the Japanese vessels, creating destruction and panic amongst the Japanese crews. By nightfall, the Japanese fleet has been effectively destroyed by the superior Korean tactics and gunnery.

4 As soon as the Japanese ships are within range, the Korean vessels open fire with their superior cannon, devastating many of the enemy before they can themselves get within firing range.

1 A Japanese fleet gathers around Sacheon, one of Korea's major harbours. The deployment threatens Korean control of its southern waters, and gives Japan greater control over it naval logistical support for the land campaign.

3 29 May. After reconnoitring the Japanese forces around Sacheon, Admiral Yi launches a feint attack. His ships race towards the harbour and then turn seaward, luring the Japanese vessels out of their protective anchorage and into open waters.

A statue of Admiral Yi Sun-shin stands in Seoul, South Korea. Admiral Yi is one of the heroes of Korean military history. Crucially, he invested in maritime military technology at a time when other Korean armed services were declining in power.

create the transport fleet necessary for its amphibious operation. The key to the outcome of future Japanese–Korean naval clashes, however, lay in the respective warship designs.

The principal Japanese warships were the *Atakabune* and *Sekibune* classes. The former was the larger and heavier of the two; it typically carried up to 170 sailors/marines, while the *Sekibune* complement was roughly half that number. Both classes were very much seagoing vessels, with V-shaped hulls, deep draughts and large turning circles.

Both relied on a mix of oar and sail to provide power, but when under sail they generally performed poorly against unfavourable winds because of a square-rigged configuration. Structural integrity was also questionable – the Japanese ships used relatively thin planks of lightweight cedar and fur, held together by iron nails that eventually rusted in sea water and weakened the structure.

These inadequacies in the Japanese vessels meant that only limited numbers of

cannon – usually 1–3 – were carried on board. Instead, the Japanese navy used musketry to provide its direct fire, and grappling, boarding and on-deck fighting by marines as the principal methods of overcoming an enemy ship.

KOREAN TECHNOLOGY

The Koreans had gone down a very different route with their naval technology. Their primary vessel was the *panokson*, a two- or three-deck ship with a typical

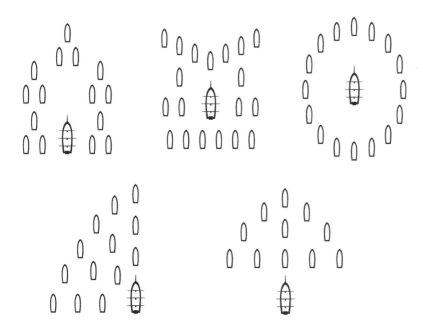

Japanese naval formations, the larger vessel denoting the flagship. The two formations at top left are essentially advance and attack configurations, while the remaining three focus more on defence, giving all-round (top right), flank (bottom left) and frontal (bottom right) protection for the flagship. Yi's battle tactics fractured such formations.

complement of around 50 sailors and 125 marines, and powered once again by a combination of oar and sail.

Combatant personnel were stationed on the upper deck, where there was a basic castle structure, while non-combatants such as rowers were positioned on lower decks, keeping the ship's 'powerplant' safely tucked away from enemy musket fire. Unlike the Japanese vessels, the Korean warships had relatively flat, shallow-draught hulls, which were more suited to the tidal characteristics of Korean coastal and inland waters. This design, along with a better double-sail configuration that gave good performance against adverse winds, meant that the Korean warships were extremely manoeuvrable – with correct use of the oars, they could even turn within their own radius.

These Korean vessels were also much tougher than the Japanese ships. Typically, they were constructed of very thick pine boards, fastened together by large wooden pegs that swelled in the water to tighten the structure and, obviously, suffered from no rust problems.

KOREAN FIREPOWER

Unlike the Japanese, with their preference for boarding operations, the Koreans focused their attention on long-range naval firepower. The wide, open deckplan of the *panokson*, as well as the vessel's sturdy design, made it ideal for cannon, and the ship carried a least a dozen such weapons, sited to give all-round (360°) fire capability.

Korean cannon were labelled by type rather than by calibre, from the smallest to the largest: Yellow, Black, Earth and Heaven. At the large end of the scale, the Heaven cannon could fire a *daejon* (a type of arrow) or a *chulwan* (a round shot) to a distance of up to 1km (1094 yards) – although the arrow tended to have a lesser range than the shot. The smaller cannons commanded the intervening distances. *Wangu* naval mortars also provided a short-range indirect-fire capability, their shells having a 20cm (7.9in) calibre and a weight

SAMURAI ARCHER

Archery was as integral to sixteenth-century Japanese naval warfare as it was to land warfare. Bowmen would engage enemy vessels from a range of several hundred metres, not only inflicting casualties but also suppressing the enemy sailors' ability to operate and manoeuvre their ship. This archer has a classic composite bow, plus a katana *sword on his hip for boarding engagements. The riveted body armour extends downwards into* haidate *thigh guards, and footwear is a simple pair of cloth sandals. Naval personnel were often less heavily armoured when compared to land soldiers, principally because naval crews needed greater freedom of movement in their life aboard a ship.*

At the Battle of Sacheon, however, skilled Japanese archery proved less decisive than the heavily-armoured and armed kobukson *turtle ship of the Korean navy.*

that was sufficient to smash through deck boards.

Panokson formed the bulk of the Korean fighting fleet in the late sixteenth century, but from 1591 a new type of warship made an appearance – the *kobukson*, or 'turtle ship'. Firepower aboard the *kobukson* was substantial, delivered from around a dozen cannon ports each side of the hull plus further ports at the stem and stern. The bow also featured a carved dragon's head from which could be pumped a sulphurous smoke, which served both to lay down a screen and as a weapon of psychological warfare. Alternatively, an extra cannon could be fitted in the dragon's head. Although only some three to six *kobukson* were in commission in 1592, they were to make an important military contribution, and their appearance had a demoralizing effect on the Japanese navy.

SACHEON

The young Toyotomi Hideyoshi leads a night attack on a castle on Inaba Mountain in 1564. Hideyoshi was supreme naval commander at the time of the Battle of Sacheon, and later went on to become first supreme lord of all Japan. However, his imperial ambitions on China and Japan were curtailed by, amongst other thing, Korean naval supremacy.

Alongside the technological investment, Admiral Yi had made strides in training and tactics. Discipline aboard ships was improved, as was the quality of the officers, while at the same time Yi fostered patriotism and an *esprit de corps* amongst the ranks by giving them confidence in their tactics and weapons.

PRELIMINARY ACTIONS

Even as the Japanese land forces were pushing northwards, Yi was working on a strategy to strangle the invasion. The Japanese were acutely reliant upon naval logistics to fuel the army's advance, and Yi saw that he could use his superior naval power (superior in technology, not numbers) to interdict the supply routes from bases around his naval headquarters at Yeosu, on the far southern coast.

The first major naval clash came at Okpo Harbour on Geoje Island, where the Japanese were already engaged in sacking the coastal town. On 5 May 1592, Yi sailed from Yeosu, assembling his fleet along the way, so that by the time he reached Okpo he had some 50 vessels, including about 24 *panokson* and some *kobukson*. Anchored in Okpo Harbour were about 70 Japanese vessels. On 7 May, the Korean fleet sailed at speed into the harbour waters in a broad enveloping attack.

Korean tactics frequently favoured a 'crane's wing' tactic – a line of ships in double concave formation that would wrap around enemy vessels in an envelopment manoeuvre. The Japanese, caught by surprise, were overwhelmed, their arquebus fire proving utterly inadequate against the Korean cannon. By the end of the battle, some 45 Japanese ships had been sunk and 4000 Japanese mariners and soldiers killed.

Additional actions at Happo and Chokjinpo on the Korean return journey resulted in a further 16 Japanese ships

destroyed. Nervous tremors went through the Japanese high command, and the scene was set for the Battle of Sacheon.

THE BATTLE

Reports of a large fleet of Japanese ships in the area around Sacheon, just to the west of Yeosu, gave Yi reason to fear for the safety of his headquarters. Favouring the

offensive, Yi set off with a force of 26 warships, including one of his *kobukson*. He would be facing a far superior force of up to 70 Japanese ships. Yi reached the area around Sacheon on 29 May, and reconnoitred the harbour where the Japanese ships were anchored. Yi noted that a high cliff overlooking the anchorage would provide a superior fire base for

Japanese musketmen if the Koreans allowed themselves to be drawn into the harbour itself. Therefore, Yi would have to draw the Japanese out to the open sea, where the Koreans would have the advantage in gunnery and manoeuvre.

To lure the Japanese seaward, Yi had his force sail at speed towards the harbour, then reverse direction, as if suddenly alarmed by the sight of the Japanese warships. The Japanese fell for the ruse, and dispatched up to 40 vessels for a pursuit action. It would be a fatal mistake. The deployment took time, hence the light was fading even as the Japanese put to sea.

Once the Japanese ships were out of the harbour, the Koreans went into action, turning rapidly and using their oars to drive their ships quickly into gunnery range. Korean gunners were taught to begin engaging as soon as they entered cannon range, and soon the Japanese ships were being smashed by shot and arrows. The Japanese could only respond with peppering arquebus shots, but one such shot nearly changed the course of the entire war when it struck Yi, although the ball did nothing more than deliver a flesh wound to the admiral's left arm.

TURTLE SHIP ATTACK

Now the Koreans played their ace card. The turtle ship sailed into the heart of the Japanese fleet, its cannon delivering crushing broadsides against the lightweight enemy vessels while Japanese musket balls bounced harmlessly off the upper deck and thick hull. The appearance of the *kobukson* caused panic. Its unusual layout and heavy firepower startled the Japanese sailors and marines, who struggled to see how the ship could be taken and were alarmed at the grinning, smoking dragon's head.

By nightfall, every Japanese warship that had sailed out to engage the Koreans was sinking or critically damaged. On the Korean side, casualties amounted to just a handful of sailors injured.

Sacheon gave the Japanese a salutary lesson in modern naval warfare, particularly in the advantage of long-range professional gunnery over the tactics of grapple and board. More importantly, the Koreans had found a way to tackle the Japanese invasion

– naval interdiction of supply lines. In 1592 alone, the Koreans sank nearly 400 Japanese vessels. It was this strategy, combined with a guerrilla war and the intervention of Chinese forces, that saved Korea from Japanese domination. Hideyoshi's army was forced back into the south and steadily evacuated in 1593. It would be another four years before it returned.

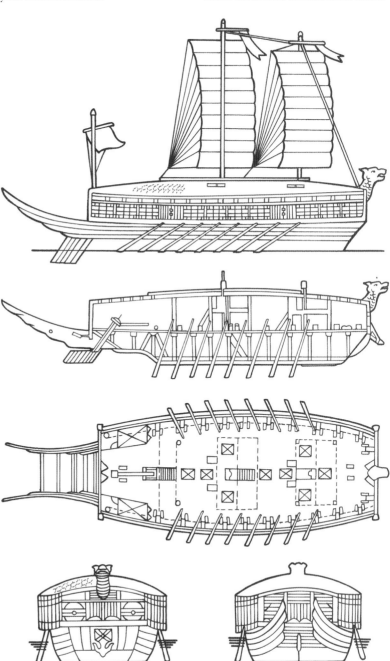

Multiple views of the kobukson *turtle ship. Note how the large square sails, the plentiful oar power and flat hull profile would have made the vessel extremely manoeuvrable. Such manoeuvrability was ideally suited to the close-in war around the Korean coastline.*

THE DUNES
3 JUNE 1658

THE ENGLISH NEW MODEL ARMY BROKE WITH TRADITION IN FAVOUR OF EFFICIENCY IN COMBAT. AT THE TIME, ARMIES WERE NORMALLY RAISED ON AN AD HOC BASIS AND LED BY POLITICAL RATHER THAN MILITARY FIGURES. THE NEW MODEL ARMY PROMOTED PROFESSIONALISM AND DEMONSTRATED A NEW AND BETTER WAY TO FORM A MILITARY FORCE.

WHY DID IT HAPPEN?

WHO An Anglo-French army numbering about 15,000, opposed by around 14,000 Spanish and (British and Irish) Royalist troops.

WHAT A Spanish relief force attempted to relieve Dunkirk, which was under siege by the Anglo-French force.

WHERE Around 6.4km (4 miles) east of Dunkirk, today in France, then in the Spanish Netherlands.

WHEN 3 June 1658.

WHY After the English Civil War (1642–51), the exiled King Charles II (1630–85) received support from Spain, embroiling English Parliamentarian forces in fighting on the Continent.

OUTCOME The Spanish army was driven off and decisively defeated.

The tumultuous events that took place in Britain between 1642 and 1651 are generally placed together under the heading of the English Civil War. The events and politics of the period were complex, but essentially the war was fought for control of the country, pitting King Charles I (1600–49) – and later his son, Charles II – against the forces of Parliament.

There were three main phases to this conflict. What is normally termed the First Civil War ran from 1642 to 1645 and was followed by a short lull. During this pause, King Charles I consolidated his hold on the territories that had remained loyal to him, and rebuilt his forces. The Parliamentarians undertook a more radical shake-up of their military, resulting in the New Model Army.

In 1648–49, the conflict flared up again, in what is now termed the Second Civil War. This ended with the defeat and execution of Charles I. The third phase of the war was fought between Parliamentarian forces and Royalists loyal to Charles II, son of the executed king. The fighting came to an end with a Parliamentarian victory at Worcester in 1651, but this was by no means the end of the matter.

While the kingdom of England became first the Commonwealth of England and then the Protectorate under the Lord Protector, Oliver Cromwell (1599–1658), Charles II sought allies overseas. He found support from Philip IV of Spain (1605–65), who provided arms and money to raise troops. Charles's position was weak and his forces were not large, but he was still able to contribute to Spanish campaigns in Europe.

Oliver Cromwell at the Battle of Marston Moor, 1644. This was the largest action of the English Civil War and the Parliamentary victory helped to establish Cromwell as a respected commander. It was also the first decisive victory of Cromwell's embryonic New Model Army.

Meanwhile, England was allied with France and sent forces to the Continent to assist King Louis XIV of France (1638–1715) against rebels who had thrown in their lot with Spain. This served Cromwell's purposes. Charles II was hoping to raise an army to invade the English mainland, and if there was going to be fighting, better it were done on someone else's territory.

The force sent to Europe was part of the New Model Army that had been created by Parliament in 1645. The army was the result of a realization that the conventional way of raising and organizing a military force was insufficient to ensure victory over the Royalists. This was no overnight revelation, but the result of battlefield experience gained throughout the First Civil War campaign.

For example, at the Battle of Edgehill in 1642, the Parliamentarian cavalry was seen to be inadequate. Not only did some units defect to the Royalist side but the remainder underperformed in action. The infantry, too, needed reorganizing.

One major problem facing the Parliamentarian forces was that although they had good sources of recruits, and potentially more men than their enemies could field, the current system of recruitment meant that many units could legitimately refuse to serve outside a given area – and such refusals were quite common. This placed unacceptable limitations on the Parliamentarian forces.

As a result of this and other factors, such as the problem of paying for the army, the whole Parliamentarian military set-up was revised. In April 1645, the Self-Denying Ordinance was passed, under which members of the House of Lords and the House of Commons were to resign any military commands they held. Command therefore passed to professional officers. Meanwhile, the organization of the army itself was completely changed, creating a professional force that was both affordable and capable.

The reorganization allowed a great number of ineffective officers to be removed. These were mainly noblemen with no real talent, experience or training,

who commanded by birthright rather than merit. Logistics, pay and training were all improved under the new system, which had profound effects on morale and efficiency.

NEW MODEL ARMY

The infantry of the New Model Army followed the pattern used successfully in the Thirty Years War (1618–48). Infantry of two types were employed, enabling their capabilities to complement one another.

Firepower was provided by musketeers armed with matchlock arquebuses. Their weapons had a short range and were very heavy – sufficiently so that a forked stand was used to support them when aiming; but

ENGLISH CAVALRY OFFICER

Nick-named 'the Ironsides' by Royalist commander Prince Rupert when they first appeared on the battlefield in 1645, the New Model Army cavalrymen typically wore 'lobster-tail' iron headpieces and chest armour over a thick leather coat. The troopers were armed with a sword and two pistols. The horses were the key to the success of this new formation, since an attack by any unit of the New Model Army was based on surprising the enemy with speed – hitting the enemy hard and decisively and then moving on. The cavalry were a key element of these shock tactics.

LOCATION

Geography dictates that some areas become battlegrounds over and over during history. The region around Dunkirk has been fought over several times due to its importance as a Channel port.

THE DUNES

they were also hard-hitting. Charges of gunpowder, along with ball and wad, were carried in clay pots on a string or belt around the musketeer's neck. The normal 'combat load' was 11 rounds, and it became an adage that a musketeer 'carried 11 souls around his neck'. Whether or not they were as deadly as this implies, musketeers were well-respected combat troops.

About a half to two-thirds of the infantry were musketeers. Their firepower could be decisive, and service as a musketeer was considered very desirable – perhaps because musketeers were paid more or had to carry less armour, or perhaps because they rarely became involved in hand-to-hand fighting. However, the musket-armed troops were very vulnerable to close assault by infantry or, especially, cavalry.

Protection from such attack, along with the capability for shock action, was provided by the second type of infantry – pikemen. Protected by a heavy metal helmet and a leather coat with back- and breastplates

A company of Spanish pikemen is shown in three distinct formations, as it would have appeared in a military manual of the seventeenth century. On the left, the formation is loose, for marching order; in the centre, the unit closes up to create a tight-packed formation capable of repelling cavalry (right).

over it, pikemen were armed with a 4.9m (16ft) pike and were well drilled in its use. Soldiers of both infantry types also carried a sidearm, usually a sword but sometimes a dagger, with which to defend themselves in close combat. Musketeers and pikemen were organized in mixed units, enabling them to provide each other with mutual support.

The infantry benefited from a common uniform of a red coat (the colour most likely chosen as the cheapest dye that would not run in wet weather) and from good training, which increased the troops' confidence in one another as well as their skill at weapons drill. The infantry of the New Model Army were thus disciplined professionals led by experienced officers, which gave them an advantage over the more usual short-term levies led by high-born amateurs.

CAVALRY

The cavalry of the New Model Army were hard-hitting shock troops trained to fight in the manner demonstrated so effectively by King Gustavus Adolphus of Sweden (1594–1632) a few years before. Not for them the elegant caracole, in which heavy cavalry rode close to an enemy and discharged pistols at them.

The New Model cavalryman was trained to charge home and overturn his enemy with his primary weapon – his sword – and most of a cavalryman's actual fighting was done with the blade. Nevertheless, he usually carried a pair of pistols, and standard tactics were to use one pistol just before charging home, to soften up the enemy, and to keep one in reserve for emergencies, such as when trying to disengage from a superior foe.

Wearing similar protection to a pikeman, of plate-covered leather coat and metal helmet, plus high boots, a cavalryman was a potent force on his own, but it was as a unit that the New Model cavalry excelled. The horsemen of the time, normally minor nobles and gentlemen, were commonly an ill-disciplined lot. They would charge bravely enough and fight hard, but they had

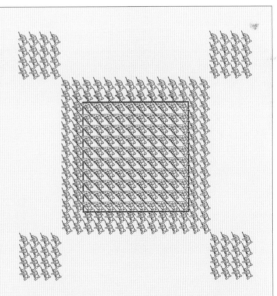

THE OPPOSED FORCES

ANGLO-FRENCH (estimated)

Total:	**15,000**

SPANISH AND ROYALISTS (estimated)

Total:	**14,000**

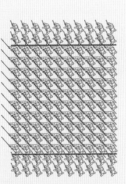

Right: When viewed from above in this formation, the pikemen appear to be the 'torso' and the firearm-equipped musketeers the 'sleeves' of a coat. This formation concentrated the fighting power of the pikemen and musketeers but still provided good protection for the shot so long as the ratio of pike to shot favoured the former.

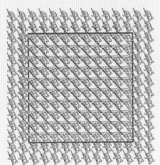

Left: The formation of a pike square surrounded by arqubusiers allowed troops armed with firearms to shelter themselves from the enemy, especially cavalry, while deployed in the open and without the benefit of protection from fortifications.

Above: A deployment of a pike square surrounded by shot, and supported by 'horns' of shot at each of its four corners, allowed for a substantial volume of fire from the shot in every direction. However, it was primarily a defensive formation since it was not easy to move while maintaining its cohesion.

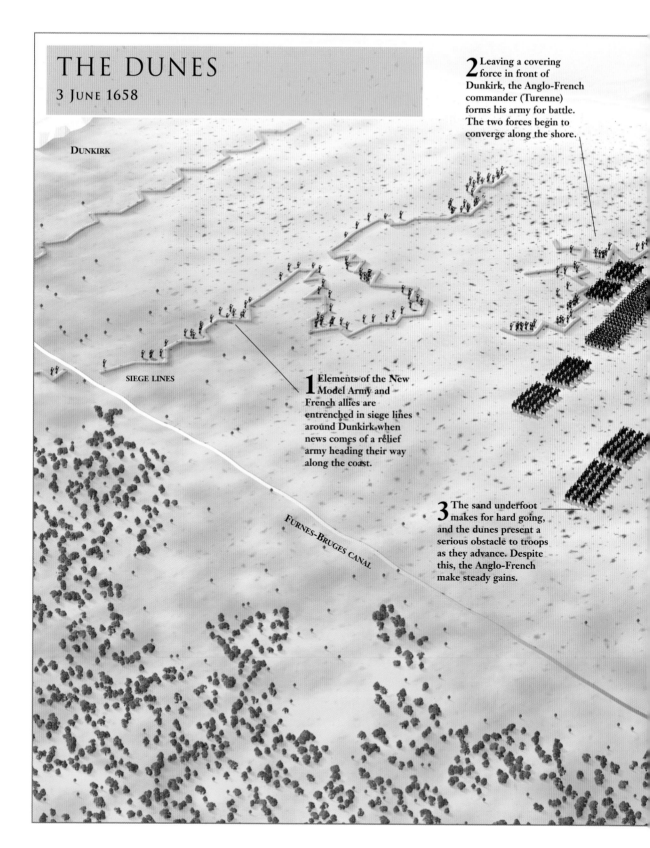

THE DUNES
3 JUNE 1658

DUNKIRK

SIEGE LINES

FURNES–BRUGES CANAL

2 Leaving a covering force in front of Dunkirk, the Anglo-French commander (Turenne) forms his army for battle. The two forces begin to converge along the shore.

1 Elements of the New Model Army and French allies are entrenched in siege lines around Dunkirk when news comes of a relief army heading their way along the coast.

3 The sand underfoot makes for hard going, and the dunes present a serious obstacle to troops as they advance. Despite this, the Anglo-French make steady gains.

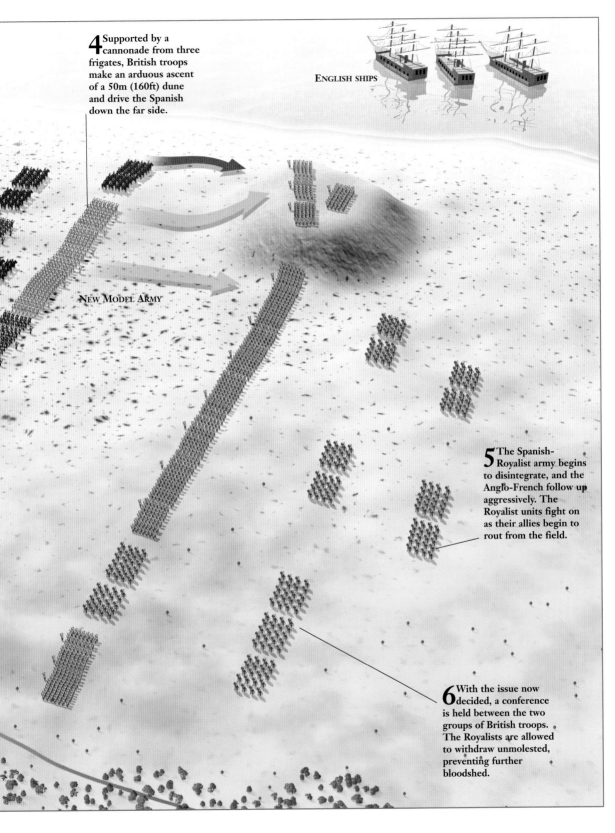

4 Supported by a cannonade from three frigates, British troops make an arduous ascent of a 50m (160ft) dune and drive the Spanish down the far side.

ENGLISH SHIPS

NEW MODEL ARMY

5 The Spanish-Royalist army begins to disintegrate, and the Anglo-French follow up aggressively. The Royalist units fight on as their allies begin to rout from the field.

6 With the issue now decided, a conference is held between the two groups of British troops. The Royalists are allowed to withdraw unmolested, preventing further bloodshed.

THE DUNES

Opposite: This portrait of Louis XIV by Charles Le Brun (1619–90) shows the French monarch in all his pomp. Twenty years old at the time of the Battle of the Dunes, Louis did not assume personal control of government until the death of his First Minister, Jules Cardinal Mazarin, in 1661.

a tendency to get carried away and pursue a broken enemy off the field, ending up scattered and useless. The Royalist cavalry of Prince Rupert of the Rhine (1619–82) were notorious for this sort of free-for-all. The New Model cavalry, by contrast, were better disciplined and thus less of a one-shot weapon. They could be relied upon to rally and attack a new opponent rather than wasting their potential on just one charge.

The New Model Army also contained numbers of dragoons. These were not the medium or heavy cavalry of later times but essentially infantry mounted on cheap and inferior horses. They served as odd-job troops, screening flanks and scouting ahead, as well as acting as a mobile reserve or even as assault infantry.

Artillery was also an important weapon, though it was more effective in siege warfare than in the field. The New Model Army implemented a practice of assigning a small number of infantrymen to artillery batteries to protect them. These men were

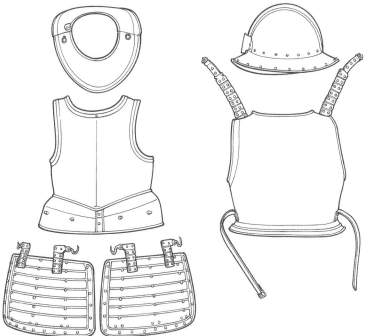

fusiliers, armed with flintlock weapons rather than matchlocks, as the presence of burning slow-matches was not desirable in proximity to artillery gunpowder.

AFTER THE CIVIL WAR

The New Model Army continued to give good service after the Civil War ended.

Armour worn by a well-equipped infantryman of the seventeenth century might include the gorget (on the top left), used to protect the throat; the breastplate; and a pair of tassets worn over the upper thighs. On the right is the soldier's backplate and helmet. This type of armour would have been typical of a pikeman of the period, especially one expected to fight in the front ranks.

Cavalry charging across the sand dunes, the French and English forces defeat the Spanish at the Battle of the Dunes, as portrayed in this nineteenth century magazine illustration of the battle.

Despite occasional mutinies (caused at least partly over pay, a common enough occurrence in the period), the army put down rebellions and tried to contain banditry and border reiving.

War with Spain broke out in 1654, and despite setbacks (mainly caused by disease) in the Caribbean, the New Model Army performed well on the world stage. Deployed to Flanders, the army found itself fighting alongside French troops against the Spanish and a British and Irish Royalist force under the command of Charles II's brother, James (1633–1701), later King James II of England.

In May 1658, elements of the New Model Army were engaged in besieging Dunkirk, which was at that time occupied by Spanish troops. A Spanish relief force was marching on the town, so the Anglo-French made preparations to meet them. Leaving a small covering force to watch Dunkirk, the Anglo-French army under the overall command of the Vicomte de Turenne (1611–75) marched eastwards to meet the enemy as they came along the coast.

BATTLE OF THE DUNES

The Spanish force included around 3000 British and Irish Royalist troops, plus a number of French rebels who held the left flank. Their aim was to break the siege of Dunkirk and drive off the Anglo-French force conducting it.

However, the Anglo-French allies had other ideas. Advancing to meet the relief force, they offered battle in terrain

A re-enactor 'gives fire'. The flash of powder so close to the firer's face was unpleasant, but this was compensated for by being further way from the enemy than a soldier armed with hand weapons need be.

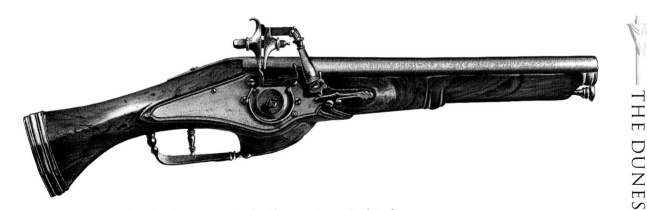

The wheel-lock pistol was preferred by cavalrymen of the age because of its efficient mechanism. Not only were such pistols easy to load, but they could be fired without the complicated process of using a match for ignition.

characterized by sand dunes – hence the name of the ensuing battle. The units of the New Model Army gave good account of themselves, using the standard tactics developed by training over some time.

Protected by the hedge of pikes on their flanks, the musketeers of the English units could move up and 'give fire' against the enemy, gradually wearing them down. Units maintained a steady fire by the constant rotation of men.

After firing, the front rank retired to the rear of the formation and began the lengthy process of reloading. Meanwhile, men with weapons ready moved up to the front of the unit and, using the forked stand to support their heavy weapon, took aim and fired at the enemy before pulling back in turn. Thus a constant, rolling fire was maintained without exposing the unit to countercharge, the covering pikemen always ready to repulse anyone who got too close.

When an enemy unit was seen to waver, the pikemen advanced to decide the matter with a 'push of pike', providing shock action to seal the victory set up by the fire of the musketeers. In some cases, English units charged up the dunes at their enemies. Moving uphill on loose sand is never easy. Charging in such circumstances to dislodge a determined enemy is quite an achievement, so the exploit of the men who ascended a 50m (164ft) sand dune to chase the occupying Spanish force off it and down

the far side was an impressive feat of arms. The Anglo-French force, particularly the elements of the New Model Army, fought an aggressive battle that threw the Spanish and their French rebel allies back on the defensive and then sent them routing from the field after two hours of hard fighting.

The British and Irish Royalist units with the Spanish army were permitted to retire after a conference with their Parliamentarian opposite numbers. Thus although the Parliamentarian and Royalist factions were deadly enemies, they agreed to live and let live, and the Royalists retired from the field in better order than many of their allied units. The French rebels made a similar withdrawal when their Spanish allies broke.

OUTCOME

The New Model Army impressed all of Europe with its fighting power, aggression and discipline at the Battle of the Dunes. About 500 casualties were incurred on the Anglo-French side, against around 6000, including prisoners, among the Spanish force, mainly from units that broke during the battle.

With the siege unbroken and no relief possible, Dunkirk surrendered to the French on 14 June. Under the terms of the Anglo-French alliance, it was then handed over to the English, who sold it back to the French soon after.

The New Model Army showed the world what could be achieved by a well-led professional fighting force, and it served as the basis for other, later, professional armies. However, the New Model Army itself was disbanded in 1660 after the restoration of the monarchy in England.

SADOWA (KÖNIGGRÄTZ)
3 JULY 1866

AUSTRIA AND PRUSSIA WERE THE TWO BIGGEST PLAYERS IN THE GERMAN CONFEDERATION, BUT WHILE AUSTRIA WAS IN FAVOUR OF THE STATUS QUO, BISMARCK'S PRUSSIA SAW ITSELF AS THE LEAD NATION OF A FUTURE UNITED GERMANY, WITH AUSTRIA ON THE OUTSIDE. THE RIVALRY SPARKED THE AUSTRO-PRUSSIAN WAR OF 1866, WHICH REACHED ITS CLIMAX AT SADOWA, WHERE THE NEWLY-INTRODUCED NEEDLE RIFLE PLAYED A DECISIVE PART IN THE PRUSSIAN VICTORY.

WHY DID IT HAPPEN?

WHO Prussian armies under Helmuth von Moltke (1800–91), opposed by the Imperial (Austrian) Army commanded by Ludwig von Benedek (1804–81).

WHAT The battle showed the effectiveness of modern breech-loading artillery and the Prussian needle rifle and also demonstrated the importance of railways, the telegraph and a professionalized officer corps and GHQ staff.

WHERE Near the village of Sadowa to the northwest of the town of Königgrätz, in northern Bohemia, now in the Czech Republic.

WHEN 3 July 1866

WHY The German states had traditionally been ruled in name only by the Austrian emperors, but in 1866 Prussia, Austria's most dangerous neighbour and enemy, sought to eliminate its influence once and for all.

OUTCOME A decisive Prussian victory that cost Austria its position as the greatest power in Central Europe (*Mitteleuropa*).

On 8 April 1866, Count Otto von Bismarck (1815–98), Minister-President of Prussia, signed a secret alliance with Italy to ensure that in a war against Prussia, Austria would have to fight on a second front to defend its outpost of Venice. In early June, Bismarck occupied Holstein, and on 15 June invaded and crushed

The real victor of Sadowa: Crown Prince Frederick William (1831-1888) whose army saved the day for the Prussians. He was the liberal hope that ruled for only 99 days, in 1888, as Emperor Frederick I.

Austria's weak German allies – Hanover, Hesse-Cassel, Nassau and Frankfurt-am-Main. Only Saxony remained, lining up its small but tough army under Prince Albert (1828–1902) alongside that of Austria.

This situation allowed General Helmuth von Moltke, chief of staff of the Prussian Army, to concentrate three armies for the invasion of Bohemia. The First Army (95,000 troops) was under the command of Prince Frederick Charles (1828–85), whose military talents were highly overrated and whose decisions were to cost Moltke and the Prussians dear. Then there was the small 40,000-strong Army of the Elbe under the dithering and slow General Herwath von Bittenfeld (1796–1884), whose skills were mired in the Napoleonic past. Finally, there was the Silesian, or Second, Army, commanded by the capable and mature Crown Prince Frederick of Prussia (1831–88), later Emperor Frederick III, the father of Kaiser William II (1859–1941) and affectionately known to his troops as 'Our Fritz'. The Second Army numbered 120,000 men.

Facing these forces was the Imperial (Austrian) Northern Army and its Saxon allies; in total, this force, with 250,000 men, was as large as the Prussian armies combined. Unfortunately, the Imperial War Council in Vienna had picked the wrong man for the commander's job – the Hungarian-born general Ludwig von Benedek. He came highly recommended, having established his reputation in 1859 against the armies of Napoleon III of France (1808–73) at Solferino, where he had earned the dubiously merited title of 'Lion of Solferino'. During the Battle of Sadowa, however, his behaviour was to be anything but lionlike.

THE ENEMIES

Austria was a multi-ethnic empire that was creaking at the seams and increasingly becoming an anachronism in the age of nations. Its army reflected this weakness, along with the empire's unimaginative and stale bureaucracy, economic backwardness and the traditional Austrian *Schlamperei* – a unique word to describe the combination of slackness, complacency, incompetence and sloppiness that permeated the Austrian

state. Yet the soldier material, especially the Hungarians and German-speaking Austrians, was good, and under effective command the Slavs, Romanians and Italians could perform well. The artillery was also equipped with modern pieces far superior to the ageing Prussian artillery park.

The Prussians, on the other hand, were a single nation with a simple stated ambition – to be masters of Germany; they were led by a political genius (Bismarck) backed by a military one (Moltke). Prussia possessed, in Silesia and the Ruhr, two huge industrial regions; it also had a modern arms industry (epitomized by Krupp) and continental Europe's most efficient and well-developed railway system, which was under strict military control in wartime.

The Prussians had also perfected the use of the field telegraph – technology that,

The small town of Sadowa lies in the heart of the Bohemia, in the present-day Czech Republic, on the road to Vienna – the capital of the Hapsburg Empire in 1866.

PRUSSIAN INFANTRYMAN

The building block of the Prussian war machine was the simple infantryman, very like the Russian soldier in appearance, with his flat field cap, half-length leather boots with hobnailed soles and rolled-up field blanket used to store paraphernalia and field coat. By tradition, the Prussians wore dark blue uniforms and the characteristic **Pickelhaube**, *or spiked metal helmet, designed for effect rather than real protection. It says something for the durability of this equipment that German soldiers in two world wars wore the same design of uniforms and boots. The soldier is carrying a Dreyse needle gun with detachable socket bayonet. It got its curious name from its needle-shaped firing pin. The first models were crude, and the blast and velocity of the rifle was reduced because of the defective gas seal; additionally, a leaky breech had a tendency to blast sparks into the face of the handler. Yet with its bolt action it could be loaded and fired in any position, unlike the muzzle-loaded musket; it also had anything between four to six times the rate of fire of a musket, and a far longer range.*

Prussian needle rifle: The Prussian victory at Sadowa was in no small measure due to the superior and flexible firepower of this bolt-action rifle.

thanks to Austrian *Schlamperei*, Benedek did not have at his field HQ during the Battle of Sadowa. Instead, he had to rely on the telegraph station in Königgrätz, which meant that he lost valuable time.

Critically the Prussian infantryman also carried modern breech-loading rifles. In 1849, the Prussian firm of Dreyse had developed the so-called *Zündnadelgewehr*, or needle rifle, for the Prussian Army. Hence the Austrian superiority in artillery firepower was balanced by a Prussian firepower advantage at closer ranges, an advantage that proved deadly during infantry clashes. In the hands of the hard-trained Prussian infantry, the needle gun was to decide the outcome of the battle.

THE BATTLE BEGINS

Showing a decided lack of judgment, Benedek placed his entire army between the small, sluggish Bystrice River and the Elbe to the east. The army was strung out in a weak crescent-shaped formation with its right flank mired in a sunken piece of ground dominated by hills to the north, thus making it vulnerable to enemy fire should that higher ground be seized. The left 'hung in the air' between the Problus and Prim Heights, while the centre was deployed along the Bystrice, leaving the pivotal point, Chlum, open to a possible Prussian attack from the northeast.

Then again, for their part the Prussians also had their problems. Their scouts had run into the vast Austrian camp by chance. Prior to that, Frederick Charles had given instructions that his cousin, Crown Prince Frederick, was not to advance beyond the

Elbe. This order was motivated by Frederick Charles's jealousy of his rival and his unwillingness to share the glory of defeating the Austrians, and was to cost his force dear when it faced the full brunt of the Northern Army without Second Army support. The order was immediately countermanded by Moltke, but it delayed the Second Army's westward march for several crucial hours.

By 04.30 on 3 July, having marched in pelting rain since 02.00, the Prussian First Army was in place. Moltke's order countering Frederick Charles's command to his cousin had arrived half an hour earlier at Second Army HQ, and Crown Prince Frederick ordered his infantry (III Corps) to march on Sadowa, 20km (12.4 miles) away. It would take most of the day for the footslogging troops to get there.

These Austrian Field Jägers are wearing great coats, standard service dress in the 1860s. The plumes on their hats made them very distinctive targets. They are armed with 1844 pattern smooth-bore muskets.

THE OPPOSED FORCES

IMPERIAL (AUSTRIAN) ARMY
Total: 250,000 men and 500 guns

ROYAL PRUSSIAN ARMY
Total: 255,000 men

Opposite: Francis-Joseph, Emperor of Austria, King of Hungary (1830-1916), in his favourite Imperial white uniform, sought to save his ramshackle realm from Prussian aggression and German nationalism.

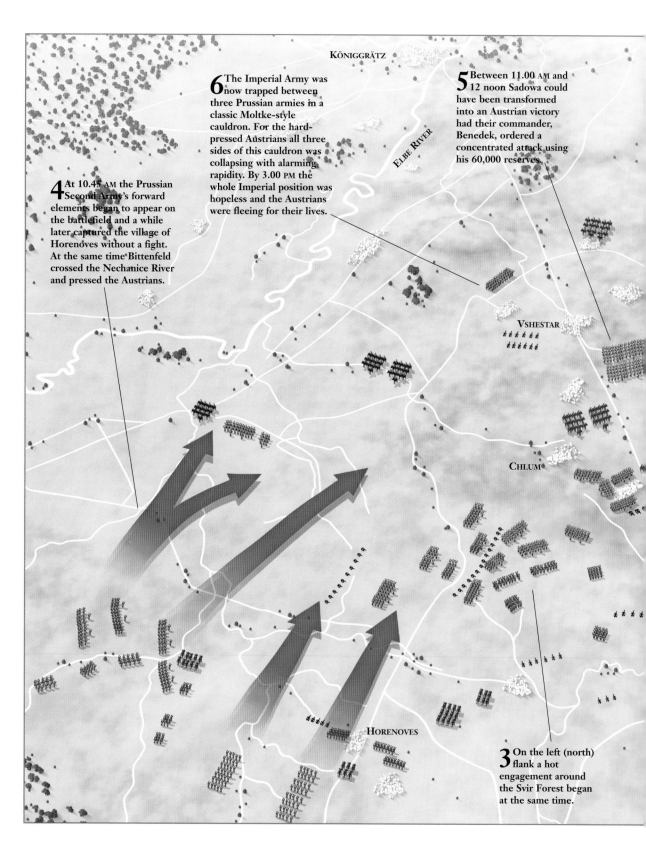

KÖNIGGRÄTZ

6 The Imperial Army was now trapped between three Prussian armies in a classic Moltke-style cauldron. For the hard-pressed Austrians all three sides of this cauldron was collapsing with alarming rapidity. By 3.00 PM the whole Imperial position was hopeless and the Austrians were fleeing for their lives.

5 Between 11.00 AM and 12 noon Sadowa could have been transformed into an Austrian victory had their commander, Benedek, ordered a concentrated attack using his 60,000 reserves.

ELBE RIVER

4 At 10.45 AM the Prussian Second Army's forward elements began to appear on the battlefield and a while later captured the village of Horenoves without a fight. At the same time Bittenfeld crossed the Nechanice River and pressed the Austrians.

VSHESTAR

CHLUM

HORENOVES

3 On the left (north) flank a hot engagement around the Svir Forest began at the same time.

SADOWA (KÖNIGGRÄTZ)

3 JULY 1866

2 On the right, General Bittenfeld's Army of the Elbe reached the Nechanice River, captured a bridge intact but failed to press home their advantage.

NECHANICE

SUCHA

1 The battle begun at 6.30 AM with 135,000 Prussians facing 250,000 Imperial (Austrian) troops. Instead of remaining on the defensive, Moltke ordered his army to cross the Bystrice River and capture the village of Sadowa. Their offensive faced, however, intense Austrian artillery fire.

SADOWA

BYSTRICE RIVER

The Prussian blues – in this case, the 27th and 67th Infantry Regiments that made up the 'Gordon' Brigade – defended Sviep woods near Ciskoves at the centre of the battlefield against several fierce Austrian attacks. They are armed with the fast-loading needle rifles.

Two hours later, at 06.30, the biggest battle on European soil since Leipzig in 1813 began, pitting a mere 135,000 Prussians against twice as many Austrians. Moltke realized that his armies would be lucky to hang on even by their fingernails along the Bystrice, and could only hope, nay pray, that the Second Army would arrive in

time to outflank the enemy. The Prussian centre advanced towards the Bystrice, taking Sadowa and other villages along both sides of the river, only to come under a ferocious pounding from the Austrian artillery, which outmatched the Prussian guns for range, accuracy and rate of fire. Bittenfeld, meanwhile, on the Prussian right

the 7th Division and two full Austrian corps raged around and inside the dense foliage of the Svib Forest.

VICTORY SQUANDERED

Between 11.00 and noon, the battle entered its most crucial phase. The Prussians, especially those units in the centre, were pinned down and badly shaken by the relentless Austrian artillery fire. Bittenfeld finally crossed the Bystrice, but his Army of the Elbe did not advance with any aggression or purpose. A disgruntled and nervous King Wilhelm I (1797–1888) turned to his chief of staff and said, 'Moltke, we are losing this battle.' Indeed they were. During this hour a massed, concentrated attack would probably have secured an Austrian victory and ensured that Prussia's military might was broken for years. Moltke turned to the king: 'Here there will be no retreat. Here we are fighting for the very existence of Prussia.' He wasn't exaggerating.

At 11.45, however, came the welcome news that the 1st Guards Division of the Prussian Second Army had appeared on the northeastern edge of the battlefield, coming to the aid of the 7th Division. Having beaten off a series of Austrian attacks in Svib Forest, the division was desperately short of manpower. An Austrian brigade was on its way for yet another attack when the Guards intervened, cutting the Austrian formation to ribbons from its right flank.

Benedek still refused to take the risk of an attack, even though urged to do so by VI Corps commander General Wilhelm Ramming and IV Corps second-in-command Lieutenant-General Anton Mollinary. They pleaded with Benedek to attack the First Army before the Second Army began to pour onto the battlefield. They pointed out, to no avail, that with a massive 50,000 infantry and 10,000 cavalry troops in reserve, the Austrians could crush the Prussians through sheer numbers alone. But the time to strike was now and not later. With every passing minute, hope of an Austrian victory grew dimmer. By 1230, when Benedek at his Lipa HQ made the decision not to attack, it was probably already too late.

A Prussian Uhlan lancer. Cavalry played a subsidiary role at Sadowa, but the legendary Uhlans were still a respected fighting force and in a massed attack upon infantry could still cause havoc.

flank, had reached the river at Nechanice, where the Austrians' Saxon allies, despite valiant efforts, had failed to burn the bridge. In the face of murderous fire from the Saxons, who had pulled back to higher ground, the Prussian general failed to press home the attack. In the north, on the Prussian left, a fierce local battle between

SADOWA (KÖNIGGRÄTZ)

MOLTKE'S TRAP

At 13.00, five Prussian Guards companies from the Second Army seized Horenove without resistance and the army's forward artillery units were already firing at Chlum. The balance had shifted decisively away from the Austrians, and Moltke turned to the Prussian king and burst out, 'The success is complete. Vienna lies at Your Majesty's feet.' Shortly afterwards, the Prussian Second Army began to cross the Trotina River on the Austrians' right flank, encountering scant resistance and capturing Trotina village.

Prussian artillery was now striking deep inside the Austrian crescent, and Benedek's defensive battle lay in tatters as his massive army began to waver and break. The situation on the Austrian left was no better. Bittenfeld's Army of the Elbe had swung into action again, moving on Problus, its artillery shooting the counterattacking Saxon infantry to pieces.

In the early afternoon, the Saxons and two Austrian corps were dislodged from the village. Now an ominous gap appeared between the Austrian left flank and centre, exposing the Austrians to a double envelopment from the south and north. Once again, however, Bittenfeld failed to exploit the situation. Nevertheless, Benedek was, by then, losing control over his crumbling army.

COLLAPSE

To the north, the Prussian 1st Guards Division, having driven into the Austrian right flank, had pushed back the Austrian artillery and taken the village of Chlum and the hamlet of Rozberic.

As a consequence, the Prussians were deep within the enemy's positions behind the Austrian centre. By 15.00, the Austrians were fleeing for their lives along the road to Königgrätz as Benedek admitted all was lost. The Prussian First Army, until now simply holding its positions, began to advance as well. It was as if three walls were collapsing atop the Austrians simultaneously.

Ramming, meanwhile, ordered his corps to attack and retake Chlum–Rozberic.

In this romanticized battle scene, the Prussian armies are finally united and are able to put to flight the Austrians as Crown Prince Frederick's troops relieve their hard-pressed comrades at Sadowa.

This painting of an abandoned battery brings home the total rout of the Austrians and what a complete catastrophe Sadowa was for the Habsburg Empire's military reputation.

Whereas Chlum remained in Prussian hands, the hamlet on the road fell to the Austrians. This saved much of the fleeing mass from capture. It cost VI Corps dearly, nevertheless, and Ramming himself was almost killed. Some 6000 of his men and 125 of his officers were not so lucky. Benedek now ordered a series of cavalry charges to try and keep the Prussians at bay a little longer while his army withdrew; they succeeded in buying him time, but at the cost of a further 2000 officers and men.

As the shattered Austrian army fled towards Königgrätz on the far side of the Elbe, its tribulations were not yet over. Some survivors of the battle plunged into the river and drowned, while some of those lucky enough to reach the walls of Königgrätz were fired on by the town's garrison. They had mistaken the Austrians' blue-coated Saxon allies for Prussians – in response, the infuriated Saxons fired back!

Luckily for the Austrians, though, their enemies ended the battle in as much confusion as they did. In any case, Bismarck had no wish for a battle of annihilation since he wanted to reconcile Austria, and at 7.30

PM Moltke called off the pursuit. This bloody day saw the Prussians lose 10,000 dead; the Austrians lost 22,000 killed and wounded and a further 18,000 taken prisoner.

AFTERMATH

With Austria's defeat at Sadowa went any hope of its winning the Austro-Prussian War. The Peace of Prague was signed on 23 August and, despite Bismarck's sentiments, was no gentle affair for Austria. It lost Holstein and all influence in Germany, and saw its German allies absorbed into Prussia – a territory of some 33,670 square kilometres (13,000 square miles) and four million inhabitants. It was curious that Austria–Hungary and Imperial Germany became such staunch allies a few decades later.

The Prussian Dreyse-made needle rifle exacted such a fearful toll against the Austrians at Sadowa – especially against the cavalry – that the days of effective massed cavalry charges were truly at an end. Soon, every European power would develop breech-loading rifles of their own.

SEDAN
1 SEPTEMBER 1870

CHANCELLOR OF THE NORTH GERMAN CONFEDERATION, COUNT OTTO VON BISMARCK USED THE SPANISH SUCCESSION CRISIS IN EARLY 1870 TO PROVOKE A WAR AGAINST FRANCE RULED BY NAPOLEON III, WHO WAS FORCED AGAINST HIS BETTER JUDGMENT TO DECLARE WAR ON PRUSSIA ON 15 JULY 1870.

WHY DID IT HAPPEN?

WHO French Army of Châlons under Napoleon III (1803–73) and Marshal Patrice MacMahon (1808–93) versus Prussian Third Army and Army of the Meuse under General Helmuth von Moltke (1800–91).

WHAT The superior Prusso-German armies brilliantly led by master strategist Moltke manoeuvred to trap, encircle and annihilate MacMahon's army. Superior Prussian artillery played a key role in securing a Prusso-German victory.

WHERE Sedan, France, near the Franco-Belgian border.

WHEN 1 September 1870.

WHY Bismarck sought to crush France, which was suspicious of a united Germany under Prussian control; victory at Sedan helped realize this political ambition.

OUTCOME Sedan led to the collapse of the Second Napoleonic Empire of France (1850–70). The war continued until early 1871 and ended with a draconian peace that left France a vanquished, but vengeful, enemy.

The Franco-Prussian War of 1870–71 is something of a forgotten war. Yet the conflict, which saw the French defeated under humiliating circumstances, would leave deep scars and contribute to the outbreak of the Great War in August 1914. Ultimately the war, engineered by Bismarck (1815–98), was about power and the chancellor's ruthless ambition that Germany should be united under Prussian control. Only by defeating France and eliminating that country's obvious opposition to a unified Germany could Bismarck realize his dream.

Bismarck therefore pushed a cousin of King William I (1797–1888) of Prussia to seek the Spanish throne, and France, unable either to accept a Hohenzollern as king of Spain or to persuade Berlin to retract the candidacy, declared war on Prussia on 15 July 1870.

Officially France was branded the aggressor; in reality, it was the other way around – in the infamous Ems Dispatch, Bismarck manipulated the Prussian reply to France's request for a withdrawal of the candidacy in a way certain to provoke the proud and prickly French into fury.

As matters now stood, in late July, the politically divided and weak France, ruled by an ailing emperor and lacking allies or even friends, faced a stronger, better-equipped German enemy, champing at the bit to fight and with a ruthless political and

A Hessian infantry regiment stands firm to prevent the breakthrough of the French Chasseurs d'Afrique cavalry, battle of Sedan. This painting is based on an original by Professor Georg Koch.

military leadership. The omens for France and for Europe were dire.

WAR PREPARATIONS

Caught unawares with its best troops in Algeria, the vaunted Imperial French Army was in no fit state to fight the Prussians. The French had rested upon their laurels since the Crimean War (1853–56) and made too much of their Napoleonic legacy; they had grown complacent while their hereditary enemies to the east sharpened their swords. The army had no reserves to speak of, and the supply, support and engineering services were in a poor state. Furthermore, it was armed with obsolete artillery and muskets, and relied upon outdated notions of élan and frontal attack. A mere 220,000 French frontline troops were strung out along the Rhine and German frontier in an almost slapdash manner and lacking direction. The question of whether to remain on the defensive or attack remained unresolved, and the French generals did not even have good maps of the frontier region.

If chaos and indecision reigned in France, the same was not true on the other side of the border. In 1866, the Austrians had almost defeated the Prussians at Sadowa with their modern artillery. Four years later, the French were still equipped with light smooth-bore muzzle-loaded artillery, while the Prussians had equipped themselves with the finest artillery in the world. The Krupp-manufactured 6-pounders, for field service, and 24-pounders were superior in all meaningful ways to the French 4- and 12-pounders. With their better rifling, breech-loading mechanism and percussion-detonated shells, the Krupp guns were three times as accurate, had twice the rate of fire, a third longer range and many times the destructiveness of the French guns.

In addition, troops in the Prussian Army were issued with breech-loading rifles; their commanders were professional and dedicated to their 'art'; their NCOs were numerous; and the men themselves, besides being well armed and supplied, were battle-hardened and experienced. Morale – after the victories over Denmark and Austria in 1864 and 1866 respectively – was at a peak. France was the hereditary enemy and the Germans itched to give the French a bloody nose. The 380,000 German troops (mainly Prussians but also Saxons and Bavarians) were divided into three armies – the First Army (60,000) at Mosel, the Second Army (190,000) around Mainz and the Third Army (130,000) on the Rhine.

MOLTKE'S MOUSETRAP

The fighting got under way at the beginning of August with minor early actions at Saarbrücken and Weissenburg before the Germans defeated the French at Wörth on 6 August, the battle costing the French 11,000 dead and 9000 men taken prisoner. The cost for the Germans was 10,000 – an expensive victory. What shocked the French most was the accuracy and rate of fire of the German artillery. French attacks were literally torn to shreds by the breech-loading guns, not to mention accurate rifle fire. News of this unexpected defeat left Paris in a state of denial.

Napoleon III divided his frontline armies into two – the Army of Châlons under Marshal Patrice MacMahon and the Army of the Rhine under Marshal François Achille Bazaine (1811–88). It was to no avail. Moltke defeated Bazaine at Gravelotte and sealed his army of 180,000 men inside a

LOCATION

Sedan lies in the strategically crucial northeastern French region of the Ardennes close to both the Belgian and German borders.

PRUSSIAN FIELD GUN C64 (8CM)

Prussia had already begun manufacturing steel-barrelled rifled breech-loaders in the 1850s and the Prussians were fully equipped with these artillery pieces model C64s from 1867. In 1870, her allies were similarly equipped. The strong new barrels allowed for a longer range and stronger charges to be used by the field artillery. In general use was the 4 pounder C64 with a 77 (3.03in) or 80mm (3.15in) calibre, and in 1867 a new breech-block was introduced, given the designation C64/67. The gun was very effective within 900m (981 yards) and had shells with reliable percussion fuses. Shrapnel was also being used with range of 2.2km (1.36 miles) with deadly effect.

This colour chromolithography from the late nineteenth century shows French cavalry attacking German infantry (formed up on the right) at the battle of Sedan, 1 September 1870. French cavalry did launch some desperate attacks during the battle, and suffered heavy casualties as a result.

pocket, or cauldron (*Kessel* in German), around Metz.

Paris – or rather, Empress Eugénie (1826–1920) – responded by ordering MacMahon to relieve Bazaine. What he should have done was to retreat westwards, trading space for time and weakening the advancing Germans while gaining numerical strength. This 'offensive' towards Metz was soon mired in mud, with rain and grumbling, plundering troops. Hoping to gain time to re-form his army, MacMahon moved to the small frontier town of Sedan, 145km (90 miles) from Metz.

MacMahon could not have chosen a worse spot for a battle from a French point

of view. Sedan was in a sunken valley where the Meuse made a loop before turning north; the area to the north was wooded, rough terrain, and to the east lay the brook of Givonne, with a series of hamlets, orchards and fields blocking the field of fire. It was the perfect spot for the French Army to be trapped against the rapidly manoeuvring and advancing Germans and the nearby Belgian frontier.

When told the news by a courier, Moltke could not believe his luck. Without much effort on his part, the French marched right into the cauldron, where he would simply wipe them out. He told his staff, 'We have them in a mousetrap! We attack at dawn!'

THE BATTLE BEGINS

A thick white mist shrouded the valley around Sedan at 0400 on 1 September as General Ludwig von der Tann's (1815–81) Bavarians advanced across the Meuse bridges. This sector was held by the French XII Corps under General Barthélémy Lebrun (1809–89), who had been up all night waiting for the inevitable German assault. There were no French pickets, so the Bavarians captured a few houses and the main street of the village of Bazeilles without a single disturbance. Even so, they were headed for the toughest soldiers on the French side – the *Infanterie de Marine*, or Marine Infantry. These elite troops had erected barricades and taken up positions in the village's remaining houses, intending to fight for each street and building. The Marines' gallant defence of Bazeilles rescued France's military reputation from being completely tarnished that day.

Two hours later, the mist had lifted and the Bavarian artillery opened fire from the far side of the Meuse in support of the three brigades and the XII Saxon Corps, which now began a bloody fight for Bazeilles. Lebrun was, like his men, astonished at the range, rate of fire and accuracy of the German breech-loading artillery. The fighting for the village raged around the church, marketplace and Montvilliers Park for hours with unabated ferocity, forcing von der Tann to call up reserves. By contrast, the village of La Moncelle fell to the XII Saxon Corps after it had been strewn with artillery shot from the Saxon batteries. Lebrun came to call this

The loser of Sedan: Field Marshal Patrice MacMahon (1808–1893) went on to become President of the Third Republic of France between 1875 and 1879.

THE OPPOSED FORCES

PRUSSO-GERMAN ARMY

Troops	250,000
Artillery pieces	500

IMPERIAL FRENCH ARMY

Troops	100–120,000
Artillery pieces	420

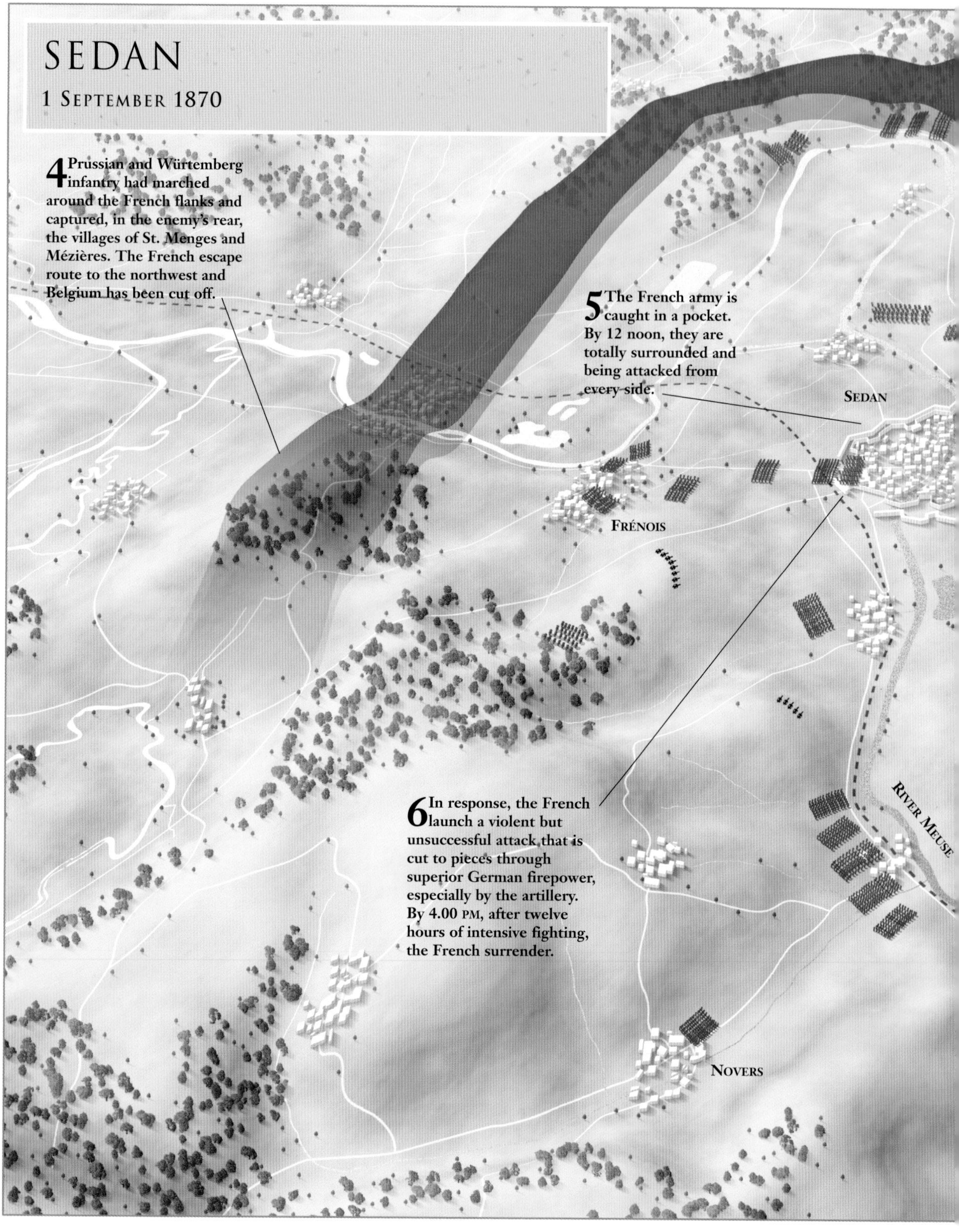

SEDAN
1 SEPTEMBER 1870

4 Prussian and Würtemberg infantry had marched around the French flanks and captured, in the enemy's rear, the villages of St. Menges and Mézières. The French escape route to the northwest and Belgium has been cut off.

5 The French army is caught in a pocket. By 12 noon, they are totally surrounded and being attacked from every side.

SEDAN

FRÉNOIS

6 In response, the French launch a violent but unsuccessful attack that is cut to pieces through superior German firepower, especially by the artillery. By 4.00 PM, after twelve hours of intensive fighting, the French surrender.

RIVER MEUSE

NOVERS

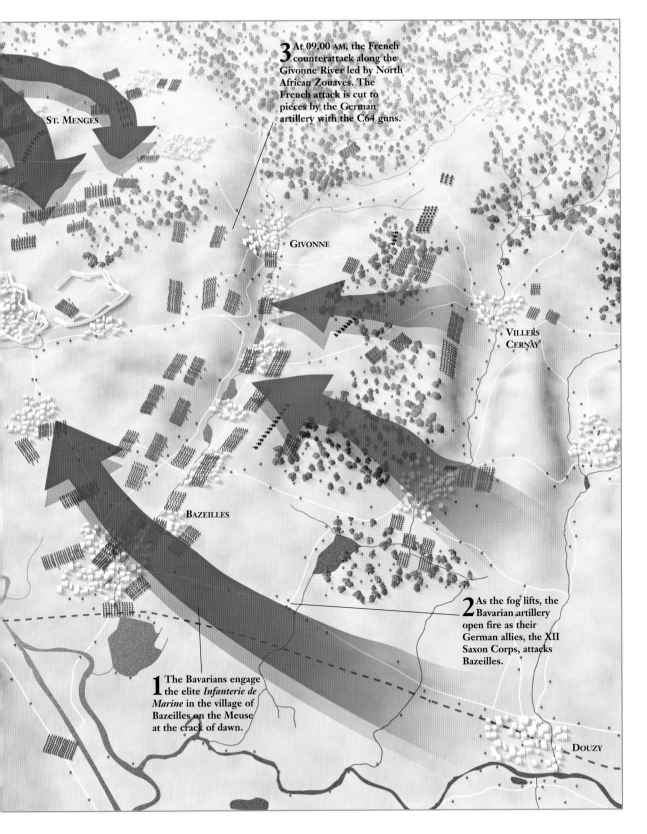

St. Menges

3 At 09.00 AM, the French counterattack along the Givonne River led by North African Zouaves. The French attack is cut to pieces by the German artillery with the C64 guns.

Givonne

Villers Cernay

Bazeilles

2 As the fog lifts, the Bavarian artillery open fire as their German allies, the XII Saxon Corps, attacks Bazeilles.

1 The Bavarians engage the elite *Infanterie de Marine* in the village of Bazeilles on the Meuse at the crack of dawn.

Douzy

143

The French infantryman's uniform of baggy trousers, knee-length coat and characteristic kepi remained unchanged, with the exception of the rifle, until 1914.

unremitting German bombardment '*avalanche de fer*' (avalanche of iron), and it almost killed him and his entire staff.

Lebrun was fortunate. Not so MacMahon, who was hit at around 05.00 by a German shell fragment. This forced him to relinquish his command to General Auguste-Alexandre Ducrot (1817–82), commanding I Corps, who now gave the order to retreat. Had this order been issued earlier in the morning, MacMahon's army might have been saved, but now there was

no choice but to fight to the bitter end. General Emmanuel Félix de Wimpffen (1811–84), who had been given secret orders to take over if MacMahon was incapacitated, now did so – and immediately countermanded Ducrot's order to retreat. These changes of order inevitably enfeebled the French defence of the Givonne Line, leaving it vulnerable to a full-scale German attack.

THE BATTLE SPREADS

By 0900, the fighting had spread up the Givonne as the Royal Prussian Guards began to advance just as the French decided to do so as well. Ducrot's I Corps and Lebrun's XII Corps launched an attack with all the dash and élan that only the French seemed able to muster. The offensive was soon pushing back the hard-pressed Saxons, who buckled and reeled under the onslaught. But with the Saxons reinforced by the Prussians and Bavarians, especially the deadly *avalanche de fer*, French resolve collapsed under the withering fire. One unit of Zouaves fled into Belgium. The combination of 96 German guns and Bavarian and Saxon infantry broke the French.

Soldiers from the 3rd Westphalian Infantry Regiment advance in line, armed with their distinctive 1857 'needle carbines'. The pioneering breech-loading bolt action system of the needle carbine offered a much faster rate of fire than the old muzzle-loading muskets, giving the Prussian infantry a distinct advantage over their enemies.

At Bazeilles, the Marine Infantry not only held but also gained ground. But when the Saxons cut their way through Montvilliers Park with billhooks, and fresh Bavarian troops attacked, this proved too much even for the Marines. Their stronghold, a villa in the northern part of the village, was broken into by the Bavarians, driving them out. Meanwhile, the Prussian Guards had pushed the French out of their remaining villages along the Givonne, forcing them to set up a new line west of the small river. At 09.00, there were six Prussian Guards batteries firing at the French; just two hours later, no fewer than 14 batteries were firing away – with deadly effect.

FLANK ATTACK

While the main German army set out to tie up the French along the Givonne, with Wimpffen swallowing the bait whole, Moltke had sent Crown Prince Frederick (1831–88) with the Württemberg Division and two Prussian corps to intercept the French and prevent their escape west via Mézières. At 07.30, this force crossed the Meuse while the battle for Givonne was

raging to the northeast. At this point, they received orders from Moltke for V and XI Corps to march on St Menges and thereby trap the French completely. French scouts failed yet again to notice the advancing enemy, who took St Menges by surprise. The French cavalry launched a dashing but doomed attack that was cut to pieces by a renewed *avalanche de fer* from 24 German batteries (some 114 guns). Having toppled the German skirmishers, French horses and men fell in a bloody heap well before they reached the German main line.

THE TRAP IS CLOSED

By midday, the Germans had effectively won the battle. They held both banks of the Givonne plus the villages of Balan, Bazeilles and Illy, while Sedan was cut off. The French were now caught inside Moltke's 'mousetrap'. Facing a total of 71 artillery batteries, they had no hope of escape. The German guns opened up, silencing the French artillery despite their best efforts to answer the enemy's deadly and accurate fire.

Cornered, the French lashed out. General Jean-Auguste Margueritte (1823–1870) launched a cavalry attack so

This contemporary illustration showing French troops surrounded by Prussian forces represents in figurative terms how the French army became trapped and slowly annihilated by the Prussian rifle and artillery fire at the battle of Sedan.

In this painting by Paul Louis Narcisse Grolleron (1848–1901), French Zouave infantry defend a damaged farm house under pressure from Prussian troops. They are armed with the distinctive Chassepot rifle.

By 16.00, the French attack had spent itself, and German corps were converging from all directions on Sedan. Napoleon III now in turn overrode Wimpffen – it was obvious that the bloody and increasingly pointless slaughter had to end. A white flag was hoisted.

There were parleys, and the returning German staff officers told Moltke, Bismarck and King William that among the French was Emperor Napoleon III himself. They were thunderstruck. The following morning, 2 September, Bismarck and Napoleon III met alone along the road to

ferocious and desperate that it carried all before it – the Chasseurs d'Afrique light horse rode down the Prussian infantry and almost captured a battery, but after half an hour they, including their commander, lay scattered on the battlefield, dead and dying. By 14.00, the cavalry had retired – less than half of it survived – and Napoleon III, who was with his army at Sedan, ordered the white flag raised. Wimpffen, as was his prerogative, overrode his emperor's command. With the Germans advancing from all sides, the French fought on with the determination of the damned, especially in the east.

Wimpffen belatedly adopted Ducrot's idea. He massed what remained of his army for an assault against Balan and an attempt at a breakout towards Carignan and the west. The French attacked with such fury that the Germans were stunned and almost overwhelmed, but their discipline, their steady rifle fire in massed columns and, above all, their artillery stemmed the tide of men and horses.

the German field HQ. The French surrendered 104,000 troops, 6000 horses and 419 artillery pieces.

AFTERMATH

Napoleon III chose to share his army's captivity in Germany. On 4 September, the Third Republic was proclaimed in France, and continued the struggle against Prussia and its allies despite dwindling hopes of victory. The Germans advanced, laying siege to Paris, and under the Treaty of Frankfurt of May 1871 forced a humiliated France to cede Alsace–Lorraine and to pay the new German Empire (declared at Versailles on 18 January) five billion francs in indemnity. It is little wonder that this 'peace', imposed on France despite Bismarck's objections, was a contributory factor to the outbreak of World War I (1914–18) two generations later.

The mobility of the Prussian artillery arm and the superior accuracy and rate of fire of the breech-loading guns proved decisive in the victory at Sedan, and was to announce the dominance of artillery in the wars of the early and middle parts of the twentieth century.

In this chalk lithograph by W. Loeillot depicting the events of 2nd September 1870, Napoleon III (left) is shown handing over his rapier to German Emperor William I (centre) as a sign of capitulation. Otto von Bismarck is third from right.

OMDURMAN
1–2 September 1898

HAVING ABANDONED SUDAN IN 1885 FOLLOWING THE MAHDIST UPRISING, BRITAIN LATER SOUGHT TO RECONQUER THE TERRITORY AND IN 1895 AUTHORIZED SIR HERBERT KITCHENER TO UNDERTAKE THE TASK. KITCHENER, WHO HAD WITNESSED THE AFTERMATH OF THE SIEGE OF KHARTOUM, EXECUTED A CAMPAIGN THAT REACHED ITS CULMINATION OUTSIDE OMDURMAN IN 1898. THE CAMPAIGN SAW MODERN MACHINE GUNS USED WITH DEVASTATING EFFECT IN A MAJOR ENGAGEMENT FOR THE FIRST TIME.

WHY DID IT HAPPEN?

WHO Major-General Sir Herbert Kitchener (1850–1916) led the Anglo-Egyptian Army, opposed by the Mahdist Khalifa Abdallahi (1846–99).

WHAT The battle demonstrated the enormous technological gap between the European and African powers and showed that artillery and machine guns would dominate the battlefield from now on.

WHERE The village of Egeiga, on the plains of Kerreri, north of Omdurman, Sudan.

WHEN 1–2 September 1898.

WHY The British Government wanted to remove the Mahdist threat to Egypt once and for all, while Kitchener and the Army wanted revenge for the fall of Khartoum in 1885.

OUTCOME Sudan became a British colony, thinly disguised as an Anglo-Egyptian protectorate.

From the spring of 1884, Major-General Sir Charles 'Chinese' Gordon (1833–85) was besieged in the Sudanese capital of Khartoum. He had a garrison of 6000 to defend its 30,000 inhabitants from the followers of the Sudanese Islamist leader Muhammad Ahmad (c. 1844–85), also known as the Mahdi ('Divinely Guided One'). The British Government eventually dispatched a relief force – the Nile Expedition, led by General Lord Wolseley (1833–1913) – which arrived in the Sudan from Egypt around the turn of the year. Attacked by Mahdist forces at Abu Klea on 17 January 1885, the relief force reached Khartoum on the 28th.

Unfortunately, it arrived too late. Two hours before dawn on 26 January, the Mahdist, or 'Dervish', army investing Khartoum had attacked the city and sacked it with great savagery. Among the 4000 butchered was Gordon himself, whose head was placed on display and his body dumped in the Nile. One of Wolseley's officers, Herbert Kitchener, swore revenge, and vanquishing the Mahdists became an obsession.

SLOW ADVANCE

In 1896, Kitchener, by now a brigadier-general and the Sirdar, or commander-in-chief, of the British-controlled Egyptian Army, began his slow, painstaking advance up the Nile to take on and destroy the Mahdist forces. In May, his troops captured the small fortified village of Firket, the

Sudanese troops in Anglo-Egyptian service proved superb soldiers and are seen in this photograph taking up position in a trench just before a Mahdist attack.

Mahdists losing 1000 killed and 600 taken prisoner. Kitchener noted how well his Egyptian conscripts had performed.

In September, the heavily fortified Mahdist outpost of Krema was taken without resistance. The following day the Anglo-Egyptian Army (AEA), numbering 12,000 troops, defeated 6000 Mahdists at Hafir across the Nile. The combination of gunboats, the Maxim machine gun and artillery firing high-explosive shells had not been to the Dervishes' liking.

The following year, the great challenge was finding a solution to the logistical problems of keeping the Anglo-Egyptian Army supplied as it marched on the Mahdist heartland. Kitchener, who had trained as an engineer, ordered the construction of a railway across the 380km (235 miles) of flat desert between Wadi Halfa and the Mahdist stronghold of Abu Hamed.

From May to the end of July 1897, the construction crews, despite atrocious climatic and physical hardships, laid 185km (115 miles) of line. In September that same year, when Abu Hamed and then Berber fell, there was only one stronghold between Kitchener and Mahdist capital of Omdurman – Atbara.

Kitchener's adversary, the Khalifa Abdallahi, was not an experienced military commander; he had no idea of the destructiveness of modern weaponry and was guided by something other than military logic. He claimed that the Mahdi, who had died in June 1885, had appeared to him in a vision, telling him that he should meet and defeat, with divine assistance, the infidels on the plains of Kerreri, north of Omdurman.

Kitchener, for his part, did not underestimate the enemy – a British infantry brigade under the command of Major-General W.F. Gatacre (1843–1906) was sent to reinforce the Anglo-Egyptians. Gatacre's men were equipped with the rapid-fire Lee Metford II rifle, giving them three times the rate of fire and range of the Mahdists, who, if they had a firearm at all, were armed with old Remingtons.

ATBARA

In the spring of 1898, the Khalifa sent his relative, the Emir Mahmud, to make a stand at Atbara, where the Nile met its tributary Atbara River. Mahmud constructed a camp, protected by trenches and a *zeriba* (wall of thorns), inside which his army was massed. For two weeks, Kitchener dithered. Most of his officers urged caution; Gatacre encouraged the Sirdar to attack with all force. On Good Friday, 8 April, the 14,000-

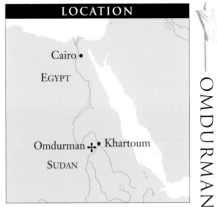

The Madhi's new capital of Omdurman was strategically located on the west bank of the confluence of the White and Blue Nile, right opposite the then abandoned Egypto-Sudanese capital of Khartoum.

MAXIM GUN

Invented in 1884 by the American-born British inventor Hiram Maxim (1840–1916), the Maxim machine gun used the energy generated from the mechanism of the recoil to eject each spent cartridge and insert a new round. This system was vastly more efficient than the Gatling gun and required less manpower. The Maxim could therefore fire 500 rounds per minute, equivalent to the firepower of 30 breech-loading bolt-action rifles, and compared more than favourably with the 200 rounds fired by the Gatling. No wonder the ditty went: 'Whatever happens, we have got, The Maxim gun, and they have not.' Never was this more true than at Omdurman. This photograph shows Egyptian infantrymen tending to their carriage-mounted Maxim during the reconquest of Sudan in 1898.

OMDURMAN

Soldiers of the British 1st Brigade leave camp at Wad Hamed, on the bank of the Nile in the Sudan, to begin their march on Omdurman, August 1898. Illustration from The Graphic *magazine, 1898.*

strong Anglo-Egyptian force marched to a ridge 2.4km (1.5 miles) from Mahmud's camp. Kitchener's army deployed in an arc 1370m (1500 yards) wide, with Gatacre's British brigade on the left. A violent 10-minute barrage from the Naval Division and the Nile Flotilla heralded a full-scale Anglo-Egyptian assault. As the dust from the artillery bombardment settled, the signal was given. The troops, shouting at the top of their lungs, 'Remember Gordon!', advanced on the emir's camp. In half an hour, it was all over. Kitchener lost 600 men; the Mahdists 3000. However, the Anglo-Egyptians had also taken the Emir Mahmud alive.

ADVANCE ON OMDURMAN

It was not until August 1898, after another British infantry brigade plus cavalry and artillery had arrived and when the Nile was rising again, that Kitchener ordered his

army to make the final advance on Omdurman. On 21 August, he inspected his 25,000-strong army. It consisted of two British brigades totalling some 8000 men and an Egyptian division of 17,000 Egyptian and Sudanese troops; it occupied a vast camp stretching 5km (3.1 miles) along the banks of the Nile. Despite its numbers, the Anglo-Egyptian Army was still outnumbered by the Khalifa's fierce warriors by a factor of two to one.

Three days later, Kitchener marched out, and on 30 August the AEA took up position at the village of Egeiga, 10km (6.2 miles) north of Omdurman. General Gordon's nephew, Major Staveley Gordon, was the first to spot the dome of the Mahdi's Tomb in the Dervish capital.

The Khalifa had prepared as well as he could to meet the enemy, constructing a line of forts to block the approach to his capital and mining the Nile to prevent gunboats from approaching by water. He put his trust, however, in the accuracy of his premonition that the infidels would be crushed at Kerreri – and left unanswered a request from Kitchener to send civilians out of Omdurman.

1 SEPTEMBER

The Khalifa should have heeded the warning, since Omdurman was built of mud bricks and would prove easy pickings for Kitchener's flotilla anchored at Halfeya. These 8–10 white-painted gunboats packed quite some punch with their aggregate firepower of 36 guns and 24 Maxims.

The flotilla opened fired on the forts and the city at 11.00 with devastating effect, the targets being enveloped in red dust. The crews took bets on who would be first to hit the Mahdi's Tomb, which was struck at 13.00.

Meanwhile, led by the Khalifa, the Mahdist army of 50,000 marched north with beating drums, blaring horns and murmuring Ansars (followers of the Mahdi). Lieutenant-Colonel Robert Broadwood's (1862–1917) cavalry spotted the oncoming host and withdrew. Broadwood sent a young officer – Winston S. Churchill (1874–1965) – to report the Khalifa's approach back to Kitchener.

General, later Field-Marshal, Sir Herbert Kitchener (1850–1916) led the 2nd Nile Expedition, defeated the Madhists at Omdurman and went on to fame and glory.

Churchill detested Kitchener, and the feeling was fully reciprocated. The young 4th Hussars officer reported to the Sirdar, who replied: 'You say the Dervish army is advancing. How long do you think I have got?' Churchill replied: 'You have got at least an hour, probably an hour and a half, Sir, even if they come at the present rate.'

By noon, the AEA was deployed for battle in a wide arc, expecting to be attacked at any moment. This situation seemed unusual to Kitchener since the Mahdists always used the cover of darkness to take their enemy by surprise. The sun rose and fell. Nothing happened, and the Mahdist army withdrew to its former positions.

Mahdist, or Dervish, infantry massed for a charge at the Anglo-Egyptian formations. The men with long, thick hair were known to the British troops as 'Fuzzy-Wuzzies'.

THE OPPOSED FORCES

MAHDIST ARMY

Warriors	**50,000**

(of which only 10–15,000 armed with Remington and Martini Henry rifles)
Some artillery

ANGLO-EGYPTIAN ARMY (AEA)

2 British infantry brigades:	8000
1 Egyptian division:	17,000
Total:	**25,000**

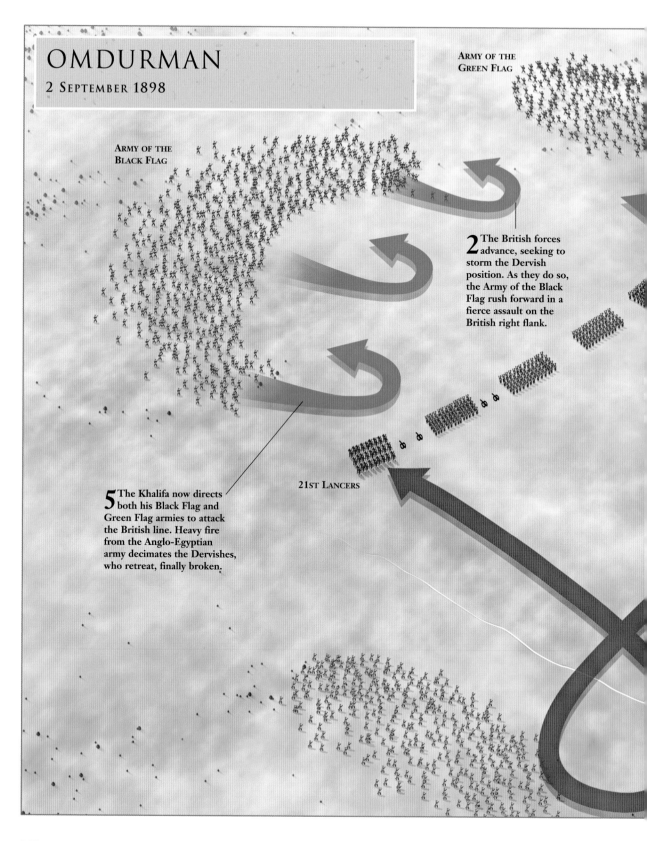

OMDURMAN
2 September 1898

ARMY OF THE
GREEN FLAG

ARMY OF THE
BLACK FLAG

2 The British forces advance, seeking to storm the Dervish position. As they do so, the Army of the Black Flag rush forward in a fierce assault on the British right flank.

21ST LANCERS

5 The Khalifa now directs both his Black Flag and Green Flag armies to attack the British line. Heavy fire from the Anglo-Egyptian army decimates the Dervishes, who retreat, finally broken.

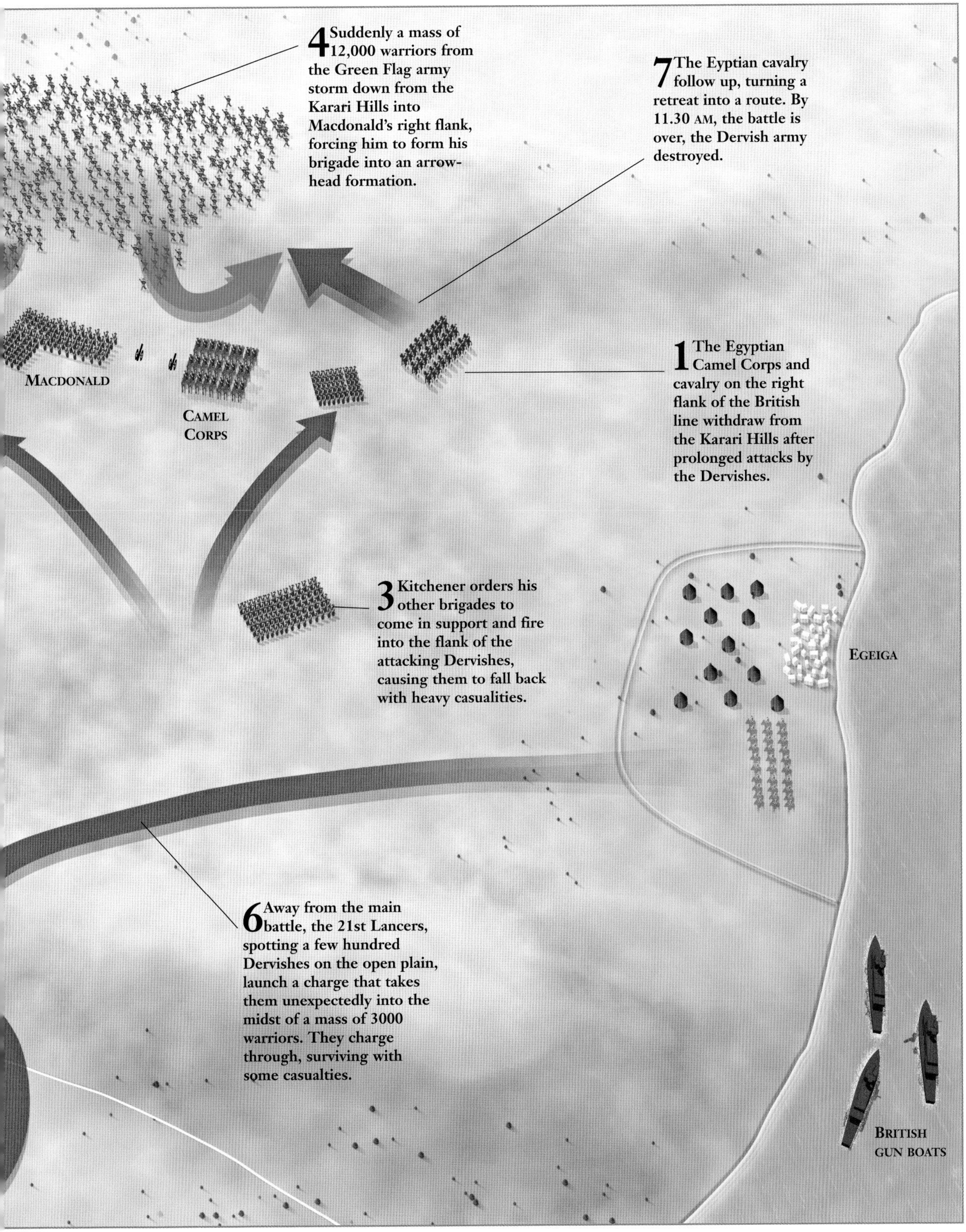

4 Suddenly a mass of 12,000 warriors from the Green Flag army storm down from the Karari Hills into Macdonald's right flank, forcing him to form his brigade into an arrow-head formation.

7 The Eyptian cavalry follow up, turning a retreat into a route. By 11.30 AM, the battle is over, the Dervish army destroyed.

1 The Egyptian Camel Corps and cavalry on the right flank of the British line withdraw from the Karari Hills after prolonged attacks by the Dervishes.

MACDONALD

CAMEL CORPS

3 Kitchener orders his other brigades to come in support and fire into the flank of the attacking Dervishes, causing them to fall back with heavy casualities.

EGEIGA

6 Away from the main battle, the 21st Lancers, spotting a few hundred Dervishes on the open plain, launch a charge that takes them unexpectedly into the midst of a mass of 3000 warriors. They charge through, surviving with some casualties.

BRITISH GUN BOATS

A night attack was just what the Sirdar feared more than anything. In the dark, his troops would be without the protection of their Maxims, which they could not use at close quarters at night for fear of hitting their own troops. This raised the spectre of hand-to-hand combat, in which the Mahdists were superior. To prevent such an attack, Kitchener asked director of military intelligence Reginald Wingate (1861–1953) to get his agents inside the Mahdist camp to spread the rumour that the AEA would be attacking during the night. The ruse worked since no Mahdist assault came.

2 SEPTEMBER

The Kerreri Plain is enclosed on three sides. To the east, lies the murky, grey Nile; to the north, the Kerreri Ridge (Daham and Abu Zeriba Hills); and to the south, the forbidding Black Hill (Jebel Surghum). In this vast natural amphitheatre, a bloody drama was about to unfold.

The Khalifa, with his brother Emir Yacub, held the Black Flag Army of 17,000 in reserve behind Jebel Surghum. Ibrahim al-Khalil with 4000 men was deployed on the right with a skirmish force of 700 under Osman Digna. The Mahdist centre consisted of 8000 men under Emir Osman Azrak, backed up by Abdallah abu Ziwar's Green Flag Army of 4000. A final reserve of 10,000, under the Khalifa's son, Sheikh Osman el-Din, was lined up on the extreme left.

In response, Kitchener had his army lined up along the perimeter of their encampment, behind the *zeriba*. From left to right were the 2nd British Brigade, 1st British Brigade, then three Egyptian brigades, with the fourth held in reserve in the centre of the camp.

Some time before dawn, the Mahdist army lined up for battle, wearing their characteristic white jibbas (cloaks) with ceremonial 'patches' and carrying firearms,

Despite the futility and losses involved, the Khalifa unleashed his fanatical soldiers in regular, open formed, frontal charges against troops armed with rifles, artillery and Maxim guns.

A young Winston Churchill, in the uniform of an officer of the 10th Hussars. He was by no means Kitchener's favourite.

knoll at the centre of the line and sick at the spectacle, shouted: 'Cease Fire! Cease Fire! Oh, what a dreadful waste of ammunition!'

Kitchener now instructed Colonel Martin to take his 21st Lancers out on the Kerreri Plain to reconnoitre as he ordered his brigades to advance on Omdurman. A scout noticed a small group of Mahdists holed up in a gorge, and Martin, ignoring Kitchener's orders, sent his 320 lancers into the attack. In just two minutes' fighting, the unit earned three Victoria Crosses, but lost 70 men killed or wounded.

LESS HASTE

Kitchener's haste in pushing on to Omdurman almost proved his undoing. The 1st Egyptian Brigade, commanded by Colonel Hector MacDonald (1853–1903), got separated from the rest of the army. With three-quarters of his force uncommitted, the Khalifa grasped the chance to turn apparent defeat into stunning victory, thanks to Kitchener's mistake. He ordered MacDonald crushed by the Green Flag Army and the Black Flag Army. Had the attacks been co-ordinated, MacDonald's fate would have been sealed.

First on the scene was the Mahdist cavalry – until now uncommitted – which simply rode straight at the brigade. The men and their fine mounts were slaughtered before they even had a chance to reach the enemy's lines. Then came the news that Yacub's huge host was bearing down on the brigade. MacDonald, nicknamed 'Fighting Mac', was determined to make a stand, so he rejected advice to retreat, called his battalion commanders to his side and formed, under fire and with only minutes before the Mahdists arrived, a new fire line. MacDonald even managed to discipline his enthusiastic but unruly Sudanese

swords, shields, spears and green, black and red banners with Koranic verses stitched into them. The metal glinted in the sharp sunlight. Sheikh Osman took a force and marched north in an attempt to outflank the *zeriba* line, only to be lured further and further north by the cavalry under Broadwood. He drew the Mahdist host down to the banks of the Nile, where they proved a juicy target for the gunboats, enabling Broadwood to escape back to the main army.

DEVASTATING FIRE

Meanwhile, forces under Osman Azrak and Osman Digna formed a massive crescent around the Anglo-Egyptian encampment and launched a frontal assault. At 2600m (2800 yards), they came under fire from the artillery, which gouged out huge holes in their advancing lines. From 1800m (2000 yards) out, the Mahdists came under volley fire from the Lee Metfords and the Maxims, and when the range closed to 730m (800 yards) the Egyptians and Sudanese opened fire with their Martini Henrys. The effect was devastating. None of the Mahdists got within 275m (300 yards) of the *zeriba*. By 08.00, the first attack had come to a bloody end, with 2000 dead and 4000 wounded Mahdists lying on the field in front of the encampment. Kitchener, standing on a

This 'Fellah', or infantryman, from the 10th Sudanese battalion, wears the standard uniform of the Egyptian army, with leather belts and pouches and a Martini-Henry rifle.

mercenaries (who had more than one score to settle with the Mahdists), getting them to fix bayonets and fire in volleys. It was these tough Sudanese rather than the Egyptians who bore the brunt of the tide of the screaming Mahdists.

Kitchener had not realized that 'Fighting Mac' was in trouble, but soon sent his other brigades to aid him. A battalion of the Lincolnshire Regiment arrived to reinforce the 1st Egyptian Brigade's right flank, and it was a combination of cold steel, superior firepower and reinforcements arriving in the nick of time that saved the brigade from annihilation.

Having reduced the Black Flag Army to tatters, MacDonald could turn his brigade around, with increasing streams of British and Egyptians arriving to join the engagement, and fix his attention on the oncoming hordes of Green Flag Mahdists. By 11.30, most of the Madhist troops had had enough, and they began to flee in ever larger numbers to the Kerreri Hills, the Sudanese mercenaries in hot pursuit. The latter spared no one in their path, and the Egyptians, having previously experienced the fanaticism of the enemy, took no chances, shooting any captured or wounded Dervishes out of hand.

AFTERMATH

The battle that destroyed the once formidable and feared Mahdist empire cost the AEA a mere 48 men killed and 434 wounded. Mahdist casualties were enormous: 11,000 killed and 16,000 wounded or captured. That afternoon, Omdurman surrendered and Kitchener had the Mahdi's bones dumped in the Nile. The Khalifa fled into the desert fastness, but was captured by Wingate 18 months later.

Modern breech-loading rifles and the Maxim gun ensured the British a total victory at Omdurman with minimal losses, and demonstrated that modern armies could not do without the destructive power of the machine-gun.

Left: Glorious folly: the charge of the 21st Lancers at Omdurman against some 2000 entrenched Madhist warriors. It was the last time an open cavalry charge of this kind was staged.

U-9 vs CRUISER FORCE
22 SEPTEMBER 1914

THE TORPEDO WAS ONE OF THE WEAPONS THAT CHANGED NAVAL WARFARE. IT PERMITTED MINOR VESSELS TO DESTROY BIG SHIPS IF THEY COULD JUST GET WITHIN RANGE. DOING SO WAS BY NO MEANS EASY FOR LIGHT SURFACE CRAFT, BUT THE EMERGENCE OF THE SUBMARINE AS A STEALTHY DELIVERY PLATFORM WAS A DECISIVE DEVELOPMENT.

WHY DID IT HAPPEN?

WHO German submarine *U-9* versus three elderly British armoured cruisers.

WHAT *U-9* sighted the British cruiser force, which was on patrol, and attacked with torpedoes.

WHERE North Sea.

WHEN 22 September 1914.

WHY The British squadron was part of a standing patrol commitment and was vulnerable to attack.

OUTCOME All three British ships were sunk for no loss on the German side. The attack demonstrated the future impact of the submarine on naval warfare.

Early submarines such as *U-9* can more properly be termed submersibles than true submarine craft. They spent most of their time on the surface and could operate underwater only for a relatively short time, and at much reduced speed. In addition, their torpedo armament was both unreliable and extremely limited.

When World War I (1914–18) broke out, the submarine was very much in its infancy and its role was still being explored, leading to ill-fated experiments like the British K-boats. These were steam-powered fast submarines intended to operate with the battle fleet, but they proved to be a liability (they were prone to accidents) rather than an asset.

However, more modest designs showed a lot of promise. A vessel that could cruise long distances on the surface and then dive to make a surprise attack with powerful ship-killing weapons was an attractive idea, especially for nations that could not afford large numbers of big-gun surface ships.

When major warships clashed, the conventional mode of warfare was for them to exchange salvos of big shells fired from huge guns. Ship design, training levels and gunnery skill could all influence the course of a battle, enabling ships to score more hits and shrug off damage and thus remain in the battle line to keep firing for longer. However, there was a certain degree of mathematical probability to such a battle, leading almost inevitably to the defeat of the weaker side.

The arrival of torpedo-armed light vessels that could charge across the gap

HMS Dreadnought. *Despite her fearsome reputation and world-changing design, her sole direct contribution to the war was to ram and sink* U-29, *killing Commander Weddigen and all his crew.*

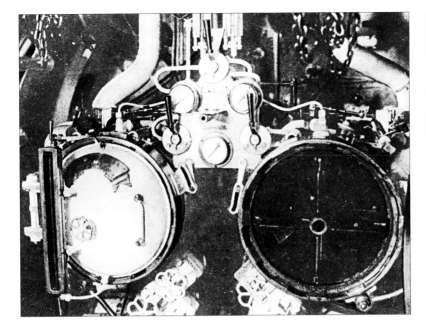

This photograph taken in 1915 shows the twin torpedo tubes of a German Unterseeboot ('under sea boat' – U-boat) of the U-9 type. Working conditions in these small submarines were cramped.

- Scapa Flow

North Sea

UNITED KINGDOM

Wilhelmshaven •

• Harwich

GERMANY

The cruiser force's patrol zone was close to the enemy shore, in easy reach of faster, more modern warships and, of course, submarines.

between two fleets upset this balance somewhat, but they could be countered by light cruisers and torpedo-boat destroyers (later shortened to 'destroyers') on the opposite side. Submarines offered new possibilities. They were useful for reconnaissance missions and might even be able to successfully attack a major warship.

The potential of submarines had yet to be proven, however. Some nations thought that they would make good defensive assets, deployed like a mobile, intelligent minefield to protect naval bases or to restrict access through narrow waters like the English Channel. Others thought more in terms of offensive action against the enemy fleet.

A third option was to use submarines in commerce raiding, traditionally the recourse of a lesser naval power when facing a greater power. At the outbreak of war, a set of fairly civilized rules of engagement existed, whereby submarines, in common with all raiding vessels, were required to reveal themselves and give the target a chance to surrender. This convention took away the main asset of the submarine – its capability for stealth – and until the advent of unrestricted submarine warfare later in the war, submarine raiders were nowhere near as effective as they might have otherwise been.

The submarine's most powerful weapon was, of course, its torpedoes, but the torpedoes of the time were unreliable, and obtaining a hit was problematic until the development of homing and guided versions, long after the end of World War I. Even in the days of unrestricted submarine

TYPE U-9 SUBMARINE

First of a class of four boats, U-9 had a crew of 35 officers and men. She was primitive by modern standards, but nevertheless a deadly weapon. On the surface she was as fast as the cruisers she engaged, though her underwater speed was only 14.8km/h, or 8 knots, and her range very limited (129km/80 miles at 9.25km/h, or 5 knots, underwater). U-9's deck gun was effective enough against unarmed merchantmen, but against a warship her only useful weapon was her six torpedoes. Commander Weddigen showed that, if cleverly and aggressively handled, a U-boat could sucker-punch even a major warship. His success did much to establish the submarine as a serious weapon of war.

A U-boat leaving port. Far less glamorous than destroyers or cruisers, U-boats were commanded by very young men – 23-year-old veterans were not uncommon.

warfare, most attacks against merchant ships were still undertaken on the surface with deck guns, commanders preferring to conserve their torpedoes until they were needed for a tough target like a warship or an escorted merchant.

The question of whether or not a submarine would be able to take on a major warship was answered in the early months of World War I, when several British cruisers were sunk by German U-boats. From that point on, the submarine was considered a very serious threat to surface combatants – and for some time it was a threat to which there were no satisfactory countermeasures.

Early World War I submarines were not fast enough to operate with even the lumbering pre-Dreadnought battleships that made up the bulk of many fleets, but they could still contribute to fleet actions, as scouting units or even directly. Tag-and-run attacks, intended to draw a pursuing force over a concealed patrol line of submarines, became a possibility, and the fear of a submarine ambush heavily influenced naval tactics throughout the war, notably at the Battle of Jutland in 1916.

One reason that the fear of ambush was so strong was the massacre of the so-called 'Live Bait Squadron' in September 1914. The squadron was part of a British

Admiralty plan to keep the German High Seas Fleet bottled up in its ports. This plan called for an aggressive forward patrol commitment, which required large numbers of cruisers and lighter warships.

'LIVE BAIT SQUADRON'

Cruiser Force C was made up of four armoured cruisers, HMS *Euryalus* (the force flagship), HMS *Aboukir*, HMS *Hogue* and HMS *Cressy*, the name ship of the class to which these vessels belonged. All the ships involved were more than 10 years old and obsolete, and the Admiralty was aware of their marginal utility. Most of their crewmembers were cadets or reservists; newer and better ships got the pick of the recruits. While their two 234mm (9.2in) and twelve 152mm (6in) guns represented a decent enough armament, the ships themselves were slow. They were being dangled within reach of fast modern German battlecruisers and dreadnoughts, earning Cruiser Force C the nickname of 'Live Bait Squadron'. The Admiralty, however, considered that the patrol was

THE OPPOSED FORCES

ROYAL NAVY

Cruiser Force C: 4 armoured cruisers

KRIEGSMARINE

U-9 (gasoline-powered submarine)

Metal warships were just 40-years-old when World War I broke out, and here HMS Aboukir *shows the influences of the days of sail with her tall masts and broadside armament.*

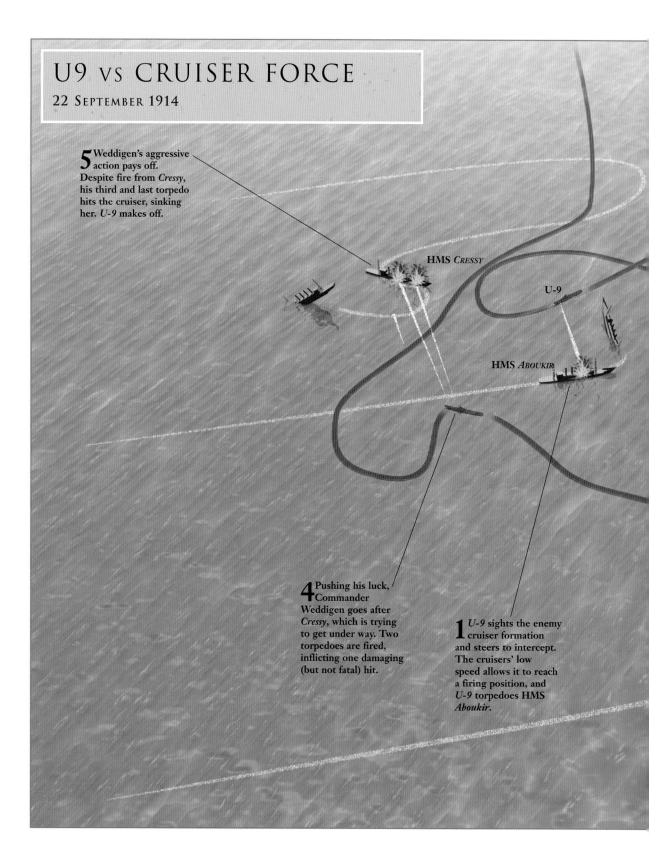

U9 vs CRUISER FORCE

22 SEPTEMBER 1914

5 Weddigen's aggressive action pays off. Despite fire from *Cressy*, his third and last torpedo hits the cruiser, sinking her. *U-9* makes off.

HMS *CRESSY*

U-9

HMS *ABOUKIR*

4 Pushing his luck, Commander Weddigen goes after *Cressy*, which is trying to get under way. Two torpedoes are fired, inflicting one damaging (but not fatal) hit.

1 *U-9* sights the enemy cruiser formation and steers to intercept. The cruisers' low speed allows it to reach a firing position, and *U-9* torpedoes HMS *Aboukir*.

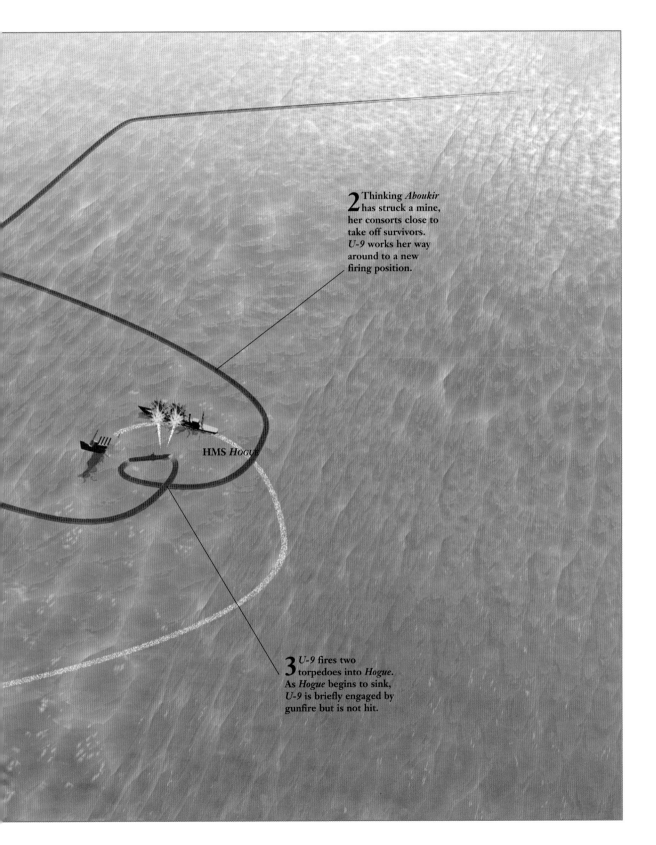

2 Thinking *Aboukir* has struck a mine, her consorts close to take off survivors. *U-9* works her way around to a new firing position.

HMS *Hogue*

3 *U-9* fires two torpedoes into *Hogue*. As *Hogue* begins to sink, *U-9* is briefly engaged by gunfire but is not hit.

necessary. It could not be mounted by destroyers in bad weather and there were too few modern ships available, so the old cruisers would have to do their best. With the traditional 'can do' spirit of the Royal Navy, the four ships prepared to put to sea despite serious misgivings.

These doubts were echoed at a high level. Indeed, the Admiralty was considering withdrawing Cruiser Force C, but events overtook it before a decision could be made.

The original plan was for the cruisers to put to sea on 20 September 1914, accompanied by a destroyer force. However, the seas were too rough for the escorts, so the bigger ships had to sortie without them. Then *Euryalus*, the flagship, was forced to return to port due to a shortage of coal and to a wireless malfunction caused by the foul weather. Ordinarily, the patrol commander, Rear-Admiral Arthur Christian, would have transferred his flag to one of the other vessels. In this case, high seas made this

impracticable, so Captain John Drummond of the *Aboukir* took command, and the three remaining ships struggled onward.

U-BOAT AT LARGE

U-9 represented the most advanced submarine technology available at the time, though by modern standards the boat was very primitive. Commissioned in 1910, it carried a total of six torpedoes, with two bow and two stern tubes through which to launch them. *U-9* could dive to 50m (164ft) safely and probably as deep as 125m (410ft) before being destroyed.

U-9 could manage 25.9km/h (14 knots) on the surface and a little over half that underwater. The boat was commanded by Lieutenant-Commander Otto Weddigen (1882–1915), and had a total crew of four officers and 25 other ranks. Just a few weeks before, *U-9* had made history by being the first submarine to reload her tubes while remaining submerged.

The weather had improved somewhat by the night of 21/22 September, and had

HMS Cressy's *ram bow is clearly obvious here, the product of a time when naval planners believed that ramming, not gunfire and certainly not torpedoes, was the future of naval combat.*

Admiral Christian been present, Cruiser Force C's destroyers might have been ordered out to take up their escort role. Since Christian had returned to port and Captain Drummond was not aware that he had the authority to call the escorts out, they were still not present on the morning of the 22nd.

Thus it was that *U-9* sighted the three cruisers sailing unescorted in the forenoon of 22 September. They were obviously unaware of the U-boat's presence and were not taking anti-submarine precautions such as zig-zagging. There was a standing order in place that all vessels were to frequently make changes of course along their general heading. This measure would make even a slow ship a difficult target, but the severity of the submarine threat was not recognized at that point, and in any case there were no reports of U-boats in the area. As a result, the order was not implemented.

The cruisers' age and generally low capabilities also contributed to their eventual undoing. They were supposed to be making 24km/h (13 knots) but simply could not keep up this speed. One of the biggest problems for submarines in both

world wars was getting into position for an attack. Many boats sighted the enemy at an awkward angle or distance and could do nothing more than report the sighting and hope that someone else was in a better position. Slower ships, however, were much easier to intercept.

FIRST ATTACK

The three vessels spotted by Lieutenant-Commander Weddigen that morning were extremely vulnerable to torpedo attack, and he resolved to make the most of his opportunity. At around 0625, after manoeuvring into position, *U-9* fired a single torpedo at *Aboukir*.

The torpedo functioned perfectly – which was not always the case at that time– and hit the cruiser on the port side, causing severe flooding accompanied by a loss of engine power. Damage control parties did what they could and some compartments were counterflooded to balance the list that developed. Nevertheless it rapidly became apparent that the ship was mortally wounded. Her captain, the acting patrol commander, had to give the order to abandon ship.

The crew of U-9 *attending a wedding. A close-knit crew was vital if such a small vessel was to be effective and not suffer a serious breakdown in morale.*

At that time, it was thought that *Aboukir* had struck a free-floating mine. As no others could be seen, and the submarine had not been spotted, the other two cruisers closed to pick up survivors. As the crew of *Aboukir* were being pulled from the sea, Captain Drummond finally realized that his ship had been torpedoed. This implied that a submarine was nearby and he ordered the other ships to get under way as quickly as possible.

Aboukir capsized at about 0700, roughly half an hour after being hit. HMS *Hogue*

was close by the sinking cruiser but on the wrong side of the vessel from the standpoint of *U-9*. The submarine had to endure a long and nerve-racking period of manoeuvring to reach a position from which to fire on the second cruiser.

Finally, *U-9* got to within 300m (328 yards) of *Hogue* and launched two more torpedoes. The cruiser was hit squarely amidships and her engine room quickly flooded. It was immediately apparent that she was sinking. For a small vessel like *U-9*, the weight lost by launching two torpedoes

in succession significantly affected her trim, and for a moment she broke the surface, giving *Hogue*'s gunners, still at their stations, a chance for vengeance. The U-boat was not hit, however, and managed to return to periscope depth to go after *Cressy*.

CRESSY vs U-9

With *Aboukir* gone and *Hogue* sinking fast, Captain Robert Johnson of HMS *Cressy* rang down for full steam and tried to get his ship moving and out of danger. The old engines took time to reach full revolutions

and acceleration was slow, so *Cressy*, too, presented an easy target. *U-9* launched two more torpedoes from her bow tubes, having reloaded underwater. One of the torpedoes missed by a small margin; the other struck home but did not inflict a killing wound. As *Cressy*'s gunners engaged *U-9*'s periscope, the only target they had, the U-boat came about and fired her last remaining torpedo. This hit the already damaged cruiser, which began to settle. Within 15 minutes, *Cressy*, too, had sunk. The U-boat, its torpedoes expended, slipped away.

A number of merchant ships and trawlers appeared on the scene and began picking up survivors of the sinkings. Although unrestricted submarine warfare was not yet in force, the risk taken by the civilian vessels that came to the rescue of the cruisers' crews was considerable.

They had no way of knowing that the U-boat was out of torpedoes and heading homewards. Slightly more than 800 men were pulled from the sea, though the death toll was still over 1400.

AFTERMATH

A court of inquiry apportioned some blame for the disaster to certain senior officers, but mostly condemned the Admiralty for authorizing the patrol. Anti-submarine precautions were taken far more seriously by the Royal Navy thereafter, though even then the order to zig-zag and maintain more than 24km/h (13 knots) was not always followed.

The practice of using slow armoured cruisers for patrols within easy reach of the enemy's forces was abandoned as a result of the inquiry, and major warships were forbidden to stop to pick up survivors in the event of an attack. Anti-torpedo protection also became an important consideration in warship design.

U-9 made it home unscathed, and under Weddigen sank another British cruiser, HMS *Hawke*, the following month. In early 1915, Weddigen took over *U-29*, but in March his new command was rammed and sunk in the North Sea by HMS *Dreadnought*, killing Weddigen and all hands. *U-9*, meanwhile, served throughout the war, carrying out seven patrols, in which it sank a total of 13 merchant vessels and five warships. *U-9* surrendered to the Allies at the end of the conflict.

Although in theory U-boats could have been useful fleet weapons against enemy naval warships, in practice they were most effectively used in an economic-warfare role, enforcing a naval blockade against Allied shipping in the North Atlantic. This they did very successfully: over the course of four-and-half years of naval warfare, 274 U-boats sank approximately 6596 merchant ships, equalling 12,800,733 tonnes (12,598,609 tons) of shipping.

A German propaganda poster. Despite losses, morale in the U-boat service remained high and several commanders were considered to be national heroes.

Left: A U-boat torpedoes a merchant ship. Unrestricted submarine warfare came closer to starving Britain into surrender during World War I than World War II.

2ND BATTLE OF YPRES

APRIL–MAY 1915

THE YPRES SALIENT WAS THE SCENE OF ENDLESS ATTRITIONAL STRUGGLE AND THREE MAJOR CAMPAIGNS, IN 1914, 1915 AND 1917. THE REGION WAS STRATEGICALLY IMPORTANT TO BOTH SIDES, AND BOTH ATTACK AND DEFENCE WERE CONDUCTED WITH GREAT DETERMINATION. AT THE SECOND BATTLE OF YPRES, A NEW WEAPON WAS DEPLOYED IN THE HOPE OF BREAKING THE DEADLOCK.

WHY DID IT HAPPEN?

WHO German Fourth Army, opposed by British Second Army plus two French divisions.

WHAT German forces used poison gas to assist a major offensive.

WHERE Ypres salient, Flanders.

WHEN 22 April to 25 May 1915.

WHY The German high command wanted to eliminate the Ypres salient and thus threaten the Channel ports.

OUTCOME German forces initially made some gains assisted by the gas, but were unable to achieve their overall objectives.

The early stages of World War I (1914–18) on the Western Front were marked by fluid action and a series of flanking attacks as both sides tried to turn the flank of the opposing forces. This resulted in the 'Race to the Sea', during which subsequent operations each tried to hook around to the north of the last. As each operation failed, static and well-defended positions were built, and these would eventually become the great trench lines that characterized the rest of the war in this theatre.

Late in 1914, the German Army launched its final attempt to break through the Allied lines and capture the Channel ports. This would have had serious implications for the Allies, making it very difficult to supply and reinforce British troops in mainland Europe, and might even have provided an 'anvil' against which the northern British forces on the Continent could be smashed.

This German offensive took place from 18 October to 30 November 1914, in the region around the city of Ypres. It began as something of an encounter battle, with both sides manoeuvring in the open and seeking a vulnerable flank. The battered British Expeditionary Force (BEF) was attacked by a German force composed largely of newly raised reserve units, many of which

A classic image of World War I: British troops at Ypres in 1915, silhouetted against the sky. The size of the packs carried, even in combat, is obvious.

contained great numbers of extremely young soldiers.

The resulting First Battle of Ypres has become known as the 'Massacre of the Innocents', as the scantily trained but enthusiastic young troops suffered immense casualties. They were backed up by more experienced troops, including elements of the elite Prussian Guard, but in the end the offensive bogged down and failed. Casualties among British troops were also extremely high. It has been said that the BEF died at Ypres; many of its units were reduced to skeleton strength.

The result of the Ypres offensive was a salient in the Allied line, which bulged eastwards towards the Belgian capital, Brussels. As the fighting in the area subsided, both sides spent the winter digging in along the line. Meanwhile, the Germans planned an operation for the spring, in which they would attempt to encircle the Allied troops in the salient and cut them off. By the spring, though, both sides were becoming skilled at trench warfare and the impressive strength of their defensive systems was apparent. Some way to give the attackers an advantage had to be found. It was decided to use gas.

GAS EXPERIMENTS

The Second Battle of Ypres was not the first use of gas in warfare, though it was to be the first large-scale offensive in which it was deployed. German forces had experimented with gas in 1914, firing shrapnel shells containing an irritant at French troops at Neuve Chapelle in October. The experiment was not a success; the defenders did not even notice the gas.

In January 1915, the German Army tried again, this time firing tear-gas shells at Russian troops on the Eastern Front. The extreme cold prevented the gas from being effective, but the Germans were not deterred. They now decided to try an even more virulent agent, chlorine, for use in the Ypres operation.

Exposure to chlorine was not usually immediately fatal, but even a relatively mild dose caused serious effects, including irritation of the eyes, vomiting, coughing and respiratory difficulties. This was terrifying and limited the ability of troops to

fight. A more serious dose would result in a slow and agonizing death, the victim's lungs filling with fluid, drowning him slowly. Being heavier than air, the gas would sink into trenches and shell holes, endangering troops sheltering there. Chlorine gas was highly visible and had a severe effect on morale, even for troops who were not directly affected by it.

The initial means of delivering gas as a weapon was to release it from cylinders at the front line and then rely on a favourable wind to carry it to the enemy. This was a somewhat random method, and later in the war gas shells became more common. These normally used mustard gas rather than chlorine. Mustard gas was less lethal than chlorine, though it could kill. Normally, it was used to wear down the

BRITISH 'TOMMY'

By 1915, troops of all nations involved in the Great War were equipped in a similar fashion – a uniform of dowdy colour, a rifle with a bayonet and a pack filled with a great weight of equipment. Early in the war, caps and soft hats were common, but these were quickly replaced by steel helmets. A helmet would not stop a bullet but it would prevent the commonest of combat wounds: a head injury caused by shell fragments. Rifles of the sort issued to most nations' troops were less than ideal for trench warfare. They were unwieldy at close quarters, and their long range was wasted in the prevailing conditions.

LOCATION

ENGLAND

BELGIUM
+ Ypres

GERMANY

• Paris

FRANCE

The critical location of the Ypres salient: had the German army reached the Channel Ports, the British forces on the Continent would have been cut off from supplies and reinforcements.

enemy, since it produced irritant effects and would persist in some areas for weeks after delivery, making life even harder for the miserable troops in the trenches. Other gases were used at times, such as the mix of chlorine and phosgene known as White Star. Although gas did cause significant casualties, its main effect was psychological, since the troops' fear of gas and a lack of effective countermeasures could drive them from their positions even when the threat was minor.

In April 1915, a number of iron cylinders were delivered to the German front-line trenches. This was noted by Allied forces, but they were not unduly concerned about a large-scale gas attack. For one thing, such a measure was outlawed by the 1907 Hague

A German flamethrower team – another 'new' weapon to be developed in World War I. Used to dig a determined foe out of good positions, early flamethrowers were so unreliable they posed a threat to everyone around them, not just the enemy.

Convention. Even when a German prisoner, captured on 14 April, stated that a gas attack was imminent, the threat was not taken seriously. Perhaps it was simply unthinkable, or perhaps no effective countermeasure could be conceived of. In any case, the Allies did not react. As it happened, the attack was scheduled for the following day but had to be postponed until the wind was favourable. Finally, on 22 April the operation, and the Second Battle of Ypres, began.

FIRST GAS ATTACK

The 1915 Ypres offensive opened with a gas attack delivered by a little fewer than 6000 cylinders, adding up to 160–180 tonnes (157–176 tons) of chlorine gas. This resulted in a five-minute flow of gas that rolled slowly towards the Allied lines on the afternoon wind.

The troops facing the attack were French, with Canadians on their flank and British troops farther from the centre of the cloud. As the gas crossed the front line, thousands of men abandoned their positions. Those who stayed on the relatively high ground of the firing step fared better than those who jumped into the trench or tried to flee and ended up running inside the cloud. However, those who stood their ground – and they were a minority – suffered enough.

Within an hour, the French line was more or less deserted. The German infantry were able to advance pretty well unopposed. Field Marshal Sir John French (1852–1925), commanding the British Expeditionary Force, did not blame the French for breaking under what he saw as an appallingly barbaric assault. He wrote that if any troops could have withstood what he called an 'unexpected' and 'treacherous' onslaught, the French division would have held their positions. His comments reinforce the view that the Allies simply did not think they would be attacked with gas.

Despite the catastrophic effects of the gas, the assault was not quite as successful as it might have been. Although the French had suffered terribly and been driven from their positions, the Canadians on their flank were in somewhat better shape. They, along with reinforcements hurriedly pushed into

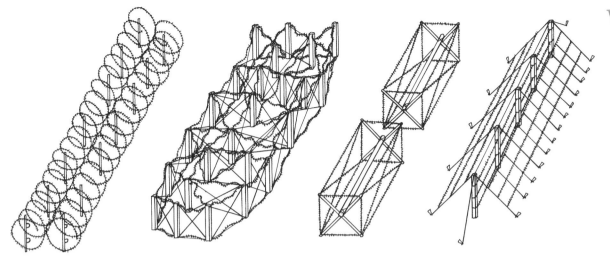

2ND BATTLE OF YPRES

the gap, were able to put up a stubborn defence and even launched a counterattack to seal off the breach. Despite heavy casualties and a great deal of confusion, the situation was stabilized.

The German infantry were understandably reluctant to advance into the gas, and dug in to consolidate their gains rather than punching deep into the enemy lines. Thus the result was a spectacular success for the German forces, but not a total victory.

French troops with improvised gas masks. A damp cloth over the face offered a measure of protection from gas, while the goggles prevented some eye irritation.

OFFENSIVE CONTINUES

The Germans were now in possession of a segment of the Allied line about 8km (5 miles) long, but the Allies were not yet beaten. On 23 April, the Allies worked out that the gas used against them had been chlorine and improvised a partial countermeasure. Since chlorine was soluble in water, a wet cloth tied over the mouth and nose offered a measure of protection. More importantly, a man who thought he was protected – rightly or otherwise – was more likely to stand and fight, denying the enemy an easy victory like that of the previous day.

Thus when gas was used against the Canadians on 24 April, they were able to

Barbed wire came in many different varieties, including the coiled 'Dannert' wire (far left), the virtually impenetrable high wire entanglements (centre left), and the apron fence, both square and pyramid shaped (right and far right). The gas attacks of 1915 were intended to overcome the static trench warfare which was beginning to develop on the Western Front.

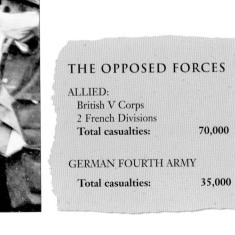

THE OPPOSED FORCES

ALLIED:
  British V Corps
  2 French Divisions
  Total casualties: **70,000**

GERMAN FOURTH ARMY

  Total casualties: **35,000**

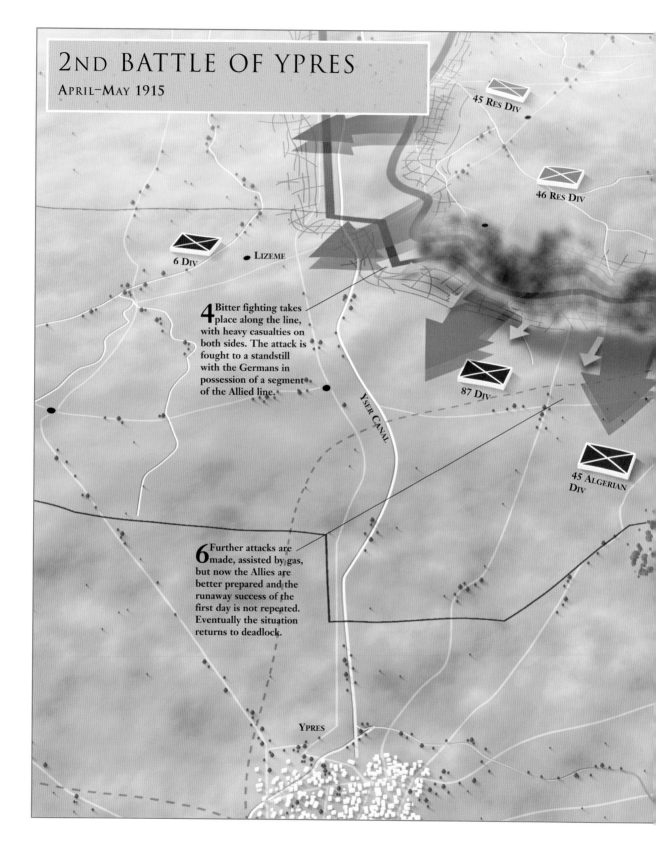

2ND BATTLE OF YPRES
APRIL–MAY 1915

45 RES DIV

46 RES DIV

6 DIV

LIZEME

4 Bitter fighting takes place along the line, with heavy casualties on both sides. The attack is fought to a standstill with the Germans in possession of a segment of the Allied line.

87 DIV

YSER CANAL

45 ALGERIAN DIV

6 Further attacks are made, assisted by gas, but now the Allies are better prepared and the runaway success of the first day is not repeated. Eventually the situation returns to deadlock.

YPRES

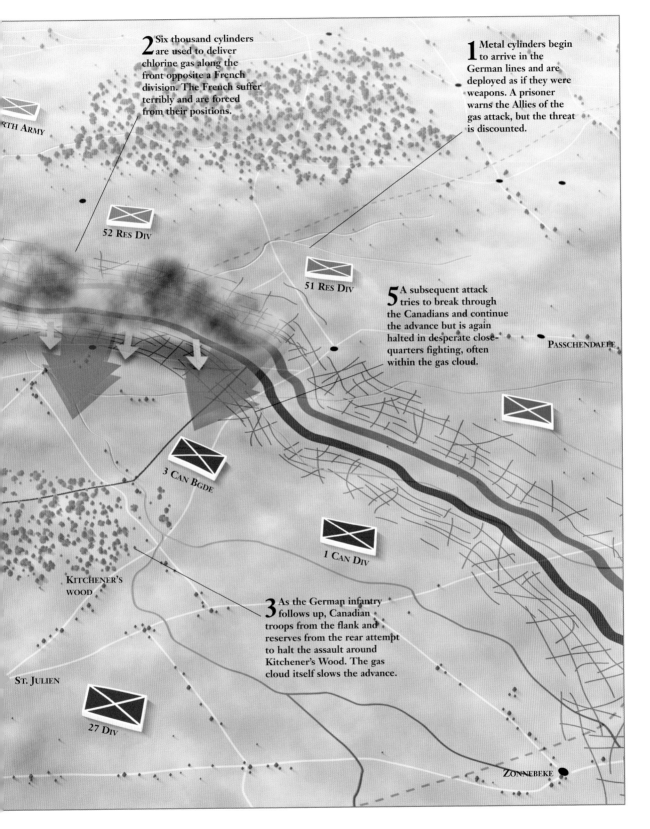

2 Six thousand cylinders are used to deliver chlorine gas along the front opposite a French division. The French suffer terribly and are forced from their positions.

1 Metal cylinders begin to arrive in the German lines and are deployed as if they were weapons. A prisoner warns the Allies of the gas attack, but the threat is discounted.

RTH ARMY

52 RES DIV

51 RES DIV

5 A subsequent attack tries to break through the Canadians and continue the advance but is again halted in desperate close-quarters fighting, often within the gas cloud.

PASSCHENDAELE

3 CAN BGDE

1 CAN DIV

KITCHENER'S WOOD

3 As the German infantry follows up, Canadian troops from the flank and reserves from the rear attempt to halt the assault around Kitchener's Wood. The gas cloud itself slows the advance.

ST. JULIEN

27 DIV

ZONNEBEKE

A gas attack on the Western Front. The delivery of gas in this manner, from canisters, depended very much on wind conditions. Generally, with weather fronts coming off the North Atlantic and blowing in an easterly direction, these favoured the Allies more than the Germans.

somewhat resist its effects – both physical and psychological. This resilience is all the more extraordinary for the fact that the 1st Canadian Division had arrived in its positions on 17 April – just a week earlier – without any experience of trench warfare. Despite having seen their allies shattered two days before, the Canadian division reacted with firmness and good sense.

Forced to retire from the front line of trenches by the gas cloud, the Canadians fell back and took cover while their supporting artillery pounded the former Allied trench

line, hampering the enemy advance. Despite suffering considerably from the effects of the chlorine – and many men incurred serious long-term damage from their exposure – the Canadians, thanks to their improvised gas masks, were able to hold out even during those few minutes when the gas was thickest, which meant that the division was able to stay in the battle. The gas made it difficult to see and fight effectively. This affected both sides, resulting in a series of short-range brawls as units stumbled upon one another.

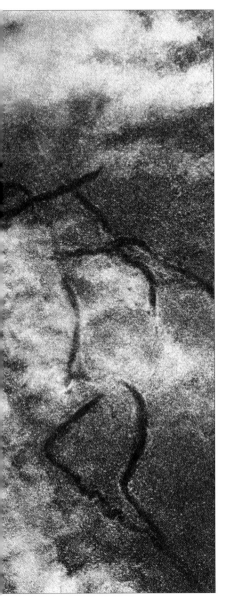

the situation. His superior, Sir John French, in overall command of the BEF, was unimpressed and dismissed him.

Smith-Dorrien was replaced by General Sir Herbert Plumer (1857–1932), who also pushed for a withdrawal to a more secure position. After a counterattack launched on 29 April failed, French agreed and the Allies fell back over the period 1–3 May.

On 3 May, the Canadian division was pulled out of the line. It had lost almost a third of its 18,000 men, killed or wounded, and more than half of those had fallen on the first day in the desperate fighting to seal the breach. The Canadians were replaced by British troops and were hailed as heroes wherever they went for having put up such a stiff fight under appalling conditions.

FURTHER OFFENSIVES

A renewed German attack – once more preceded by gas – was launched on 8 May and continued for five days. By now,

Gas pours into a British trench in this newspaper illustration. Troops are depicted bravely fighting back or dying in place; in reality, gas drove many units entirely from their trenches.

The combination of Canadian stubbornness and the availability of more reinforcements, plus the reduced effects of the gas, enabled the Allies to repulse the assault. Although some ground was lost and casualties were serious, the line was held.

ALLIED CHANGES

General Sir Horace Smith-Dorrien (1858–1930), commanding the British Second Army, proposed a withdrawal closer to Ypres, feeling that a major counteroffensive was necessary to restore

Emperor Wilhelm II and Prince Eitel Friedrich observe troops in action from a safe distance. The days of heroic leadership were long gone.

Below: British soldiers blinded by gas assist one another to the rear. While many men recovered their sight after a time, some had their eyesight permanently damaged and a good proportion were blinded for life.

however, the Allies were better able to cope with the silent assassin, both mentally and physically. Although they were pushed off the high ground east of Ypres, they ceded little territory and there was no spectacular collapse.

Another assault took place on the 24th and continued into the next day. It was again accompanied by the use of gas, and succeeded in pushing the Allies back a little further. Although the Ypres salient had been reduced in size, it remained more or less intact, and the initial shock of being subjected to gas attack had by now worn off. The fighting wound down as the Germans ran low on supplies and reinforcements, and gradually the Ypres sector returned to the usual trench stand-off, with artillery bombardment and minor infantry operations taking the place of grand offensives.

AFTER YPRES

Surprise is a great asset to military commanders, and it takes many forms. So-called 'technological surprise' exists when a weapon is deployed that the enemy either does not have a counter to or of which the enemy is unaware. Like all other forms of surprise, its effect is limited in duration, however devastating it might be at the time.

The Ypres offensive of 1915 made extensive use of gas for the first time, and the technological surprise it created was expended in the first few days, for fairly limited results. Gas would be used in various forms – by both sides – throughout the rest of the war, but it would never again catch troops utterly unprepared. It remained a factor and sometimes a decisive one, but the initial advantages had now been lost.

With the emergence of gas as a battlefield weapon, it became obvious that troops must be protected from it, and so a system of sounding gas attack alarms was implemented, along with training for troops to enable them to resist the psychological effects of a gas threat.

Most important, however, was the provision of gas-protection equipment to troops. Initially rather primitive, gas masks became standard equipment for soldiers within months of the Second Battle of Ypres. Indeed, such was the impact of gas at Ypres that although the use of chemical weapons (including but not limited to chlorine and phosgene gas) was outlawed after World War I, chemical-protection equipment and the training to use it has remained a part of military preparedness ever since.

In the final analysis, the use of chlorine gas at Ypres was not decisive, but it was extremely effective for a short time. Like many other innovative weapons, gas was deadly until an effective counter was found. After that, it became just one more factor to be considered by planners and commanders. In the long run, it just added one more ingredient to the misery experienced by soldiers in the trenches.

By the end of the 1914–18 conflict, little remained of the town of Ypres. Artillery fire had reduced much of the town to rubble and then turned it over again and again. Some smaller settlements vanished entirely.

CAMBRAI
NOVEMBER–DECEMBER 1917

ON 20 NOVEMBER 1917, AT THE BATTLE OF CAMBRAI, THE TANK CAME OF AGE. AS A WEAPON SYSTEM, ALONG WITH AIR POWER, IT WOULD FUNDAMENTALLY CHANGE THE NATURE OF LAND WARFARE AND DOMINATE THE CONVENTIONAL HIGH-INTENSITY BATTLEFIELD FOR THE REST OF THE TWENTIETH CENTURY.

WHY DID IT HAPPEN?

WHO The British Third Army commanded by Lieutenant-General Sir Julian Byng (1862-1935) and the Tank Corps under Brigadier-General Hugh Elles (1880-1945) against the German Second Army led by General Georg von der Marwitz.

WHAT The Tank Corps deployed its tanks *en masse* over suitable terrain. The tanks were supported by infantry trained in co-operation with armour and supported by artillery using new 'Silent Ranging' techniques. On the first day, the British made unprecedented advances at minimal cost.

WHERE The Hindenburg Line, west of Cambrai in Northern France.

WHEN 20 Nov – 3 Dec 1917.

WHY To maintain pressure on the Germans after the tremendous efforts of the Third Ypres offensive and, perhaps, to salvage something from the campaigns of 1917, General Sir Douglas Haig authorized the attack.

OUTCOME Although the British achieved spectacular success on 20 November, the gains were lost to a German counterattack. However, the tank-infantry-artillery tactics used presaged the combined-arms approach that would break the German line in 1918.

At Cambrai, tanks were concentrated on a large scale for the first time on suitable terrain, using specially developed tactics. The result was an 8km (5-mile) penetration through German lines at minimal cost in comparison to the lengthy and extremely costly offensives that had preceded the battle. Although the gains were short-lived, the Battle of Cambrai demonstrated the immense potential of the tank, which would be instrumental in breaking the deadlock of trench warfare and then, 20 or so years later, revolutionize warfare itself.

Despite the technological advances of the late nineteenth and early twentieth centuries, such as rapid-firing artillery, the magazine-loading rifle, the machine-gun and barbed wire, all armies entered World War I in August 1914 expecting a war of movement. Therefore, cavalry still made up a substantial proportion of the forces deployed, even though a century, perhaps a century and a half, of experience pointed to

An aerial reconnaissance photograph showing the deep trenches, mine craters and shell strikes on an important sector of the Hindenburg Line. The relatively unscathed terrain at Cambrai made it more suitable for the employment of tanks.

the vulnerability of mounted men in combat. In the opening weeks of the war, whenever cavalry met well-formed infantry, they were shot from their horses in droves. Within six weeks, the horse was banished from the Western European battlefield.

Although cavalry were maintained in order to exploit the hoped-for breakthrough, and remained useful in the East and subsidiary theatres such as the Middle East, a key element of tactical and strategic mobility had been driven forever from the battlefield.

Even less expected was the fact that the firepower which shattered the cavalry proceeded to do the same to the bayonet charges of the infantry. At a terrible cost to themselves, the outnumbered British, French and Belgium armies managed to fight to a standstill the invading Germans. The shovel became the essential weapon as the exhausted armies dug in and the war settled into a stalemate.

BREAKING THE STALEMATE

The problem of breaking that stalemate was to exercise the generals for the next three years. Initially, a heavy reliance was placed on artillery, but unfortunately there were usually enough of the well dug-in defenders left, or enough men in reserve, to repulse the infantry following the barrage or recapture any lost ground. Yet, the High Commands persevered through Vosges, Lorraine and Neuve Chappele in 1915; Lozono, Verdun and the Somme in 1916; and Arras, Chemin des Dames and Ypres in 1917, at the cost of hundreds and thousands of their men's lives. There were some attempts at innovation, such as the introduction of poison gas or large-scale mining operations, but none proved decisive. The Battle of the Somme provides a suitable example of the difficulties and costliness of attacking on the battlefields of World War I. Despite a seven-day bombardment that preceded the battle, the attacking British sustained some 60,000 casualties on the first day. Over the following four months of the Somme offensive, at a cost of 400,000 men, British troops advanced no further than 16km (10 miles). Modern technology had reduced mobility to almost nothing.

In the midst of the slaughter of the Somme, however, the British introduced a new weapon, the tank. Development of a tracked armoured fighting vehicle capable of crossing trenches and overcoming barbed wire began in early 1915. A prototype tracked armoured vehicle, 'Little Willie', was ready by December, and 'Mother', an actual vehicle intended for combat and based on the famous rhomboid shape, was trialled in late January 1916.

Its performance was impressive enough for the vehicle to be put into production: 100 were ordered, half of them 'males' armed with 6-pounder (57mm) guns in sponsons on the sides; and half of them 'females' armed with machine-guns. The vehicles were referred to as 'Water Tanks' for security reasons, and the name stuck. An entirely new weapon system had been conceived, designed, built and put into production in less than 12 months. The driving force behind the programme, Colonel Ernest Swinton, had specific ideas about how the new weapon should be used:

Not only...does it seem that tanks will confer the power to force successive comparatively unbattered defensive lines, but...the more speedy and uninterrupted their advance the greater the chance of their surviving sufficiently long to do this. It is possible, therefore, that an effort to break right through the enemy's defensive zone in one day may be contemplated as a feasible operation.

Swinton was determined that the tank 'should not be used in driblets...but in one great combined operation'. Unfortunately, a mere 36 crossed the start-line and were deployed to prop up the Somme Offensive at Flers-Courcelette on 15 September 1916. There was no big breakthrough that day. Yet, despite the fact that the tanks achieved very little – most broke down, became stuck in the appalling terrain or were quickly knocked out – the British

LOCATION

ENGLAND

GERMANY

Cambrai

Paris

FRANCE

Cambrai lies to the south of the battlefields of the 3rd Ypres offensive. It was a important railhead and a key part of the German communications network in northern France.

TANK OFFICER

This Lieutenant of the Tank Corps has a tank qualification badge on his right sleeve. His equipment includes a 1914 leather pattern belt and a holstered .455 revolver. He carries a box respirator slung to his left and wears a standard British helmet and an anti-splash mask to protect against fragments of the interior of a tank knocked lose by bullet strikes.

A colourized photo of Mark IV 'male' tanks in action. These made up the bulk of Tank Corps forces at Cambrai. The 'male' Mark IV was armed with two 57mm (6 pounder) guns, one in each sponson, and had armour ranging in thickness from 6mm (0.24in) to 12mm (0.47in). The tank was manned by a crew of eight.

THE OPPOSED FORCES

ALLIED ARMY
2 Infantry Corps
Tanks: 476

Tanks knocked out   **179**
Total casualties: **42,000**

GERMAN ARMY
1 Infantry Corps

Total casualties: **45,000**

commander in France, General Sir Douglas Haig, decided to order 1000 more.

THIRD BATTLE OF YPRES
The next major commitment of tanks was at Arras in April 1917. Sixty Mark I and II tanks were employed in conditions similar to the Somme, in terrible weather, across ground churned up by preliminary bombardment, and with similar results. There were some local successes: six tanks operating in support of 37th Division captured a very heavily fortified village at very little cost. As the Corps Commander Lieutenant General Aylmar Haldane remarked: 'I certainly never again want to be without tanks, when so well commanded and led.' Although it had achieved little thus far, the tank had been accepted, at least temporarily, as a useful weapon system and was deployed by the British across the front and other theatres.

The Tank Corps, as the new arm became in July, was committed to the major British offensive of 1917: the Third Battle of Ypres,

often known as Passchendaele, which lasted from 31 July to 6 November. Again, the conditions for tank operations were not ideal and they added little to the conduct of operations. At great cost, the British broke into German defences, but were unable to convert these occasional tactical successes into a strategic breakthrough. Yet, as the Third Battle of Ypres petered out, plans were being made that might provide some hope for the future.

There had been a couple of small tank actions in the midst of the slaughter of Ypres that had proved the weapon had some potential, and after an attack on German pillboxes in St Julien area on 19 August, the General Staff approved a plan for larger tank operation on Cambrai. The Chief of Staff of the Tank Corps, Colonel JFC Fuller, proposed a large-scale tank raid, with the reasonably limited aim of getting the tanks onto the German gun-line. His ideas were seized upon and expanded into a major offensive by the commander of the Third Army, General Sir Julian Byng (1862-

1935). Fuller and the commander of the Tank Corps, Brigadier-General Hugh Elles (1880-1945), had their doubts about this, given the commitments made at Ypres, but, knowing the Corps desperately needed a success, they concurred.

In Operation GY, as the offensive was codenamed, the Third Army intended to break the German line with tanks and then push cavalry across the St Quentin Canal to seize Bourlon Wood and the town of Cambrai. Haig, however, made it clear to Byng that, should results prove disappointing, he would close the offensive down quickly.

A LEARNING EXPERIENCE

It had taken some time and bitter experience to learn the lesson that tanks needed to be used on suitable ground. The rolling, firm chalk downland in the Cambrai sector, relatively untouched by artillery fire, had drawn Fuller to the area in the first place. Despite this, the tanks still faced a considerable task in terms of breaking through the German defences. The approach to the first line of trenches was through linked outposts and strong points. The forward trench itself, full of dugouts and machine-gun posts, had been widened to more than 4m (12ft) across, making it tank proof in German eyes. Beyond that, at a distance of 274m (900ft), were the similarly constructed support trenches. To counter this, the Tank Corps developed new tactics. It equipped its tanks with large brushwood fascines strapped to their roofs.

The tanks would advance in sections of three in an arrowhead formation, with the infantry following in file 23m (75ft) behind them. The tanks were responsible for crushing the wire in front of the trenches for the infantry. The leading tank, when it reached the forward trench, would turn left and fire into it with its starboard guns. The second tank would drop its fascine into the trench, cross it, turn left and fire on both the forward and support trenches. The third tank would drop its fascine into the support trench, turn left and fire on the defenders from their rear. Then, the first tank would come forwards with the infantry, while the tanks and infantry would regroup on the objective and resume the advance.

Co-operation between tanks and infantry was vital because, if machine-guns held up the infantry, the tanks would deal with them; and if artillery stopped the tanks, it was up to the infantry to suppress the gunners. The tanks and infantry trained extensively together prior to the opening of the offensive.

COMMITMENT TO BATTLE

The entire Tank Corps was committed to the battle, divided between the two British corps that would take part: III Corps (four infantry divisions, including the reserve) on the right flank, and IV Corps (two divisions) on the left, at a rate of 64–72 tanks per division. This was a total of 476 tanks. The bulk of these were 378 Mark IVs, the main combat type of the time. The Mark IV still resembled the original Mark I, but was up-armoured, had an external fuel tank in effort

General Julian Byng commanded the British Third Army and was responsible for the attack at Cambrai. He was an effective leader and had commanded with some success at Gallipoli and Vimy Ridge.

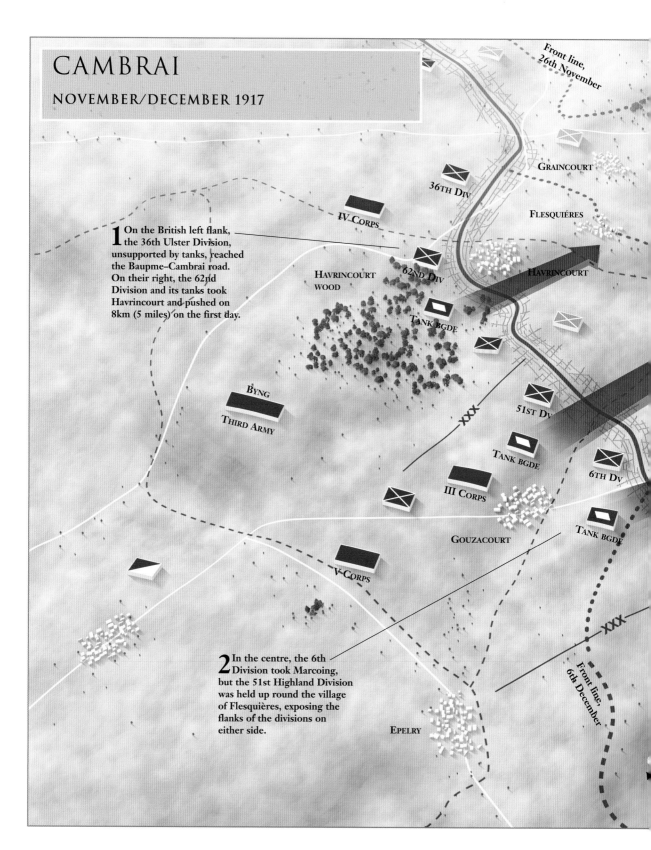

CAMBRAI

NOVEMBER/DECEMBER 1917

Front line,
26th November

GRAINCOURT

36TH DIV

FLESQUIÉRES

IV CORPS

HAVRINCOURT

1 On the British left flank, the 36th Ulster Division, unsupported by tanks, reached the Baupme–Cambrai road. On their right, the 62nd Division and its tanks took Havrincourt and pushed on 8km (5 miles) on the first day.

HAVRINCOURT
WOOD

62ND DIV

TANK BGDE

BYNG

THIRD ARMY

51ST DV

TANK BGDE

6TH DV

III CORPS

GOUZACOURT

TANK BGDE

V CORPS

2 In the centre, the 6th Division took Marcoing, but the 51st Highland Division was held up round the village of Flesquières, exposing the flanks of the divisions on either side.

EPELRY

Front line,
6th December

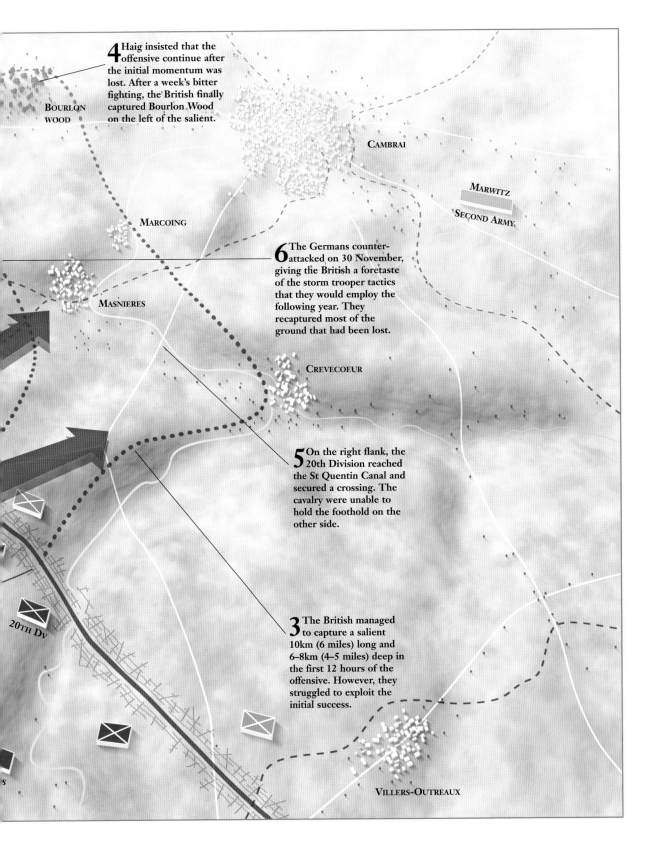

4 Haig insisted that the offensive continue after the initial momentum was lost. After a week's bitter fighting, the British finally captured Bourlon Wood on the left of the salient.

BOURLON WOOD

CAMBRAI

MARWITZ

SECOND ARMY

MARCOING

6 The Germans counter-attacked on 30 November, giving the British a foretaste of the storm trooper tactics that they would employ the following year. They recaptured most of the ground that had been lost.

MASNIERES

CREVECOEUR

5 On the right flank, the 20th Division reached the St Quentin Canal and secured a crossing. The cavalry were unable to hold the foothold on the other side.

20TH DV

3 The British managed to capture a salient 10km (6 miles) long and 6–8km (4–5 miles) deep in the first 12 hours of the offensive. However, they struggled to exploit the initial success.

VILLERS-OUTREAUX

to improve crew safety, and a new engine and transmission, which proved surprisingly quiet. The remainder were more lightly protected Mark Is and IIs, which had been converted to act as specialist support tanks for supply, communication and laying bridges. Many carried grapnels for pulling wire out of the way of the cavalry. Nine were equipped with radios. After dark, on the evening of 19 November, the tanks were moved up to the start line, their noise masked by overflying aircraft and sustained machine-gun fire. Quite apart from the innovative use of tanks, Cambrai would also reintroduce the concept of surprise to the Western Front.

Cambrai is rightly remembered for the achievement of the tank arm used *en masse* for the first time, yet much of the initial success was down to the innovative use of British artillery. There would be no long 'Somme-style' bombardment. Indeed, there were no preliminary ranging shots, as the guns were ranged 'silently', based on intelligence, air reconnaissance and ballistic data, a method pioneered by Brigadier-General Henry Tudor, the commander

Royal Artillery in 9th Division. The purpose of the short, sharp opening barrage was to keep the enemy's head down and neutralize his artillery, and then shift to a 'creeping barrage' 274m (900ft) in front of the advancing troops and tanks. A large number of smoke shells were to be fired to mask the attackers. The British had mustered about 1000 guns, and these opened up at 0620 on 20 November 1917. At the same time, the tanks and infantry began to move forwards.

Reeling from the opening bombardment, the German outpost line put up little resistance to the tanks and infantry looming out of the early morning mist. The British were soon into the forward trenches, crushing paths in barbed wire, dropping their fascines into the trenches, and crossing and swinging left as the infantry followed. Many Germans were captured and some desperate counterattacks broken up as the Germans moved across open ground.

On the extreme right of the British assault, the 12th (Eastern) Division captured Bonavis and Lateau Wood, dug in on the flank and allowed the cavalry to pass

German troops pose beside a captured British tank. The British lost 65 tanks to enemy action on the first day of Cambrai.

Commonwealth troops clear Germans from their position on Passchendaele Ridge. The attack at Cambrai initially made similar gains but at far less cost.

Below: The German response to the deadlock was to improve their infantry tactics. Elite storm trooper units made an appearance when the Germans counterattacked at Cambrai.

through as intended. Next to them, the 20th (Light) Division advanced as far as the St Quentin Canal and managed to secure a bridge at Masniéres, which promptly collapsed under the weight of a crossing tank. Some cavalry managed to cross the canal but were driven back. The 6th Division captured Marcoing, but the 5th Cavalry Division that passed through them did not get much further. In the centre, the 51st (Highland) Division faired less well. The Division took its first objectives to schedule, but was slowed by the stiff German defence of the village of Flesquières, where there were a couple of German anti-tank batteries still intact. Its commander, Major-General George Harper, has been blamed for introducing tank-infantry tactics of his own, particularly for holding his infantry further back than was the norm.

It seems that there was poor co-operation between his infantry and tanks. That said, the 51st was assaulting the strongest point of the German line and the defenders might well have halted any division. Whatever the case, the 51st did not take the village on the first day. The 62nd (2nd West Riding) Division fought its way through Havrincourt and pushed on 8km (5 miles) by nightfall. This was a remarkable achievement. On the left flank, the 36th (Ulster) Division reached the Baupme–Cambrai Road.

BREAKTHROUGH

It had been an extraordinary day's fighting. The British had carved out a salient 9.6km (6 miles) long and 6–8km (4–5 miles) deep in a mere 12 hours, taking 7500 prisoners and 150 guns. This had been achieved at the cost of 4000 casualties. Sixty-five tanks were lost to enemy action, 71 broke down and 43 were ditched or abandoned. To put this into perspective, similar territorial gains of the Third Battle of Ypres had taken three months and cost 250,000 casualties. Little surprise, then, that bells were rung in England for the first time in the war. The celebration proved premature, however, as the Germans rapidly recovered. Their defences stiffened the following day and, despite the loss of momentum, Haig ordered the offensive to continue. The Germans counterattacked on 30 November, recapturing most of what they had lost.

The importance of Cambrai lay not so much with the outcome, but rather in demonstrating that the tank, supported by new artillery tactics and in close co-operation with the infantry, could achieve the long-sought breakthrough on the Western Front. The modern combined-arms battle was not far away.

PEARL HARBOR
7 DECEMBER 1941

THE JAPANESE ATTACK ON PEARL HARBOR DEMONSTRATED SPECTACULARLY THE POSSIBILITY OF CARRIER-BORNE AIRPOWER. AIRCRAFT OF THE JAPANESE IMPERIAL NAVY'S STRIKE FORCE SUNK SIX US BATTLESHIPS AND NUMEROUS SMALLER WARSHIPS, DESTROYED 164 AIRCRAFT AND KILLED 2403 US PERSONNEL. THE ATTACK CONFIRMED THE AIRCRAFT CARRIER AND NAVAL AVIATION AS THE DOMINANT WEAPON SYSTEM IN MARITIME WARFARE.

WHY DID IT HAPPEN?

WHO The Japanese Combined Fleet's Air Fleet 1, aboard a task force commanded by Vice-Admiral Chuichi Nagumo (1887–1944), against the US Pacific Fleet and various land installations commanded by Admiral Husband Kimmel (1882–1968) and Army and USAAF units in Hawaii under Major-General Walter Scott.

WHAT The Japanese Combined Fleet assembled six fleet carriers to launch an audacious attack on the US Pacific Fleet base of Pearl Harbor, 5472km (3400 miles) away.

WHERE Pearl Harbor, on Oahu, one of the Hawaiian Islands in the middle of the Pacific Ocean, west-southwest of the United States mainland.

WHEN 7 December 1941.

WHY In the face of both US and British sanctions, Japan needed to neutralize US naval power in Pacific, at least temporarily, in order to seize British and Dutch resources in the region, particularly oil.

OUTCOME Tactically, Japan caused considerable damage at little cost to itself, but, in the words of Vice-Admiral Nagumo, it managed only 'to awaken a sleeping giant and fill her with a terrible resolve'.

Despite the brilliant execution of the Japanese plan in attacking Pearl Harbor on 7 December 1941, it had landed a stunning, not a knockout, blow. Japan was subsequently drawn into a struggle of attrition in the Pacific, against an adversary it could not hope to defeat.

Almost as soon as the Wright Brothers made the first controlled flight by an aeroplane in 1903, sailors could see the possibilities that aircraft had for maritime warfare. The US Navy was the first to fly a plane off a naval vessel in 1910. By the outbreak of World War I, specialized aircraft, usually seaplanes, and seaplane carriers were in service, primarily for fleet reconnaissance. Nonetheless, a year later, in August 1915, Flight Commander CHK Edmonds made history by sinking a Turkish transport ship with an airborne torpedo launched from his Shorts seaplane.

Subsequently, a number of merchant ships and cruisers were converted to carry aircraft. Ship-launched Sopwith Pup fighters had some success against German Zeppelins over the North Sea. However,

Taken on 18 January 1941 in Honolulu, Hawaii, this photograph shows Rear Admiral Husband E. Kimmel in a good mood on hearing that he was to be appointed Navy commander of the US Fleet at Pearl Harbor. Kimmel would be relieved of duty after the Japanese attack on 7 December.

after take-off, these aircraft had to be ditched or landed ashore. It was not until 2 August 1917 that Squadron Commander EH Dunning landed his Sopwith Pup on HMS *Furious*, making the first deck landing on a ship at sea. More ambitious operations followed.

On 19 July 1918, Sopwith Camels, operating off *Furious*, attacked the airship base at Tondern, destroying two German Zeppelins. The Admiralty, however, shelved plans for a concerted carrier-borne air offensive against German naval bases. In September 1918, HMS *Argus*, the first carrier with an unobstructed flight deck or flush deck, was commissioned, setting the pattern for modern aircraft carrier design.

THE WASHINGTON TREATY

Britain, the United States and Japan continued to experiment with naval aviation after the war, with Japan launching its first carrier, the *Hosho*, in 1921. The Washington Naval Treaty of 1922 limited Japan's carrier tonnage to 82,300 tonnes (81,000 tons), in comparison to Britain and the United States with 137,000 tonnes (135,000 tons). Each carrier was restricted to 27,500 tonnes (27,000 tons), but Japan and the United States were permitted to convert two battle cruisers each to carriers of up to 33,500 tonnes (33,000 tons). Increasingly powerful aircraft made larger carriers more appealing, so the Treaty was allowed to lapse in 1936.

However, reasonably scrupulous observance of its terms meant that the three carrier-operating fleets went into World War II with relatively few of these vital weapons, and Japan faced something of a deficit, if it was to face the European powers and the United States in the Pacific. Thus freed of constraints, the Japanese Navy launched an ambitious naval construction programme the following year.

By 1939, the Commander-in-Chief of the Japanese Combined Fleet, Admiral Isoroku Yamamoto (1884–1943), was faced with this problem. He was a keen proponent of naval aviation, had worked in the Naval Air Corps and captained carriers earlier in his career. He was determined to move his navy's emphasis away from the battleship and towards a modern force with airpower

as its key component. He ordered new 30,400-tonne (30,000-ton) carriers capable of taking 80 aircraft. He was instrumental in the design and development of the Mitsubishi A6M Zero, a carrier-borne fighter far superior in performance to British and US equivalents. Japan also had its first carrier-borne monoplane attack aircraft in the shape of the Nakajima 97 Kate. Priority was given to the training of combat fliers. Though Yamamoto reorganized the Combined Fleet, he was well aware that challenging the United States was a dangerous game. He told Japan's Prime Minister Prince Konoe: 'We can run wild for six months or a year, but after that I have utterly no confidence, I hope you will try to avoid war with America.'

AN INEVITABLE CONFLICT

Yet Yamamoto was well aware that the aggressive policies of his government made such a challenge quite likely. The Japanese Army had been engaged in an intractable war in China since 1937. There had also been clashes with the Soviet Union on the Mongolian border in 1938 and 1939. After the Fall of France in 1940, Japan joined Germany and Italy in the Tripartite Pact and used the weakness of France and Britain to close down supply routes to Nationalist Chinese forces.

Yet the defeat of the democracies in Europe led the United States to look to its own defence. Accordingly, Congress passed the Two-Ocean Expansion Act in June

LOCATION

Pearl Harbor was the forward base and home of the Pacific Fleet since May 1940. Basing the fleet there placed US naval power deep in the Pacific, and it became the logistical hub of subsequent US operations in this theatre.

PEARL HARBOR

A portrait of Vice Admiral Chuichi Nagumo of the Imperial Japanese Navy, who commanded the carrier group that bombed Pearl Harbor.

1940, a massive naval building programme that would eventually dwarf Japanese sea power. Relations with the United States deteriorated further as Japan occupied French Indo-China and the United States and Britain imposed sanctions. An increasingly desperate Japanese leadership accepted that it would have to go to war with the United States if it was to secure the resources of the British and Dutch Eastern Empires. As early as the winter of 1939, Yamamoto, although he doubted the wisdom of such a course, began thinking about just such an eventuality.

PREEMPTIVE STRIKE

The only hope was first to reduce the superiority of the US battle fleet. Yamamoto reckoned that he needed a plan to destroy the US Pacific Fleet in one devastating strike, and he drew on a number of inspirations. Ironically, in 1938, the United States had staged a mock attack on the Pacific Fleet's base in the Hawaiian Islands, at Pearl Harbor. A total of 150 aircraft from the attack wings of the aircraft carriers *Lexington* and *Saratoga* managed to make a completely undetected and unopposed pass over the anchorage and thereby, in theory, destroy the fleet.

The US Navy may have been unimpressed, but Yamamoto had taken note. If a similar stroke could be pulled off by the Japanese Navy to cripple US military power, Japan should gain enough time to seize the Dutch and British possessions that were its main objectives. Of course, the British and Dutch forces in the region had to be dealt with too, but the United States was the real long-term threat to Japanese plans. The hope was that by the time the United States had recovered, Japan would

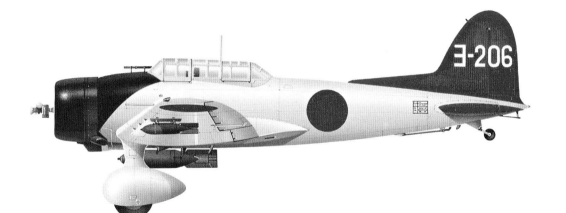

PEARL HARBOR

have secured its gains, forcing a weakened US Navy to come forwards and fight in Japanese-dominated seas. Alternatively, the United States might be dragged into the European war and possibly seek some sort of compromise with Japan.

The Naval General Staff did not universally accept Yamamoto's proposal. However, his case was immeasurably strengthened by the British attack on the Italian Fleet at Taranto in November 1940. British carrier-based aircraft succeeded in sinking three battleships, half the Italian capital strength. Surely, the larger and more modern Japanese Naval Air Arm was equally capable of such a coup? Indeed, Yamamoto's naval building programme,

initiated in the late 1930s, was beginning to pay dividends. The Naval Air Arm had grown to six large and three smaller carriers, equipped with the most advanced carrier-borne aircraft in the world.

By May 1941, a plan had been drawn up, and one that Yamamoto believed would guarantee success, as long as he could use six carriers and absolute secrecy was maintained. Although final authority had not been granted, rehearsals were undertaken at Kagoshima Bay on the southern island of Kyushu, which bore a striking similarity to Pear Harbor.

Torpedoes were modified to operate in the shallow waters of the US base. The Japanese Navy had plenty of information on

The Aichi D3A 'Val' bomber was a carrier-borne, single-engine dive bomber. Single-engine bombers made up nearly a third of the attacking aircraft at Pearl Harbor. It is credited with sinking more Allied shipping than any other Axis dive bomber in World War II.

Mitsubishi A6M5 Zero fighters prepare to take off from an aircraft carrier (reportedly Shokaku) *to attack Pearl Harbor during the morning of 7 December 1941.*

PEARL HARBOR

7 DECEMBER 1941

3 At 07.55, Kate torpedo bombers target ships to the northwest of Ford Island. This was where the missing carriers were normally berthed.

6 The USS *Nevada* attempted to make for the safety of open water, but was attacked by wave after wave of torpedo and dive bombers.

MIDDLE LOCH

FORD ISLAND
NAVAL AIR STATION

USS *CALIFORNIA*

US NAVY
YARD

5 Attacked by both the first and second waves, Hickam Field suffers the heaviest damage of Oahu's airbases.

SOUTHEAST
LOCH

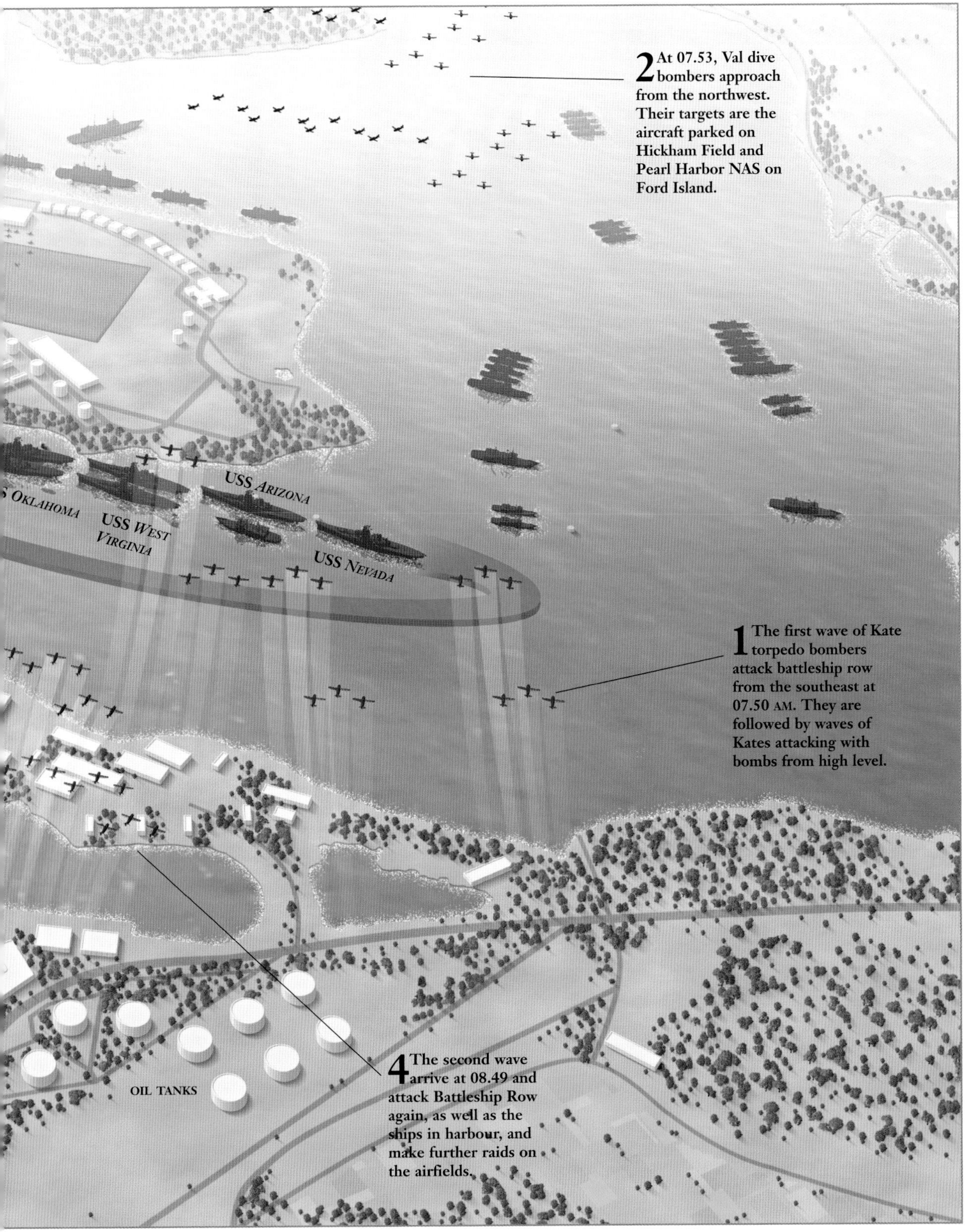

2 At 07.53, Val dive bombers approach from the northwest. Their targets are the aircraft parked on Hickham Field and Pearl Harbor NAS on Ford Island.

1 The first wave of Kate torpedo bombers attack battleship row from the southeast at 07.50 AM. They are followed by waves of Kates attacking with bombs from high level.

USS OKLAHOMA

USS WEST VIRGINIA

USS ARIZONA

USS NEVADA

4 The second wave arrive at 08.49 and attack Battleship Row again, as well as the ships in harbour, and make further raids on the airfields.

OIL TANKS

US personnel man air defences at Pearl Harbor. These men are armed with 7.62mm (0.3in) Browning medium machine guns. The Browning was a multipurpose machine gun used by all US forces during World War II, and could be seen mounted on tanks, aircraft and infantry trucks.

The 20,574 tonne (20,250 ton) aircraft carrier Hiryu took part in the Pearl Harbor attack. Slightly small for a fleet carrier, she could carry 70 aircraft. The Hiryu was sunk at the Battle of Midway on 5 June 1942.

flagship *Akagi*, led out the fleet carriers *Kaga*, *Shokaku*, *Zuikaku*, *Hiryu* and *Soryu*. These six carriers made up the largest concentration of naval airpower ever assembled. They boarded a total of 423 Zero fighters, Kate torpedo-bombers and older Aichi D3A Val dive-bombers.

Their supporting force consisted of two battleships, two heavy cruisers, a light cruiser, nine destroyers and eight replenishment tanks and supply ships. Negotiations with the United States were continuing, though neither side seems to have expected a successful outcome.

On 27 November 1941, all US Army and Navy commanders received a final war warning. Despite the heightened tensions, life at the US base continued much as normal. The Commander-in-Chief of the Pacific Fleet, Admiral HE Kimmel, was more concerned with the nearest Japanese possession, the Marshall Islands to the southwest, the likeliest launching point for any Japanese assault. Not that the United States anticipated an air attack, its main concern being sabotage or, perhaps, submarines.

Indeed, the fact that a large number of P40 fighters had just been transferred to Wake and Midway Island confirmed the extent to which the United States did not consider it a serious threat. Anti-aircraft positions around the harbour had no ready ammunition and the USAAF fighters lay undispersed on their airfields. Because of the shallowness of the harbour, torpedo nets were considered unnecessary. Worrying intelligence gleaned from Japanese diplomatic ciphers, which indicated a Japanese interest in the islands, was not even passed on to Hawaii.

Pearl Harbor, as it was in plain view of the city and aerial sightseeing trips across it were permitted.

THE HAWAII OPERATION
The Naval General Staff finally accepted Yamamoto's plan, known as the Hawaii Operation, on 3 November 1941. A week later, the first minor units of the fast carrier striking force under Vice-Admiral Chuichi Nagumo sailed for a secret rendezvous at Tankan Bay in the Kurile Islands. At the same time, a force of 16 submarines, five of which carried a number of midget submarines, left harbour to co-ordinate their attack with the main carrier force. On 26 November 1941, Nagumo, aboard the

'CLIMB MOUNT FUJI'
Nagumo's force sailed for five days under cover of a weather front moving at a similar pace to the fleet. The route took them well

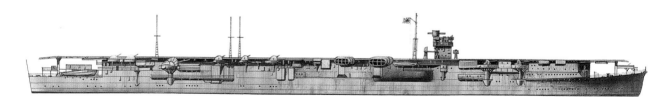

clear of shipping routes. The task force successfully refuelled on 28 November. On 2 December, Nagumo received a fleet signal from Yamamoto, 'Climb Mount Fuji', meaning that the attack was to go ahead as planned. On 4 December, the weather improved, and by 6 December the seas were clear at last. By the time the task force had reached the attack point, 443km (275 miles) north of Pearl Harbor, the conditions were perfect. This seemed so miraculous that both Nagumo and the first strike wave's leader, Air Commander Mitsuo Fuchida (1902–1976), believed that it signified divine intervention.

On 7 December, Nagumo received the disappointing news that the US carriers were absent, but Yamamoto, well aware of the implications, allowed the attack to go ahead. Fuchida briefed his pilots one final time. The torpedo-bombers were to go in first, followed by the dive-bombers. The

fighters would concentrate primarily on the two USAAF bases, Hickam and Wheeler Field, strafe the ships and deal with any US planes that managed to get into the air. If they failed to gain the surprise, Fuschida would fire two flares, indicating that the dive-bombers should go in first to cause maximum confusion. He and his aircrews boarded their planes at 0600. Fuschido's force of 183 aircraft took off, assembled in formation, climbed to 3048m (10,000ft) and headed southwards towards Pearl Harbor.

The United States' first indication of an enemy presence was a contact made with a submarine at 0342. That or another was depth-charged at 0645 at the entrance of the harbour. Yet it was only at 0725 that Admiral Kimmel was informed. American radar had also picked up an earlier Japanese float plane reconnaissance mission, but for some reason no action was taken. Even when the main assault wave was detected,

The carnage at the Ford Island Naval Air Station following the Japanese raid. Smoke from the USS Arizona *billows behind the Catalina and Kingfisher aircraft in the foreground.*

A rescue launch plucks a man from the water, as the
USS West Virginia *burns in the background. The*
USS Tennessee *lies behind her.*

no report was made because a flight of B17s was expected from the same direction. In harbour that Sunday morning were some 70 warships, including eight battleships.

The Japanese formation flew over Oahu Bay at 0749, having achieved complete surprise. Due to a mix-up, Fuschida fired two flares, which meant the Val dive-bombers and Kate torpedo-bombers made their attack at the same time, though it seems to have made very little difference to the effectiveness of their attack. Five battleships were torpedoed, as well as two cruisers. Armour-piercing bombs hit two more. The fighters strafed the Army and Marine air bases. By 0825, the first wave had withdrawn. Fuschido remained, waiting for the second wave, which arrived

24 minutes later. Some 170 planes led by Lieutenant-Commander Shegekazu Shimazaki now attacked Battleship Row, as well as the ships moored in docks, and then made further runs on the airfields. Despite the fact that smoke obscured the target, they were able to cause serious damage, and the fleet flagship USS *Pennsylvania* was hit, as were several destroyers.

By 0945, the attack was over and the Japanese planes were on their way back to the carriers. Nagumo, pleased by the reports of the action, refused to launch a third strike. This decision ignored the advice of Fuschido and it proved to be a serious mistake; in particular, he missed the opportunity to attack the port repair facilities and fuel installations. The task

Right: The shattered remains of aircraft at Wheeler Field in the aftermath of the attack. Amongst the wreckage are the remains of a Curtis P-40 Warhawk fighter and an amphibian.

force steered away for a replenishment rendezvous and then back to Japan.

NEW ERA OF NAVAL WARFARE

In less than two hours, Japan had sunk six battleships and damaged two others, sunk three destroyers and three light cruisers; four other vessels had also been sunk. The battle squadron of the Pacific Fleet had ceased to exist.

On the airfields, 164 planes had been destroyed and 128 damaged. Altogether, 2403 Americans had been killed and a further 1176 wounded. The cost to Japan was just 29 aircraft and 54 pilots and aircrew. It had been a carefully planned and superbly executed raid.

Yet, there were a number of flaws in what appeared to be a perfect operation. The base facilities of the base remained intact, as did the vast oil-storage tanks full of fuel. Therefore, the US Pacific Fleet could remain at, and operate out of, Pearl Harbor

rather than having to retreat to San Diego. Furthermore, amongst all the ships sunk and damaged, there were no carriers. Longer term, six of the battleships would be repaired and returned to service.

Japan had ushered in a new era of naval warfare, but it had also brought upon itself war with a nation that would eventually ensure it suffered a comprehensive defeat of terrible proportions.

Below: Japanese torpedo bombers attack Battleship Row at about 0800 on 7 December, seen from a Japanese aircraft. The ships are, from lower left to right: USS Nevada; USS Arizona with Vestal outboard; Tennessee with West Virginia outboard; Maryland with Oklahoma outboard; Neosho and California. White smoke in the distance is from Hickam Field.

SINAI

6–25 OCTOBER 1973

THE YOM KIPPUR WAR OF OCTOBER 1973 USHERED IN A NEW ERA OF WARFARE. THE DEVASTATING EFFECTS OF GUIDED ANTI-TANK MISSILES RAISED A QUESTION MARK OVER THE FUTURE OF MAIN BATTLE TANKS AS THE PRINCIPAL SPEARHEAD OF ARMIES.

WHY DID IT HAPPEN?

WHO The combined armies of Egypt and Syria, with some minor allies, against the Israeli Defense Forces (IDF).

WHAT Egypt and Syria launched an assault on Israeli-held territories in Sinai and the Golan Heights, aiming to overwhelm the Israeli defence through a two-front strategy.

WHERE Egypt attacked across the Suez Canal into Sinai, while Syria fought in the Golan Heights to the north of Israel.

WHEN 6–25 October 1973.

WHY Egypt hoped that the offensive would force Israel to the international negotiating table, where it would be forced to concede territories captured in the 1967 Six Day War.

OUTCOME After suffering heavy losses on both fronts, Israel rallied and reversed all the gains made by Egypt and Syria, inflicting massive casualties on the Arab armies before a UN ceasefire was imposed.

The seeds of the Yom Kippur War were sown six years earlier in the Six Day War of June 1967. In that conflict, Israel had stunned the world with its military brilliance, particularly in its handling of air power and armour, and had vastly expanded its territory to control the whole of Sinai, the West Bank of the River Jordan and the Golan Heights. The conquests fulfilled their intended purpose – to give the State of Israel a protective 'buffer zone' in a sea of Arab enemies – but did not bring peace. The Arab world demanded the withdrawal of Israel from its conquered territories, something Israel would contemplate only if the Arabs acknowledged Israel's sovereignty and right to exist. Neither side's requirements would be satisfied, so Israel established a string of fortified positions along the east bank of the Suez Canal. This

was known as the Bar-Lev Line, after Lieutenant-General Chaim Bar-Lev (1924–94), chief of the general staff of the Israel Defense Forces from 1968 to 1971. Not always adequately manned or protected, the Bar-Lev Line became the victim of regular Egyptian artillery bombardment from 8 March 1969, the start of what became known as the 'War of Attrition'. This war would steadily escalate into another full-scale showdown between the Arabs and Israel.

REARMAMENT

During the Six Day War and until his death in 1970, Egypt was under the leadership of President Gamel Abdel Nasser (1918–70). Nasser, smarting at the humiliating defeat of 1967, began the job of revitalizing his forces. Central to this effort was the

An Egyptian soldier holds up a portrait of President Sadat. Sadat was a skillful politician, and the Yom Kippur War did much to raise Arab morale, as it broke the myth of Israeli invincibility. Sadat was assassinated, however, in 1981.

expertise and technology of the Soviet Union, Egypt's principal Cold War backer. In particular, Egypt needed solutions to two problems – the Israeli Air Force (IAF) and Israel's armoured formations. To tackle the former problem, Egypt invested heavily in Soviet SA-2, SA-3, SA-6, SA-7 and SA-9 surface-to-air missile (SAM) systems, as well as the formidable four-barrelled ZSU-23-4 radar-controlled self-propelled anti-aircraft cannon. By forging these systems into a tight interlocking network, the Egyptians aimed to created a SAM 'umbrella' that would provide ground forces with relative freedom from IAF ground-attack missions. The different operational altitudes of the various SAM systems meant that an Israeli aircraft's efforts to avoid one type of SAM usually put it within the effective range of another.

The problem of Israeli armour was partly answered by re-equipping Arab tank forces – in total, the Soviet Union supplied over 4000 tanks to Egypt and Syria in the years between 1967 and 1973, mostly T55s and T64s. The other side to Egypt's anti-armour restructuring was to acquire huge supplies of infantry anti-tank weapons. These were the AT-3 Sagger and the now infamous RPG-7. Each had its own capabilities (see box, right).

The rearmament programme of the Arab armies seemed to put them on a secure footing for a coming war. By October 1973, Israel had 275,000 soldiers (one-third were regulars, the rest were reserves), 1700 tanks and 432 aircraft. Egypt had 285,000 men, 2000 tanks and 600 aircraft, but its ally Syria added another 100,000 men, 1200 tanks and 210 aircraft to the Arab arsenal.

CROSSING THE CANAL

Nasser died in September 1970 and was succeeded as president by Anwar Sadat (1918–81). Sadat made great efforts on the international stage to secure a diplomatic solution to the Arab–Israeli problem, but by 1971 he felt that war was his only option. Here lay a problem. Sadat knew that his forces could not match Israeli military professionalism (and that the United States would come to Israel's material aid). His plan, therefore, was to open a multi-front war that was not aimed at crushing Israel but at forcing it and the international community to the negotiating table. The plan was as follows: Egypt would launch an assault across the Suez Canal, penetrate a short distance into Sinai, then hold the ground while Israeli forces battered themselves against the SAM, anti-tank and infantry defences. A simultaneous attack by Syrian forces in the Golan Heights would stretch the Israeli response thin, preventing it from applying the focused *Blitzkrieg*-style warfare it had employed in the Six Day War.

For Israel, the Sinai provided an important buffer zone between its home territories and its Egyptian enemy. Israel was, however, surrounded by potential and real enemies on all other borders.

INFANTRY ANTITANK WEAPONS

The Sagger (see below left) fired a missile 860mm (33.9in) in length, either from a suitcase launcher or from rails mounted on an armoured fighting vehicle (AFV) or a helicopter. It had a range of up to 3000m (3281 yards) and guidance was by the Manual Command to Line of Sight (MCLOS) system. This system relied on the operator guiding the missile to the target via a joystick, a tricky job, especially under combat conditions. A 3000m (3281-yard) flight would take up to 30 seconds, during which time enemy gunners could fire at the tell-tale dust cloud generated by the missile's launch and hopefully knock the shooter off aim. Impact rate for the Sagger could be as low as 30 per cent, even in the hands of a skilled operator. Nevertheless, in quantity and with an armour penetration of over 400mm (15.7in), it remained a very dangerous weapon.

The RPG-7 was a different animal from the Sagger. This shoulder-launched weapon fired an unguided rocket fitted with a High Explosive Anti-Tank (HEAT) warhead, which had an armour penetration of around 260mm (10.2in) at close range. Being unguided, the RPG-7's PG-7V missile gave the weapon an effective range of up to 500m (547 yards), but in practical combat 100–200m (109–219 yards) was more realistic. The great virtue of the RPG-7 was, and remains, its ease of use. Every infantryman trained in the weapon could destroy any of the tanks in the Israeli inventory.

The Arab attack would be codenamed Operation *Badr*. The primary focus of our study here is the Sinai theatre of operations, although this in no way relegates the Golan Heights action to a secondary position.

Under the cloak of a highly effective deception operation, Egypt assembled five infantry, three mechanized and two armoured divisions, plus several other independent brigades, along the Suez Canal in early October 1973. (The timing of the operation was made to coincide with the most favourable tides and weather over the Suez Canal.) The deception operation was designed to make the Israeli high command, headed by Prime Minister Golda Meir (1898–1978) and her minister of defence, Lieutenant-General Moshe Dayan

(1915–81), believe that the force gathering was mere posturing. Such was the skill of its execution that only 18 of the 32 strongpoints on the Bar-Lev Line were occupied, and by fewer than 500 troops. This relaxed attitude was adopted in spite of the IDF's then chief of the general staff, Lieutenant-General David Elazar (1925–76), having stated his belief that the Arab mobilization was a definite prelude to a major offensive.

ATTACK BEGINS

On 6 October at 1400, Egyptian artillery went into action along the Suez Canal, unleashing up to 10,500 shells in the first 60 seconds alone as the Israeli positions came under fire. Meanwhile, the Egyptian

Israeli Centurions mass for the attack in the Sinai. One of Israel's greatest mistakes in the Yom Kippur War was its tendency to commit armour without infantry support, resulting in many losses to Egyptian anti-armour teams.

Air Force embarked on heavy ground-attack missions against Israeli air defence and command-and-control centres, although it quickly lost 40 aircraft to Israeli fighters and anti-aircraft fire. Then, at 1420, the first Egyptian infantry began to swarm across the canal in assault boats. Their way was paved by remarkable combat engineering, the principal challenge of which was cutting through the huge sand berms constructed by the Israelis on their side of the canal. This was accomplished by using the same high-pressure water hoses employed in the construction of the Aswan Dam; the jets of water cut through the berms, and steel matting was laid in the gap to enable armoured vehicles to pass. Huge motorized rafts ferried tanks across the water, and over the next two days 10 massive prefabricated bridges were thrown over the canal to expedite troop and vehicle transfer.

Once the force was across, the Egyptians advanced into Sinai and prepared to face the inevitable Israeli counterattack. Only 208 Egyptian troops were killed during the crossings, and by 7 October 90,000 troops and 850 tanks were on the eastern side.

ISRAELI COUNTERATTACK

Between 6 and 8 October, as fighting raged around the Bar-Lev strongpoints, the Israelis began to mount their response in earnest. Here they made their first mistakes. Self-belief within the Israeli Armor Corps was extremely high, with powerful characters such as Major-General Avraham Mandler (commander 252nd Armoured Division), Major-General Avraham Adan (b. 1926 – 162nd Reserve Armoured Division), Major-General Ariel Sharon (b. 1928 – 143rd Reserve Armoured Division) and Brigadier-General Kalman Magen

Soviet-built Egyptian SA2 anti-aircraft missiles captured by the Israelis on the western bank of the Suez Canal. SA2s provided a high-altitude anti-aircraft 'umbrella' under which Egyptian land forces could operate.

THE OPPOSED FORCES

ISRAEL (estimated)	
Total:	**275,000**
EGYPT (estimated)	
Total:	**285,000**

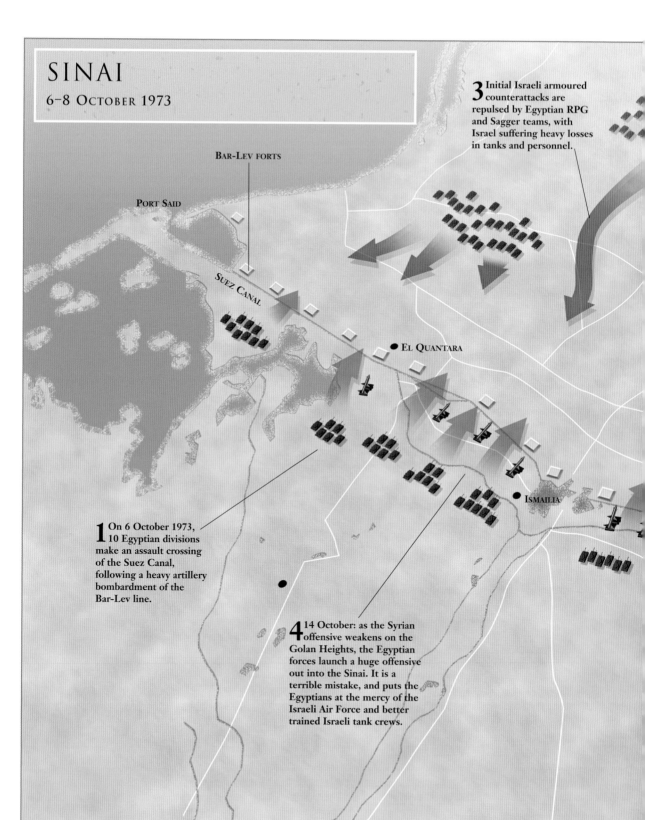

SINAI
6–8 OCTOBER 1973

BAR-LEV FORTS

PORT SAID

SUEZ CANAL

EL QUANTARA

ISMAILIA

3 Initial Israeli armoured counterattacks are repulsed by Egyptian RPG and Sagger teams, with Israel suffering heavy losses in tanks and personnel.

1 On 6 October 1973, 10 Egyptian divisions make an assault crossing of the Suez Canal, following a heavy artillery bombardment of the Bar-Lev line.

4 14 October: as the Syrian offensive weakens on the Golan Heights, the Egyptian forces launch a huge offensive out into the Sinai. It is a terrible mistake, and puts the Egyptians at the mercy of the Israeli Air Force and better trained Israeli tank crews.

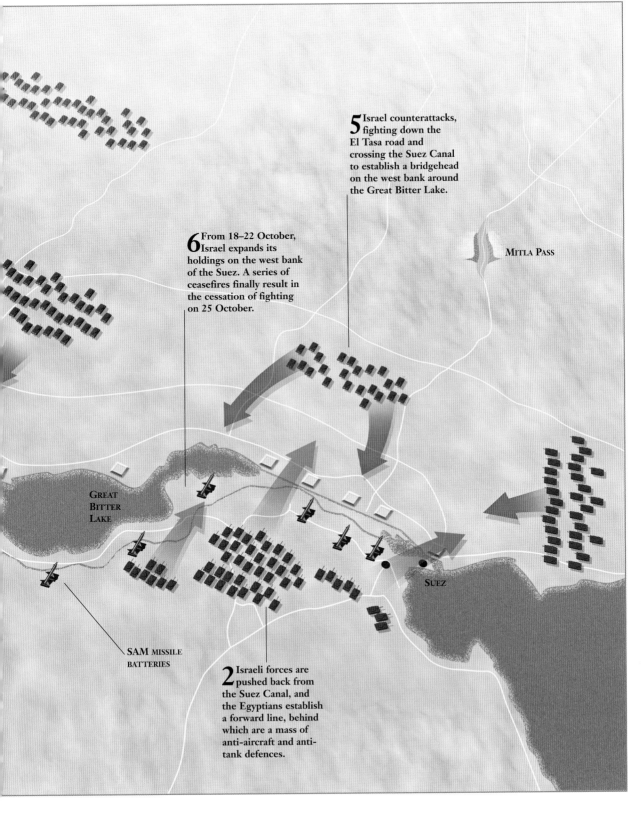

5 Israel counterattacks, fighting down the El Tasa road and crossing the Suez Canal to establish a bridgehead on the west bank around the Great Bitter Lake.

MITLA PASS

6 From 18–22 October, Israel expands its holdings on the west bank of the Suez. A series of ceasefires finally result in the cessation of fighting on 25 October.

GREAT
BITTER
LAKE

SUEZ

SAM MISSILE
BATTERIES

2 Israeli forces are pushed back from the Suez Canal, and the Egyptians establish a forward line, behind which are a mass of anti-aircraft and anti-tank defences.

(146th Reserve Armoured Division) pushing for rapid offensive action. However, the SAM umbrella was already inflicting serious losses on the IAF, and troop mobilization was taking time, so the armoured forces would largely go into action without the cover of air superiority or large troop movements. Artillery support was also slow in materializing.

HEAVY ARMOURED LOSSES

The result was that the Israeli armour threw itself against the Egyptian defences, mostly in battalion-sized packets, making 23 individual counterattacks between 6 and 8 October. Almost all were bloodily repulsed when they encountered Egypt's

anti-tank screen. The experience of Adan's division was typical.

Adan attacked with his three brigades against the Egyptian Second Army south of El Qantara, with Sharon's division ordered either to make a follow-up attack against the more southerly Third Army or to move up as a reserve support to Adan if he found himself in trouble. The overall Israeli plan was to sweep along the eastern side of the Suez Canal, breaking up the Egyptian defences in preparation for taking back the territorial losses.

Adan's manoeuvre seemed to be going smoothly, when Egyptian infantry armed with RPG-7s and Saggers suddenly broke their cover from dug-in positions and

Israeli up-armoured Shermans head to the frontline. Israeli tank commanders often fought stood up with their heads out of the turret hatch. Although this provided better tactical awareness, it resulted in terrible losses amongst the commanders.

The T-55 tank, one of the mainstays of Egyptian armoured forces during the Yom Kippur War. The T-55 had some good qualities, but its 100mm rifled gun was outclassed by the 105mm weapons mounted on Israeli M60A1 and Centurions.

unleashed dozens of missiles at the Israeli tanks. Twelve tanks were destroyed in quick succession, and more soon followed. One brigade was engaged by the anti-tank units about 1000m (1094 yards) from the canal, and 18 of its tanks were lost. By 1400, Adan's entire counterattack had been smashed, and similar stories were repeated up and down the front.

Israeli armoured counterattacks in the Sinai between 6–9 October were disastrous, with the Israelis losing more than 400 tanks destroyed or damaged in this period. Combined with the air losses to the SAM screen, and the stress of the additional fighting on the Golan Heights, a deep depression started to sink over the Israeli forces and the high command.

CLAWING BACK VICTORY

By the end of 8 October, events seemed to be going in Sadat's favour. Yet the Arab forces would eventually go on to lose the Yom Kippur War, through a combination of foolish strategic changes and the dogged resilience of the Israeli troops, who had the added motivation in the Golan of fighting to protect their homeland. The battle for the Golan Heights, which began with a Syrian assault on 6 October, turned into one of the greatest armour-versus-armour battles in history.

The Syrians unleashed some 1200 tanks against, initially, only two brigades of Israeli armour numbering around 180 tanks, obliterating them by 8 October. Nevertheless, the heroism of the Israeli defenders, plus the steady influx of other Israeli tank and infantry units, began to

inflict unsustainable losses on the Syrians and their allies. In three days of fighting on a battlefield only 16km (10 miles) deep, the Arab forces lost 1400 tanks, several other Arab countries, particularly Iraq, having also deployed tank forces in the sector. In one action alone, an Israeli unit of 50 tanks wiped out 200 Syrian tanks near Yehudia. Although fighting in the Golan would rumble on for several more weeks, the Syrians were effectively defeated by 9 October.

Alarmed by such events, Sadat made a fatal decision. It was decided that Egypt would go on the offensive, abandoning its original plans to fight a defensive battle. The decision was a critical mistake on several levels. First, it would force Egyptian units to fight the fast-moving manoeuvre engagements at which the Israelis excelled, and for which the laborious, centralized Egyptian command and control was poorly suited. Second, an advance would push the Egyptians out from under their SAM umbrella, where they would suffer the depredations of the IAF. Third, the Israelis were beginning to cope with the anti-tank threat. By pouring machine-gun and mortar fire on enemy anti-tank troops, the Israelis could either destroy the anti-tank units or disrupt their aim. Similarly, the IAF

IDF TANK CREWMAN

The personnel of the Israeli Armoured Corps (IAC) were critical to the eventual defeat of the Arab armies during the Yom Kippur War, but they paid for victory with hundreds of lives – some 400 Israeli tanks were destroyed in the Sinai. This first lieutenant (his rank is displayed on the collar straps) gives a typical image of an IAC crewman. He wears a fibre helmet, drilled through with ventilation holes, a simple lightweight fatigue uniform and a communications headset (the junction box is suspended over his chest). Israeli forces have long been known for their informality in dress, the emphasis in training being placed on combat effectiveness rather than what some might feel are minor points of military etiquette.

Above: An Egyptian infantryman showing the simplicity of his uniform. Most Egyptian equipment was of Soviet origin, hence this soldier has a Soviet-type Russian helmet and an AKM assault rifle.

began operating in larger formations, overwhelming SAM defences and utilizing US-supplied Walleye guided bombs to destroy launchers and radar systems.

The Egyptian offensive was launched on 14 October, with disastrous results. In only two hours, the attack was crushed. Four hundred Egyptian tanks were committed to battle, but 260 were destroyed by Israeli tanks and units firing US TOW anti-tank missiles. Worse still, the failed effort gave an opening for the Israelis to return to the offensive, this time with improved tactics and against a weakened enemy. On the 15th, IDF armoured formations crossed the canal

around Deversoir and consolidated a bridgehead, while more units moved across the Great Bitter Lake to the south, using assault boats and pontoon bridges.

By the 17th, the canal was effectively in Israeli hands, so much so that on the 18th, the IDF launched Operation *Gazelle*, an offensive into the Egyptian interior. Accompanied by extensive air strikes that destroyed 50 Egyptian SAM batteries over four days, three Israeli brigades pushed outwards from the western bridgehead, advancing 56km (35 miles) by the end of 19 October. Many units of the Egyptian Third Army escaped encirclement only by

Israeli troops try out a captured Egyptian Carl Gustav anti-tank weapon. The Israeli solution to Egyptian tank hunters was to saturate their positions with small arms and artillery fire, thereby disrupting their ability to aim and manoeuvre.

directly disobeying Sadat's orders and pulling out. Nevertheless, the going remained hard for the Israelis, and some of their objectives, such as Suez City, remained in the hands of the defenders.

By now, the international community was pushing hard for a ceasefire, especially when Saudi Arabia stopped oil exports to the United States, who had launched Operation *Nickel Grass*, a massive resupply operation to Israel during the early stages of the war. A ceasefire was agreed on 22 October, but it took several more UN Security Council resolutions to bring the fighting to a close on the 25th.

AFTERMATH

The Yom Kippur War inflicted heavy losses on both sides. In total, Israel suffered 2687 dead and 7251 wounded, while the Egyptian losses alone on the Arab side were in the region of 12,000 dead and 35,000 wounded. Ironically, both sides declared the action a victory, although the fact that Israel held onto all of its previously acquired territory, and indeed made some additional conquests, does make their claim appear the

more plausible. Nevertheless, the 1973 war shook the IDF to the core, and it came in for heavy criticism both in terms of its prewar intelligence and its tactical choices. What was apparent was that both armour and air force had to refresh their tactics in the light of new battlefield technology.

Some 107 IAF aircraft and 400 IDF tanks were lost in Sinai, and even though these losses were in some way offset by the 277 aircraft and 1000 tanks lost by Egypt, they were still an appalling cost for what was a small armed force.

The Israelis had been totally unprepared for the Egyptian's mass deployment of antitank weapons, such as the Sagger and RPG-7, and these had proved extremely effective against one of the best-equipped professional armies in the world. The Yom Kippur War showed that motivated infantry armed with effective antitank weapons could take on modern AFVs and win.

Arguably, Israel would never again have the total military confidence enjoyed after its 1967 victory, although the war spurred the IDF to become one of the most technologically-advanced forces in the world.

Moshe Dayan (right) was the Israeli Minister of Defence during the time of the Yom Kippur War. While his brilliance in the earlier Six-Day War in 1967 brought him fame, the tactical and intelligence failures of the 1973 conflict eventually led to his resignation in 1974.

THE GULF WAR

JANUARY–FEBRUARY 1991

THE 1991 GULF WAR SAW AN OUT-OF-DATE SOVIET-STYLE IRAQI MILITARY FACE THE FULL POWER OF WESTERN WARMAKING TECHNOLOGY, INCLUDING THE CAPABILITIES OF FORMIDABLE SYSTEMS SUCH AS THE F-117 'STEALTH' FIGHTER.

WHY DID IT HAPPEN?

WHO Iraq versus a US-led Coalition. Both sides had about the same troop numbers, but the Western forces enjoyed technological superiority.

WHAT During Operation *Desert Shield*, the Coalition built up assets for Operation *Desert Storm*, the military campaign to eject Iraqi forces from Kuwait. The F-117 'Stealth' Fighter proved invaluable in knocking out air defences and other key Iraqi assets.

WHERE Kuwait and southern Iraq.

WHEN *Desert Shield* ran from 7 August 1990 to 17 January 1991, when *Desert Storm* began. Kuwait was declared liberated on 27 February 1991.

WHY The Iraqi invasion of Kuwait threatened the security of global oil supplies and raised the possibility that Saudi Arabia would also be invaded.

OUTCOME For less than 400 casualties, the Coalition drove Iraqi forces from Kuwait and inflicted some 150,000 casualties on Saddam Hussein's (1937–2006) military.

At the end of the 1980s, relations between Iraq and its southern neighbour Kuwait were strained. When Kuwait requested the repayment of loans made to Iraq to finance the latter's debilitating eight-year war with Iran (1980–88), Iraq countered by accusing Kuwait of conducting a campaign of economic warfare. Besides Kuwait's pressure over repayments, Iraqi grievances included charges that Kuwait was exceeding its oil production quota, thereby affecting the overall international oil revenues that were so important to Iraq, and stealing oil by cross-border drilling into Iraqi reserves. Outside the realm of economics, the Iraqis also claimed that Kuwait was historically part of Iraq. As Iraqi president Saddam

Hussein massed his forces on the Kuwaiti frontier, talks between the two countries aimed at resolving their differences broke down on 1 August 1990. On the 2nd, the Iraqi Army crossed the border into Kuwait. By the end of the day, this small but oil-rich country was under effective occupation.

The international response to the Iraqi invasion was surprisingly swift and nearly unanimous. The United Nations Security Council immediately passed Resolution 660, calling for Iraq's immediate withdrawal from Kuwait, and Iraq was quickly hit with economic sanctions. By August 1990, Saddam was already well on his way to becoming an international pariah. Nevertheless, he remained a respected power player in the Middle East, with a very

A British Challenger tank makes a stop on the Iraq-Kuwait border during Desert Storm. *Coalition tanks were totally superior in terms of armour, gunnery and crew training when compared to the ageing T-72s, T-62s and T-55s used by the Iraqi forces.*

F-117 NIGHTHAWK

The on-paper specifications of the F-117 did not seem all that impressive when ranked alongside those of a fighter such as the F-15E, which was of similar size. The F-117's top speed, for example, was only 993km/h (617mph). However, it was the aircraft's stealth properties that separated it out from the pack. The peculiarly angular platform and body shape of the F-117 were designed specifically to scatter radar waves. This feature, combined with a radar-absorbent coating over all surfaces, made the fighter almost invisible to radar detection.

Furthermore, the engines, which had heat-reducing exhausts, were deeply recessed into the body, dramatically reducing the aircraft's infrared and noise signatures. Within the body were two integral weapons bays, designed to carry precision-guided munitions (PGMs) and air-to-surface missiles. The F-117 could carry air-to-air missiles, but the aircraft was best suited to ground-attack work.

large land army that had quickly engulfed any Kuwaiti resistance. There also remained the possibility that Kuwait could serve as a stepping-stone to an invasion of long-time US ally Saudi Arabia. With the entire balance of Middle Eastern power in jeopardy, and global oil interests threatened, it was time for the West to draw a 'line in the sand', known as Operation *Desert Shield*.

DESERT SHIELD

Almost immediately, a US-led Coalition, with contributions from 34 countries, began a huge military build-up in the region. Between August 1990 and January 1991, more than 500,000 troops – 74 per cent of them US soldiers – were deployed to Saudi Arabia, while major naval assets, including two US carrier battle groups, were sent to the proximate waters.

In addition to the massive build-up in land and naval forces, the Coalition also brought together an impressive volume and quality of air assets. By the beginning of 1991, there were more than 2400 fixed-wing military aircraft deployed as part of Operation *Desert Shield*. As in the case of the land forces, the United States provided the bulk of these air assets, although there were important air contributions from many more Coalition states. All were sewn

together by an enormous electronic network created by intelligence-gathering aircraft, and capably supported by the fleets of transport aircraft that were also critical to the land build-up. Most of the aircraft were based in Saudi Arabia, although some flew from Turkey while long-range B-52s operated from bases as far away as England, Spain and Diego Garcia.

Although the size of Saddam Hussein's army was causing some disquiet in the West, there was no doubting the technological superiority of the Coalition. Perhaps most emblematic of this superiority was a fighter that would occupy the vanguard of future air combat operations – the F-117A Nighthawk 'stealth' fighter.

The F-117's typical payload was two 909kg (2000lb) GBU-27 bombs fitted with the Paveway III laser guidance kit. The aircraft's primary mission was the penetration of enemy air defences to make low-level precision attacks against critical targets. To ensure accurate targeting and terrain-hugging flight at night, the F-117 had an inertial navigational system (INS) and two forward-looking infrared (FLIR) sensors; one sensor gave the pilot images of the terrain around him (beamed onto a multi-function display – MFD – in the cockpit), while the other supplied target

LOCATION

The terrain in which Operation Desert Storm *was fought was perfect for the Allied forces. The flat desert and scrub in Kuwait and southern Iraq gave the ideal conditions for rapid target acquisition.*

pictures and was coupled to a laser designator to provide guidance for the PGMs. The F-117 stood as the most advanced fighter in history, each aircraft costing over $50 million.

The Coalition's purpose was not only to protect Saudi Arabia from possible invasion but also to create the means for future offensive action in the event that Saddam Hussein were to resist all diplomatic efforts over Kuwait. That resistance looked increasingly certain as time went by. Not only did Saddam ignore the demands of leaders such as US President George Bush (b. 1924) to withdraw from Kuwait, he also seemed to be reconfiguring his forces in preparation for a showdown. On 29 November 1990, the UN Security Council passed Resolution 678, which effectively provided the Coalition with the authorization to use military means to enforce their demands if Iraqi troops had not withdrawn from Kuwait by 15 January 1991. Instead of backing down, Saddam

allowed the deadline to expire and promised the 'Mother of all Battles'.

DESERT STORM

The responsibility for taking back Kuwait lay principally in the hands of General H. Norman Schwarzkopf (b. 1934), head of US Central Command (CENTCOM), and his subordinate commanders. On the basis of four months of preparatory intelligence, a two-phase operation was planned. The first phase would be a massive and prolonged air campaign. Under the command of Lieutenant-General Charles A. Horner USAF (b. 1936), this was designed to destroy Iraqi armour, troop concentrations, supply lines, key buildings and, most importantly, the Iraqi command-and-

---

F-117 Stealth aircraft of the 37th Tactical Fighter Wing at their base in Saudi Arabia after operations into Iraqi. A indication of the F-117's heavy use is seen in the bomb-delivery motifs beneath the cockpit.

THE OPPOSED FORCES

COALITION FORCES (estimated)

Total:	**880,000**

IRAQI FORCES (estimated)

Total:	**500–800,000**

control network. The last-mentioned was especially critical, since once they were 'blinded' (in other words, once without their communications and radar networks) the Iraqi forces would not be able to coordinate air defences, thereby giving the Coalition air superiority over the battlefield. Furthermore, once the land units were without centralized instructions, they were likely to display all the poor tactical decision-making typical of armies with a dictatorial command structure that crushed individual initiative.

Once the air campaign had done its preparatory work, a large Coalition land army would strike into Kuwait and also Iraq from the west, this left wing of the attack cutting off the Iraqi forces in Kuwait from reinforcements and also trapping large numbers of troops within Kuwait itself. In both phases of what would be known as Operation *Desert Storm*, aerial surveillance would be critical.

E-2 Hawkeye and E-3 Sentry airborne warning and control system (AWACS) aircraft would monitor the skies for hostile air threats, while E-8C Joint STARS would track ground targets, transferring their

The Iraqi Republican Guard were Saddam Hussein's elite troops. Their origins were as a bodyguard force to Saddam, but by 1991 they had grown to a strength of some 80–100,000 and formed the main military concern to Coalition leaders in the Gulf War. The Republican Guard uniform was much the same as that of the rest of the Iraqi army, although they often wore red boots and red berets to distinguish themselves. They also had better access to specialist items of clothing and weaponry.

coordinates to land units or, more commonly, vectoring ground-attack air sorties. RC-135 River Joint aircraft would monitor Iraqi communications traffic. In short, the Iraqis would have nowhere to hide.

The air campaign was launched on 17 January 1991 at 0238 (Baghdad time), with a strike by eight AH-64 Apache attack helicopters on Iraqi radar sites on the Iraqi–Saudi Arabian border. Within minutes, Tomahawk cruise missiles were slamming into targets in Baghdad, and F-117s were also making attacks on the city. The air campaign was, apart from some Special Forces actions and localized border clashes,

A GBU 909kg (2000lb) penetration bomb is prepared for an aerial attack mission over Iraq. Even the most basic of such weapons could penetrate up to 1.8m (5.9ft) of reinforced concrete.

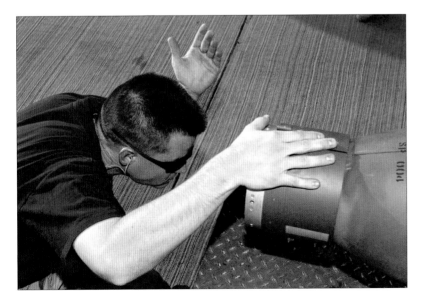

the principal method of prosecuting the war until the land campaign began on 24 February. Space here does not allow a detailed insight into one of the greatest air campaigns in history, in which more than 1000 combat sorties were flown every single day, but the contribution of the F-117 is more than representative.

STEALTH KILLER

From the outset of the air campaign, the F-117's role was critical. Although the 42 F-117As used in the war constituted just 2.5 per cent of all combat aircraft deployed to the Gulf, they actually took on 31 per cent of the key strategic targets during the first day of the conflict. The stealth fighters were contained within two squadrons (415th and 417th) of the 37th Tactical

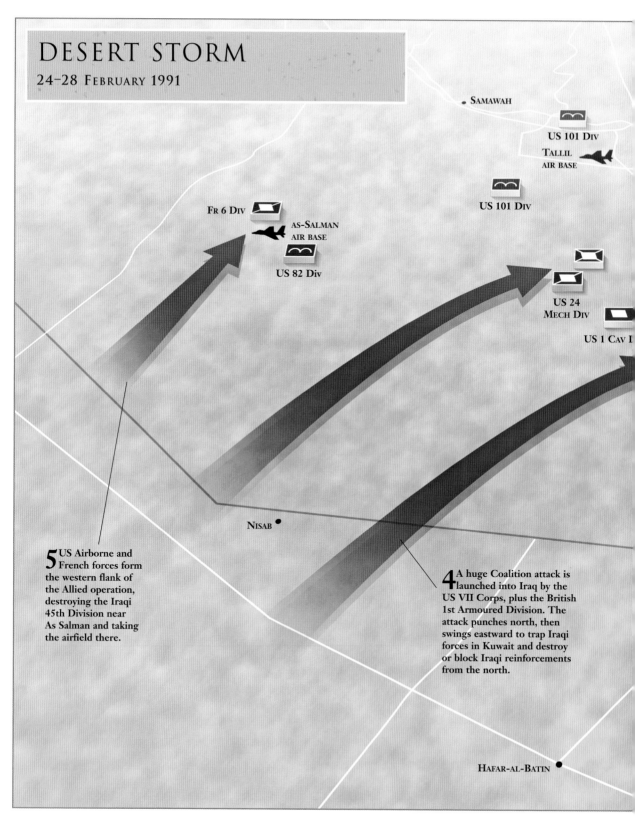

DESERT STORM

24–28 FEBRUARY 1991

SAMAWAH

US 101 DIV

TALLIL
AIR BASE

US 101 DIV

FR 6 DIV

AS-SALMAN
AIR BASE

US 82 DIV

US 24
MECH DIV

US 1 CAV I

NISAB

5 US Airborne and French forces form the western flank of the Allied operation, destroying the Iraqi 45th Division near As Salman and taking the airfield there.

4 A huge Coalition attack is launched into Iraq by the US VII Corps, plus the British 1st Armoured Division. The attack punches north, then swings eastward to trap Iraqi forces in Kuwait and destroy or block Iraqi reinforcements from the north.

HAFAR-AL-BATIN

1 Coalition air assets strike Iraqi targets in Kuwait and Iraq in support of the Coalition land operation. The air attacks destroy hundreds of armoured vehicles and command posts.

• BASRA

JALIBAH
AIR BASE

• SAFWAN

US 1 DIV

US 2
MECH RGT

BR 1 ARM DIV

• KUWAIT CITY

EGYPTIAN
DIV

KUWAITI BGDE

SAUDI BGDE

US 2 MAR DIV   US 1 MAR DIV

AL-JABEB
AIR BASE

2 A combined US and Arab force, including the US 2nd Marine Division, attack into Kuwait, heading directly north to liberate Kuwait City.

3 Saudi, Kuwaiti and Qatari troops also attack north into Kuwait, but take the coastal route towards Kuwait City.

THE GULF WAR

Fighter Wing and were based at Khamis Mushait in southern Saudi Arabia. During the course of the war, the F-117s were given a broad range of targets – command centres; communications and radar sites; nuclear, biological and chemical (NBC) facilities; powerplants; bridges; and hardened aircraft shelters. Many of their targets, however, were concentrated in the Iraqi capital, Baghdad, which by January 1991 had an air defence network of 60 surface-to-air (SAM) sites and some 3000 anti-aircraft guns.

Many details of the F-117s' combat sorties remain classified, as the capabilities and tactics of the aircraft are closely guarded secrets. Some operations did become public, however. The first bomb to be dropped on Iraq during the war was delivered by F-117 pilot Major Gregory A. Feest, who flew with nine other F-117s towards Baghdad in the very first hours of the war. Feest's first target was a camouflaged and hardened Iraqi Air Force interceptor operations centre in a town called Nukhayb. The INS helped guide Feest to the objective, although he changed course often to hamper enemy tracking efforts. Finally he was over the target, and the MFD threw up a grainy picture of the location. He locked the aiming crosshairs onto the bunker, designated the target and released a 909kg (2000lb) bomb. It flew completely true, punching through the roof of the bunker and detonating inside (Feest saw the doors of the bunker blow outwards). Heavy anti-aircraft fire opened up in response, but as would often happen through the night it quickly ceased or was wildly inaccurate, indicating that the Iraqis were unable to track the assaults. Nonetheless, it was a disturbing barrage to fly through.

The flight of F-117s began to swarm over other targets across Iraq. Another key attack – one whose MFD picture was broadcast on public television – was on Baghdad's principal telecommunications centre. As in the case of the bunker attack,

The terrible power of Coalition land assets is illustrated by this bombed-out Iraqi column. Elevated roads such as these presented targets in shooting-range clarity for helicopter gunships and strike aircraft.

An Iraqi T-55 burns in the desert. Iraqi use of armour was tactically inept. Armour relies on its mobility for survival, but all too often Iraqi forces set their tanks in static positions, there to be picked off at leisure by Coalition aircraft and armour.

the target was shattered by a 909kg (2000lb) bomb. During the war, stealth fighters dropped a total of 1814 tonnes (1778 tons) of bombs in nearly 1300 combat sorties. On average, an F-117 pilot conducted 21 combat missions, each lasting about 5 hours 30 minutes, and with about 24 hours' rest in between. In terms of both mission duration and the number of missions flown, the figures for F-117 pilots were lower than those of many other combat pilots during the conflict. However, the highly technical nature of F-117 operations, and the fact that they were always conducted at night against heavily protected targets and at low level, meant that such actions required great skill and concentration.

Of course, although it was important, the F-117's role was just a part of a massive air campaign. Day and night, Coalition aircraft swarmed over Iraq and Kuwait, delivering destruction. Iraq had no effective answer to Coalition air supremacy. Thirty-eight MiGs were shot down in the first week and up to 150 Iraqi jets were flown to Iran by pilots who recognized the futility of resistance.

Almost all command-and-control structures were wiped out, and several thousand Iraqi armoured vehicles were destroyed by A-10s, Apache helicopters, F-15Es and other ground-attack aircraft.

Possibly tens of thousands of Iraqi troops were killed when their positions were carpet-bombed by B-52s. By the end of February, conditions were right for the land campaign to begin.

ENDING THE OCCUPATION

Although the air campaign had been a resounding success, there remained an air of uncertainty over the land campaign. Iraq's army was large – with more than 600,000 troops (possibly over one million if all reserves were counted), 11,000 armoured vehicles (including 5800 tanks) and nearly 4000 artillery pieces – and many of its soldiers were combat-proven. Despite this, there were reasons for the Coalition to be confident.

The first reason was the sheer damage done by the air campaign, not only to Iraqi assets but also to Iraqi morale. Moreover, the land campaign would enjoy the cover of complete air superiority. Second, Coalition land warfare equipment – particularly

A British Special Air Service (SAS) soldier in desert camouflage holds an SLR rifle. Special forces played a crucial role in the success of the bombing campaign, provided on-the-ground markers for many of the Allies' lazer-guided bombs.

The F-15 Eagle was, and remains, arguably the world's greatest jet fighter. During the Gulf War, F-15s were mostly employed in ground-attack roles, the Iraqi air force being quickly destroyed or fleeing to safety in neighbouring countries.

armoured vehicles and battle command-and-communications systems – was generally superior to that of the Iraqis. GPS systems allowed Coalition units to manoeuvre with precision without getting lost, even in areas of featureless terrain. Finally, the airborne surveillance assets meant that the Iraqis could not move without being spotted (in good weather,

---

The Abrams M1 was at the vanguard of Coalition armoured forces during Desert Storm. *Its fire-control system enabled crews to engage Iraqi armour at distances in excess of 3000m (9842ft).*

they couldn't really stay stationary either), and their positions could be instantly relayed to fire bases or attack aircraft.

Small reconnaissance and Special Forces operations began in late January, with some larger cross-border actions around 20 February. Yet after further UN demands for an Iraqi withdrawal from Kuwait were ignored, the full force of the Coalition land army surged into Kuwait and Iraq. In effect, the land campaign consisted of three huge sweeps. To the far west, the US XVIII Airborne Corps – with flank protection from the French 6th Light Armoured Division (left) and British 1st Armoured

Division (right) – would attack into southern Iraq, sweeping upwards towards the Euphrates River and then turning eastwards towards Basra. The US VII Corps would make a similar but shorter 'hook punch' into Iraq along the Kuwait–Iraq borderlands before advancing *en masse* into Kuwait itself. US Marine and combined Arab forces would simply cross the border directly into Kuwait from the south. In effect, the Iraqi occupation forces would be crushed against the Gulf coastline.

Within hours of the Coalition invasion, it became apparent that the Iraqis were a shadow force. Poorly handled Iraqi armour could not stop the surge of US M1 Abrams or British Challenger tanks – the British 1st Armoured Division, for example, destroyed 200 Iraqi tanks, while the US 1st Armored Division took out 630. Iraq's Republican Guard units were quickly smashed; they had endured relentless bombing, which had shattered their ranks and their nerves. Mass surrenders gave the Coalition a huge logistical challenge. In addition, convoys of requisitioned and military vehicles fleeing out of Kuwait City to Iraq were shot to pieces in relentless air attacks.

By 28 February, after only 100 hours of fighting, the US president – not wanting to encourage what many would see as a purposeless slaughter – ordered the shooting to stop. The mission of expelling Iraq from Kuwait had been completed and the Iraqis were defeated, although many would rue the fact that the ceasefire allowed a couple of thousand armoured fighting vehicles and thousands of Republican Guard troops to escape. The incongruity between Coalition and Iraqi casualties was striking. Some 358 Coalition troops died from combat and non-combat causes.

By contrast, there were an estimated 150,000 Iraqi casualties, with as many as 50,000 dead. One central reason for the discrepancy is that the Coalition air power, including assets such as the F-117s, not only rendered the Iraqi forces unable to communicate effectively but reduced them to sitting ducks under the sun.

The Gulf War demonstrated the heights to which precision air attacks had ascended. This photograph shows a bridge over the Euphrates river, neatly split in two by a laser-guided bomb.

BIBLIOGRAPHY

Ashton, Robert. *The English Civil War: Conservatism and Revolution 1603–1649*. London: Wiedenfeld & Nicholson, 1978.

(Ed) Ayton, Andrew and Price J.L. *The Medieval Military Revolution*. London: I.B. Tauris &Co Ltd, 1998.

Blair, Claude. *European Armour: circa 1066 to circa 1700*. London: B.T. Batsford, 1958.

Bradbury, Jim. *The Medieval Archer*. New York: St. Martin's Press, 1985.

Clancy, Tom with Chuck Horner. *Every Man A Tiger – The Gulf War Air Campaign*. New York: Berkeley Publishing, 2000.

DeVries, Kelly. *A Cumulative Bibliography of Medieval Military History and Technology*. Leiden: Brill, 2002; Update: Leiden: Brill, 2005.

DeVries, Kelly. *Medieval Military Technology*. Peterborough, UK: Broadview Press, 1992.

DeVries, Kelly and Robert D. Smith. *Medieval Weapons: An Illustrated History of their Impact* (Weapons and Warfare). Santa Barbara: ABC-CLIO, 2007.

Dunstan, Stephen. *The Yom Kippur War 1973 (1) – The Golan Heights*. Oxford: Osprey Publishing, 2003.

Dunstan, Stephen. *The Yom Kippur War 1973 (2) – The Sinai*. Oxford: Osprey Publishing, 2003.

Ferrill, Arther. *The Origins of War from the Stone Age to Alexander the Great*. 2nd ed. Boulder: Westview Press, 1997.

Finlan, Alastair. *The Gulf War 1991*. London: Routledge, 2003.

Goldsworthy, Adrian. *In The Name Of Rome*. London: Wiedenfield & Nicholson, 2003.

Heather, Peter. *The Fall of the Roman Empire: A New History of Rome and the Barbarians*. Oxford: Oxford University Press, 2006.

Herzog, Chaim. *The War of Atonement: The Inside Story of the Yom Kippur War*. London: Greenhill, 2006.

(Ed) Holmes, Richard. *The Oxford Companion to Military History*. Oxford: Oxford University Press, 2001.

Keegan, John. *A History of Warfare*. London: Huchinson, 1993.

Keegan, John. *The First World War, An Illustrated History*. London: Random House (UK) Ltd, 2001.

Kern, Paul Bentley. *Ancient Siege Warfare*. London: Souvenir Press, 1999.

Kure, Mitsuo. *Samurai: An Illustrated History*. North Clarendon, VT: Tuttle Publishing, 2002.

Turnbull, Stephen. *Nagashino 1575 – Slaughter at the Barricades*. Oxford: Osprey Publishing, 2000.

Maenchen-Helfen, Otto J. *The World of the Huns: Studies in Their History and Culture*. Ed. Max Knight. Berkeley and Los Angeles: University of California Press, 1973.

Marsden, E.W. *Greek and Roman Artillery*. 2 vols. Oxford: Clarendon Press, 1969.

Montgomery, Field-Marshal Viscount. *A History of Warfare*. London: William Collins, Sons & Company, 1968.

Nicolle, David C. *Arms and Armour of the Crusading Era, 1050–1350*. 2 vol. White Plains: Kraus International Publications, 1988.

(Ed) Parker, Geoffrey. *The Cambridge Illustrated History of Warfare*. Cambridge: Cambridge University Press, 1995.

Perrett, Bryan. *The Battle Book*. London: Arms and Armour Press, 1992.

Putney, Diane T. *Airpower Advantage: Planning the Gulf Air Campaign, 1989–1991*. Washington, DC: University Press of the Pacific, 2006.

Richards, John. *Landsknecht Soldier, 1486–1560*. London: Osprey, 2002.

Scales, Robert. *Certain Victory – The US Army in the Gulf War*. Dulles, VA: Potomac Books, 1998.

Smith, Robert Douglas and Kelly DeVries. *The Artillery of the Dukes of Burgundy, 1363–1477*. Woodbridge: The Boydell Press, 2005.

Strickland, Matthew and Robert Hardy. *The Great Warbow: From Hastings to the Mary Rose*. Stroud: Sutton Publishing, 2005.

Taylor, F.L. *The Art of War in Italy, 1494–1529*. Cambridge: Cambridge University Press, 1921.

Troso, Mario. *L'ultima battaglia del medioevo: La battaglia dell'ariotta Novara, 6 giugno 1513*. Novara: Edizioni della Laguna, 2002.

Turnbull, Stephen. *Siege Weapons of the Far East (2) – AD 960–1644*. Oxford: Osprey Publishing, 2002.

Turnbull, Stephen. *Fighting Ships of the Far East (2) – Japan and Korea AD 612–1639*. Oxford: Osprey Publishing, 2003.

Turnbull, Stephen. *Japanese Fortified Templates and Monasteries – AD 710–1602*. Oxford: Osprey Publishing, 2005.

Turnbull, Stephen. *Samurai Invasion: Japan's Korean War 1592–1598*. London: Cassell, 2005.

Wren, Jack. *The Great Battles of World War I*. New York: Grosset & Dunlap Inc, 1972.

INDEX

PICTURE CREDITS

All maps and black-and-white line artworks produced by JB Illustrations.

AKG-Images: 8 (Peter Connolly), 14, 40 (Peter Connolly), 45, 46/7 (Peter Connolly), 47 (Peter Connolly), 64, 87, 95, 134/5, 136, 140/1, 166/7, 167, 175 (Ullstein Bild), 184 (Ullstein Bild)

Amber Books: 35t, 39, 54, 59

Art-Tech/Aerospace: 189t, 192b, 203t

Art-Tech/John Batchelor: 11b, 127

Art-Tech/De Agostini: 159b, 169, 179, 185b, 203b, 204t, 213b

Art-Tech/MARS: 9b, 119, 145, 146, 197, 198

Bridgeman Art Library: 56

Cody Images: 15, 81b, 156/7, 157, 158, 160, 161, 165, 171b, 174/5, 187, 189b, 192t, 195t, 212, 213t, 215

Corbis: 10 (Jonathan Blair), 12 (Hulton-Deutsch Collection), 13 (Bettmann), 18 (Gianni Dagli Orti), 20 (Chalil Raad), 25 (Giani Dagli Orti), 26 (Richard T. Nowitz), 27 (Archivo Iconografico, S.A.), 37 (Fine Art Photographic Library), 48 (Bettmann), 50 (Bettmann), 60 (Bettmann), 90 (Gustavo Tomsich), 98 (Dave Bartruff), 100 (Charles Lenars), 105b (Asian Art & Archaeology, Inc.), 106t (Ric Ergenbright), 106b (Werner Forman), 107 (Asian Art & Archaeology, Inc.), 108 (Kim Kyung-Hoon), 111 (Asian Art & Archaeology, Inc.), 114t (Kevin R. Morris), 116 (Asian Art & Archaeology, Inc.), 124 (Archivo Iconografico, S.A.), 126, 128 (Bettmann), 130 (Fine Art Photographic Library), 154 (Bettmann), 168 (Hulton-Archive Collection), 176t (Hulton-Deutsch Archive), 177 (Hulton-Deutsch Archive), 181, 186 (Bettmann), 188, 196 (Christian Simonpietri), 202 (Genevieve Chauvel), 204b (David Rubinger), 205 (David Rubinger)

De Agostini: 28, 30, 36t

Defense Visual Information Center: 193, 195b

Dorling Kindersley: 131t (The Board of Trustees of the Armouries)

Getty Images: 31 (Stock Montage), 44t (Hulton Archive), 66/7 (Time & Life Pictures), 68 (Dmitri Kessel), 74t (Hulton Archive), 75 (Hulton Archive), 77 (Hulton Archive), 96 (Time & Life Pictures), 118 (Time & Life Pictures), 150 (Hulton Archive), 164 (Hulton Archive), 176b, 178 (Hulton Archive), 199 (Hulton Archive)

Heritage Image Partnership: 55 (Art Media), 61t (E & E), 84 (Art Media), 85 (The British Library), 120t (The Print Collection), 141

Mary Evans Picture Library: 21t, 41b, 58, 65, 71, 78, 80, 97, 101, 125b, 148, 149, 151b, 159t, 180t, 185t

Photos12: 138 (Ullstein Bild), 146/7 (Ullstein Bild)

Public Domain: 88

Topfoto: 137

US DOD: 16, 17, 194, 206, 207, 208, 209b, 214t, 214b